Leadership Through
Strategic Planning

Leadership Through Strategic Planning

Annabel Beerel

INTERNATIONAL THOMSON BUSINESS PRESS
I⟨T⟩P® An International Thomson Publishing Company

London • Bonn • Boston • Johannesburg • Madrid • Melbourne • Mexico City • New York • Paris
Singapore • Tokyo • Toronto • Albany, NY • Belmont, CA • Cincinnati, OH • Detroit, MI

Leadership Through Strategic Planning

Copyright © Annabel Beerel

First published by International Thomson Business Press

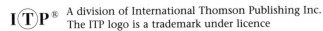 A division of International Thomson Publishing Inc.
The ITP logo is a trademark under licence

British Library Cataloguing-in-Publication Data
A catalogue record for this book is available from the British Library

First edition 1998

Typeset by LaserScript Limited, Mitcham, Surrey
Printed in the UK by TJ International, Padstow, Cornwall

ISBN 1–86152–208–8

International Thomson Business Press
Berkshire House
168–173 High Holborn
London WC1V 7AA
UK

http://www.itbp.com

Contents

List of figures

List of tables

We shall not cease from exploration
And the end of all our exploring
Will be to arrive where we started
And know the place for the first time.
Through the unknown, remembered gate
When the last of earth left to discover
Is that which was the beginning;
At the source of the longest river
The voice of the hidden waterfall
And the children in the apple-tree
Not known, because not looked for
But heard, half heard, in the stillness
Between two waves of the sea.

T.S. Eliot
Little Gidding
1942

Preface

The book *Leadership through Strategic Planning* is the product of a journey. This journey began over 40 years ago in the seedy ghetto, Doornfontein, east Johannesburg. Here I spent my early years working in my father's cold drinks factory. It was in this dark and dingy factory, situated in the centre of a dark and dingy neighbourhood, that I learned the importance of factory throughput, machine downtime, logistics and supply. I learned what it meant to market without a budget and to sell to people with little disposable income. I experienced the tensions of Sharpeville and the Soweto riots, while I, a young white girl, worked cheek-by-jowl alongside my father's all male, all black African workforce.

My father was a German-Jewish immigrant who had lost everything: family, friends, and home. While I never ceased to marvel at his ability to technically fix and refix aging, broken-down machinery, I also never ceased to be frustrated by his inability to deal with value-tensions and relationships. Maybe fleeing to South Africa in the wake of the murder of the rest of his family called on all his adaptive capabilities. Sadly, by the time I got to know him, he could no longer cope with changing new realities. It would seem that his adaptive capacities had been exceeded and that there was no more that he could call on.

After school, I spent my first seven years in business training as a chartered accountant. Here I learned about 'technical problems' and the intricacies of the rules which had been broken. Skills advancement was measured by the ability to apply ever more complex rules and as a result fix ever more complex problems. In general, proficiency as a chartered accountant was gauged by the ability to identify and resolve technical problems.

Although my work life since those early days has certainly been a disjointed one, until five years ago, the one consistent theme throughout was the emphasis on acquiring better and more sophisticated technical skills. I sought to master corporate finance, I learned the analytical techniques that seemed to belong to strategic planning, and I taught myself computer programming. Despite this dedication to more and better knowledge and techniques, I remained my father's daughter. I was always looking for new problems and took delight in 'fixing' them. This distraction, however, meant that I too was poor at handling value-tensions, at correctly reading relationships, at seeing the bigger picture and being able to adapt to new realities. All I knew and understood was that problems were there to be 'fixed'. I did not know how to put a more sensitive or nuanced spin onto my technical strategies. At some level, I did realize that technical fixes only went so far, and that something more was needed in order to move the problem or the organization in question to higher ground. I just did not know how to do it.

The last five years have resulted in a personal metamorphosis. I have learned about adaptive work as distinct from technical work. I have learned about what it means to exercise leadership, the importance of systems thinking, systemic analyses, and the significance of roles and relationships. I have been challenged to deal with value-tensions that exist when one is faced with new realities, and I have struggled with the distress and the tension that this causes. I have learned that technical fixes only go so far, and that moving to higher ground calls for greater awareness of people issues rather than skills in heuristics and sophisticated analytical techniques.

My current studies in religion and culture have made me aware, at a deeper level, of the diversity of life and the multiple realities that exist. I am also learning that in order to understand others one must first begin by understanding oneself, and that we see others the way we are and not as they are.

These are all tantalizing concepts and big questions. The answers are not found in a rule book but are rather created through a process. In this process there is nothing to be 'fixed'. Instead, there is a call to continuous adaptation, readjustment, and personal renewal. For me this process represents my own 'Long Walk to Freedom', a walk that will undoubtedly be of lifetime duration. I have chosen to embark on this walk as part of my own adaptive work, and as part of the ongoing strategic work that I hope to continue doing with those corporates that wish to move to higher ground.

Leadership through Strategic Planning synthesizes both my old and new knowledge and insights. It is intended to be a provocative reflection of what is and what might be, and I hope that it will initiate further dialogue and discussion on the topics of leadership and strategic planning. Without exception, I have tried out all the ideas and suggestions put forward in this book. Wherever they may sound abstract or unrealistic it is as a result of my limited writing capabilities or my poor execution of ideas rather than any tendency to foist abstractions or theories on the reader. In the end analysis I remain, like my father, a pragmatist. All other things being equal, what works is what is of most value.

So far, my long walk has taken me to four continents and many countries. I have lived and worked in South Africa, Europe, Asia, and the US. I have been exposed to the lives and ideas of many diverse people. Acknowledgements to those who have touched my life and who have assisted in my own adaptive process would take more pages than the rest of this book.

I would, however, like to especially thank Holly Zeeb, who immediately recognized my exceptional abilities at work avoidance, and who has expertly and patiently held me to my own adaptive work. My thanks also go to Ken Hughes SJ, who has been a guide and friend, and who has consistently reminded me, through his own person, of a reality that calls me beyond myself. I am also grateful to the wonderful professors at the Weston Jesuit School of Theology who were instrumental in starting the personal adaptive process. Ron Heifetz of the JFK School of Government was also instrumental in giving the transformative process added impetus. My thanks go to my friends whom I have tormented with impossible questions and *ad hoc* editing duties and who gave me enormous support and encouragement alongside good humour and excellent cuisine. Last and not least my thanks go to my many clients and students who have been some of my best teachers and to whom this book is devoted.

Annabel Beerel
Lincoln
Massachusetts

Introduction
Why this Book is different
from any other business book

A finished book is a great joy but the process of writing it is a torment. Part of the anguish is the many hours spent sitting in front of the computer wrestling with words that will not come. The even more difficult part, however, is remaining confident that one has something genuinely interesting and valuable to share with the reader. Reality rather than humility reminds one that there is nothing new under the sun. Usually writers know that they cannot impart something entirely new, but they fervently believe that they can provide new perspectives and insights on known ideas and themes.

Leadership through Strategic Planning aspires to provide a fresh look at the well-known topics of leadership and strategic planning. Many of the concepts and issues discussed in this book have been written about by others. What makes this book unique is not only the new ideas and perspectives, but the way in which the themes have been synthesized and converted into practical ideas for the management of organizations. What also makes this book different is the number of ideas that are conjoined into a working framework.

Here are some of the main ideas and perspectives included in this book:

- A new age, the Adaptive Age, is in the making. There is renewed emphasis on values.

- New world realities are challenging our adaptive capacities. We must develop our adaptive capacities rather than our technical capabilities. We need to distinguish between adaptive and technical work.

- Leadership should focus on exercising leadership rather than on the person of leader.

- There is a new role for the strategic planning function.

- Strategic planners have a leadership role to play in helping the organization identify its adaptive challenge.

- Findings of the new science regarding living organisms should be reflected in the way that institutions and organizations are structured.

- Businesses should adopt systems thinking and the systemic analysis approach in evaluating the environment and devising strategies.

- The business environment is characterized by new root metaphors.

- Our growing self-awareness reveals that the world is a world-wide-web. It is not just our communication links that should reflect this reality, but our attention to values and relationships.

- Scenario planning is consonant with the new understanding of living organisms and the inadequacy of cause-and-effect analysis.

- Businesses should place emphasis on co-creation, and co-evolution with partners and alliances, and devote less energy and time to 'destroying' the competition.

- The strategic planning function has a large part to play in developing the learning organization.

- Business ethics should be approached from a systemic standpoint and ethical criteria should be an intrinsic part of all decision-making criteria.

I hope that the reader will find the syntheses of these many ideas to be interesting and thought provoking. Hopefully they will inspire further new perspectives and will open up new dialogues.

CHAPTER ONE

The Adaptive Age: Reflection and Anticipation

Introduction

The evolution of the human species is different from any other species on earth in that human beings invent tools to help them along the way. This century has undoubtedly been a period of 'tool-making' par excellence. Tools have become increasingly sophisticated as they play their role in shaping humanity's future. Inventing and designing tools, which now takes the form of developing elegant technical solutions, has become the principal means of dealing with human problems. In fact, we have become so obsessed with our 'tool-making' abilities, that we are inventing and designing solutions to problems not yet experienced. Paradoxically, many of our newer problems have arisen as a consequence of our tremendous technical proficiency. We are forced to find ever-new technical solutions to compensate for the problems created by previous technical solutions.

Our modern world has become a technical fix society. Unfortunately, this devotion to technical solutions has obscured the real problems that placed us in the 'tool-making' business in the first place. While technical solutions have contributed immeasurably to our physical, and, to some extent, psychological survival, there is more at stake than that. Deep at heart, we are not looking simply for technical solutions, we are searching for meaning to our lives.

The combined events of the Industrial Revolution and the Enlightenment did much to propel us into the technical age. The Industrial Revolution stimulated and motivated our toolmaking abilities in new ways and in new domains, while the Enlightenment spirit placed the power and responsibility for the world squarely in the realm of the human intellect. This spirit has encouraged us to become self-reliant and technically proficient. It has encouraged us to place excessive emphasis on rational, analytical, and reductionistic ways of understanding the universe and its mysteries. We have come to believe that we can always find 'scientific' answers regardless of the complexity or the humanistic dimension of the problems that challenge us.

One of the consequences of this prevailing intellectual atmosphere, has been a profusion of abstract models and technical solutions in an attempt to demystify the world. This secularizing influence has been the central backdrop to the twentieth century.

The twentieth century in turn has propelled us into the heart of the technical age. It has been a time filled with new ideas, new inventions, and the emergence of new paradigms. During this century, the emphasis on the technical panacea has attained outrageous and unsustainable proportions. Whatever the problem, communally, organizationally, and individually, we reach for the technical fix. It may be called an aspirin, an abortion clinic, a welfare cheque, weight-reduction tablets, a reorganization, or a program in downsizing. It may make us feel younger, older, smarter, slimmer, or more powerful. We may have more choices and we may feel in more control, but have the root causes of the problems that we so readily 'fix' really been addressed? We have become so engrossed in our toolmaking/technical solutions, that we have forgotten that they are intended only as a means to an end. Instead they have become ends in themselves.

One example of this means-end confusion is the excessive preoccupation with the distribution of wealth found in most societies. Tinkering with wealth redistribution systems is almost always a technical fix deployed to solve complex systemic problems. Alas this approach seldom results in acceptable long-term solutions. The real 'adaptive' challenge lies in addressing the creation of new wealth rather than shuffling around the old. This new wealth is not just material wealth. It is a wealth that enables people to flourish and thrive. It is wealth that facilitates transformation. And it is wealth that is not attained at the expense of future generations. It is thus a sustainable wealth. This form of wealth is what the Chinese call 'prosperity'. It means far more than the accumulation of assets. Prosperity implies all-round well-being, a sense of groundedness, allegiance to clear values, an emphasis on relationships, and a concern for one's legacy. Prosperity seems to be a meaningful end toward which technical solutions should be directed.

The Adaptive Age

This book proposes that we are moving out of the technical age into the 'adaptive age'. In the Adaptive Age there will be a backlash against our dependence on technical fixes. There will be a return to meaning-making and a focus on the values that underlie those meanings. There will be a return to adaptive rather than technical solutions. There will be a new understanding of the complex and highly integrated systems and communities that make up the networks of life. Adaptive problems will be understood as interconnected and interdependent systemic problems that cannot be grasped or addressed in isolation. The Adaptive Age will pose new realities, new adaptive challenges, and require new responses. There will be a new language for understanding the complexities and uncertainties of life, and the old mechanistic and masculine metaphors such as 'Who is in command?', 'business is ticking over', 'entering a price war' and 'eliminating the competition' will be replaced. The new metaphors will bespeak co-evolution and co-creation while also embracing the softer and more feminine perspectives of life.

In the Adaptive Age many entrenched ideas will dissipate. Some of these ideas include viewing the universe as a mechanical system; seeing the human body akin to a machine; comparing the brain to a computer; viewing life in society as a continuous, competitive struggle for existence; upholding popular belief in the possibility of unlimited material progress; and having attitudes that subsume the female under the male (Capra 1996:6).

Leadership in the Adaptive Age

In the Adaptive Age, there is a need for leaders who can help us deal with the 'systemic' problems that go to the very core of who we are in a dynamically interrelated and interdependent world. These leaders will help us develop cross-cultural empathy that reaches beyond our tendency toward ethnocentricism whereby we denounce cultural relativism. These leaders will guide us to seek out synergistic solutions that bring out the best in all of us. The leadership focus will be on recognizing interconnected relationships, developing adaptive capacities, and developing communities that can learn through dynamic feedback. Above all, in the Adaptive Age we recognize that there are no neat and tidy answers, and that leaders certainly cannot singly provide the answers that we seek. We need to assert our own agency and actively join in the problem-solving process.

The Adaptive Age requires a systemic view of our world, our nations, and our societies. The intricate interconnectedness of all living systems, while beyond our grasp in comprehension, is not beyond our abilities for reverence, epistemological humility, and respect. There is general recognition that we have placed excessive emphasis on the 'hard' issues, and that we now need to move to the 'softer' issues. In the Adaptive Age we need to focus on meaning and values rather than on technical fixes. We need to develop our capacities rather than fixate on our capabilities. We need to understand the difference between adaptive and technical work, and we need to refrain from the repeated fallacy of misplaced concreteness. This popular fallacy upholds that all aspects of life can be converted into some number that will somehow describe their reality in definable and measurable form. Some examples include placing a numeric value on human life, or deriving an index number which describes the quality of life.

The issues raised here are not new. Western societies' dissatisfaction with the socio-economic scene in particular has been evident for a while. The future is all around us (Drucker 1989). The adaptive period has already begun. The agenda for the next century will be our response.

Strategic Planning in the Adaptive Age

The dawn of the Adaptive Age will have a great impact on the strategic planner(s) of any organization. Not only will their method of analysis have to change, but the analysis itself will require a new lens and a different focus. Strategic planners, who strive to orient organizations to anticipate and meet the challenges of the future, will need to read the times in a new way. They will also have to exercise leadership in organizations differently. Only organizations with a leadership style that suits the demands of the Adaptive Age will survive the new adaptive world. The Adaptive Age signifies a new 'Enlightenment.'

Enlightenment: West versus East

The West

During the Renaissance, a revived interest in nature led to new speculative philosophies and a new scientific movement. This fuelled a growing rift between theology and philosophy. A theocentric metaphysics was displaced by a rationalist one. Belief in the supernatural and the divine revelation of mysteries was replaced with an emphasis on what stood the test of reason.

Inspired by the scientific movement, and disillusioned with the post-Reformation 30-year carnage, thinkers and writers of the early modern period such as René Descartes, Baruch Spinoza, Jacques Rousseau, John Hobbes, John Locke, and Sir Isaac Newton ushered in a new Western world view.[1] This view rested on the newly perceived power and capabilities of man's reason. Human reason was considered to be the apt and only instrument for solving the problems connected with persons and society. Descartes placed the essence of human beings in their cognitive faculty, quite clearly setting apart mind and matter. Prompted by Descartes, other modern philosophers asserted that humanity should be free from superstitions, belief in revelation, submission to authority, and deference to tradition and institutions. The human person was assigned a new freedom. The only limitation rested on his or her ability to use reason. Ethical theory was stripped of its theological presuppositions and the new metaphysics took on rationalist characteristics.

The scientific movement, stimulated by Galileo Galilei, set the tone for a mechanistic view of the world. The nature of this mechanistic world took further shape based on the scientific insights of Sir Isaac Newton. Here nature came to be understood as a collection of atoms in which matter consisted of solid particles, each possessing its own shape and characteristics. He proposed that atoms and particles themselves are centres of force which can be identified and objectively studied. Following his discovery of the force of gravity, he claimed that if we knew the forces which act upon bodies, we could deduce the motions of those bodies mathematically.

The Newtonian view of the world holds that matter is a distinguishable substance that can be sub-divided into further distinguishable parts. These parts are seen as building blocks that can be disassembled and put together again. This belief has resulted in a foundational and analytical vision of the world. Thus the Newtonian mechanistic world is one that can be observed, measured, and analysed in discrete component parts. In this world view, space and time also tend to be considered discrete concepts. Time is perceived as linear and sequential. Consonant with this, analyses of phenomena focus on a sequential 'cause and effect' dynamic. The work of Newton effectively grounded the Western mechanistic conception of the world until the recent discovery of the 'new science' in the early decades of the twentieth century.

The methods for the development of knowledge and new truths were also radically influenced by the scientific movement of the Renaissance. The initial scientific methods used were almost exclusively experimental and mathematical in approach. Phenomena would be observed and hypotheses developed in the form of mathematical formulae to be solved by mathematical solutions. The mathematical approach served in abstracting ideas, thoughts and insights in a highly limited, defined, and value-free way. As a technique, it provided a deductive method for evaluating new data and attaining new knowledge. Using the knowledge gained by the experimental method, new knowledge can be acquired by applying known and tested formulae to similar data or similar experiments.

The next period of great influence on the development of the sciences and the use of technology was the Enlightenment. Known as the Age of Reason, the Enlightenment began in Europe during the eighteenth century. As the appellation Age of Reason indicates, during this period the human faculty of reason was further elevated in status. The scientific movement shifted emphasis from experiments based on observation to experiments designed to obtain empirical evidence based on experience. Experience, sense perception, and introspection became the new tools for unlocking the world's truths. Inductively based knowledge, confined of course to the limits of reason, acquired scientific credibility.

The Age of Enlightenment stimulated the scientific approach to all disciplines. It gave rise to the social sciences where the behaviour of human beings began to be studied using the scientific deductive and inductive methods. The Enlightenment spirit fostered the belief that, given an objective, value-free, social scientific approach to the study of all phenomena, all of the world could be made intelligible. Magic, mystery, revelation, and dogma were considered to be features of the 'pre-Enlightenment' period, when human beings were shackled to mystics, mysteries, and sacramental rituals that deflected them from their primary, superior, and worldly faculty of reason. The Enlightenment, grounded in a cause-and-effect, mechanistic world view, created a reality which added unbridled encouragement to humankind to take control of the world, analyse it, understand it, and dominate it.

Hopes for a New Enlightenment

There is, however, a new reality and a new enlightenment. The 'new science', referred to as modern physics, dispels the Cartesian division of the world and the Newtonian mechanistic world view. The Cartesian division of mind versus matter created two realms. Descartes' identification of the self with the intellect encouraged the tendency to divide the world into separate individual things where we experience ourselves as isolated egos. The influence of modern physics, however, serves to revise this conception of the world and the universe. Modern physics extends rationalistic boundaries, eliminates notions such as cause and effect, the sequence of events, and the sequential structure of our abstract concepts and symbols. The findings of modern physics reveal that the cosmos is one inseparable whole, forever in motion, alive, and organic. Motion and change are the intrinsic property of matter, and arise as a consequence of being part of force-fields, rather than as a consequence of the action of external forces. Matter itself is a field of energy not a mass of solid particles. The constituent parts of atoms, subatomic particles, have been found to be dynamic patterns which do not exist as isolated entities, but as integral parts of a separate network of interactions (Capra 1996:225).

The more scientists penetrate into the submicroscopic world, the more they find the world as a system of inseparable, interacting, and ever-moving components. The observer of the system is an integral part of the system (ibid.:25). Descartes' division between the self and the world, led to the belief that the world could be observed and described objectively. The new science has shattered the principle concepts of both the Cartesian and Newtonian world view. There is no absolute space and time; there are no elementary particles; and one cannot objectively study the causal nature of physical phenomena or devise an ideal description of nature. Nature does not comprise isolated building blocks that can be disassembled and put together again. The natural world has infinite varieties and complexities. It does not comprise straight lines or regular shapes, and things do not happen in sequence but all together. Interconnections occur as probabilities rather than as certainties, and relationships cannot be defined in a predictable or precise way.

Nature has now been discovered to be a communicated web of relations between various parts of the whole, where the observer is always included. One cannot partition the observer and the observed, as the observer participates in and affects what is being observed.

As physicist Fritjof Capra describes in his books, *The Tao of Physics*, and *The Web of Life*, the environment is engaged in a gigantic cosmic dance, animated by cascades of energy which both creates and destroys in rhythmic pulses (Capra 1996:11). In Capra's discussion of modern physics and Eastern mysticism he argues that there are strong parallels between the world view of physicists, especially as the new science unfolds, and the Eastern mystics.

The East

The Eastern view of the world is organic. Eastern mystic religions, such as Hinduism, Buddhism, Taoism, and Zen Buddhism, believe that things and events perceived by the senses are interrelated and connected, and are but different manifestations of the same ultimate reality. They emphasize the basic unity of the universe, the interrelation of all things, and the image of the Divine as the principle that controls everything from within. They reject the Western idea of a Divine as the ruler from above who directs the world.

In Eastern mysticism, the highest aim is to become aware of the unity and interrelation of all things, to transcend the notion of the individual self, and to identify with the ultimate reality. This awareness they refer to as 'Enlightenment'. Attaining Enlightenment in the East is not an intellectual act. The Eastern mystics claim that the ultimate reality can never be an object of reasoning or demonstrable knowledge. It cannot be adequately described by words, and it lies beyond the realm of the senses and the intellect. Absolute knowledge of the ultimate reality, which is deemed the source of all things, can only be 'seen' or experienced in a meditative state of consciousness. During this time the individual realizes that he or she and the ultimate reality are one. The experience of Enlightenment involves the whole person and is religious in its ultimate nature. The Eastern enlightened one does not resist the flow of life but keeps moving with it. He or she is keenly aware of flowing and ever changing reality. The universe is experienced as an inseparable web of dynamic interconnections where the ultimate reality without is identical to the reality within. All phenomena are considered to be multiple representations of the one reality, where each part contains the whole.

To the Eastern mystics, differences and contrasts are relative within an all embracing unity. They do not think in terms of opposites as these are considered to be abstract and relative concepts which belong to the realm of thought. For them the notion of opposites are polar – light and dark, winning and losing – which they consider to be different aspects of the same phenomenon. Between opposites there is a dynamic tension that holds the interplay between the two sides. They see the world through the archetypal symbols of the *yin* and the *yang*, which holds the world in dynamic balance. The *yin* represents the female, dark, intuitive, religious, mystical, occult, and psychic modes of existence, while the *yang* represents the male, light, active, rational, competitive, and aggressive modes. To the Eastern way of thinking, the *yin* and the *yang* need to remain in dynamic tension, as opposites are in effect complementary. The West undoubtedly favors the *yang* over the *yin* and views opposites as oppositional and distinct. Opposites provide occasion for dominance, oppression, and suppression, activities which form the main threads of world history as we know it.

By contrast to the West, one of the most important characteristics of the Eastern world view is the awareness of the unity and interrelation of all things and events. All phenomena in the world are experienced as manifestations of a basic oneness, emanating from one unified source. All things are seen as interdependent and inseparable parts of a cosmic whole. Everything perceived is considered to be different manifestations of the same ultimate reality.

The basic oneness of the universe is also the central characteristic of the findings of modern physics. As physicists have penetrated smaller and smaller particles of physics, the same insight is experienced. The basic constituents and phenomena of matter are all interconnected, inter-related, and interdependent. They cannot be understood as isolated entities but only as integrated parts of the whole. The idea of foundational building blocks that can be discretely taken apart and put together again has been dispelled.

East versus West

A question that we might ask ourselves is: did the Western Enlightenment really enlighten? Did it illuminate, or enhance our understanding of reality? With hindsight, it would appear that, in some respects it has achieved the opposite. Rather than encourage a holistic, integrated, and compassionate grasp of the world, it has fostered a limited, one-sided, dispassionate view of reality. Its effect has been to fragment rather than coalesce, to reduce rather than expand, and to fracture rather than heal our delicately balanced, integrated universe. It is this fragmented, reductionistic, and excessively rationalistic Western approach that is out of sync with the world's natural, organic system.

The nature of the world being uncovered by modern physics is inconsistent with the Western world view. Our nations, societies, organizations, and business institutions do not reflect the interrelated-ness which we observe in nature. By and large our approach to studying the world and its component parts remains vested in the Cartesian and Newtonian models. The manner in which we form institutional relationships is also not congruent with the natural relationships that we actually experience at a personal level. It appears that we have become so concerned with abstraction and definition that we have become detached from the real world by confusing our concepts and symbols of reality with reality itself. We have refused to accept the extreme limits of rational knowledge and we have tended to ignore the fact that our descriptions of reality are at best a mere approximation of a minute part of an infinitely indescribable whole. We have used our intellect to the extreme in order to define, distinguish, discriminate, divide, compare, measure and categorize, all in the interest of gaining rational mastery and control.

On the other hand, the Eastern idea of Enlightenment appears to be a more illuminating and holistic approach to the realities of the world. Mastery and control lies in realizing that we cannot take control and that we do not and cannot understand the fullness of reality. What we really need to master and control is our *attitude* towards our part in the *continuous, cyclical ebb and flow of life.*

It would appear that in world history, the West represents the *yang* and the East the *yin.* Since the *yang* appears to have reached its climax, the new reality may be the emergence of the *yin.* To keep in tension the world's dynamic balance, this correction seems long overdue. This is the reality of the Adaptive Age.

The New Realities of the Adaptive Age

The new realities confronting the world are no secret. As the millennium draws to a close, we observe the preoccupation of political leaders with globalization, modernization, environmental issues, communications, and technology. East and West, at both the political and economic level, are engaged in using these trends to position themselves to strategic advantage.

However, despite enormous advances in science and technology, we do not seem to have fostered the good life and the good society. Undoubtedly some benefits have accrued from our activities and the standard of living of many of the world's people has improved. But disturbing inequalities and inequities remain. Regrettably, the side effects of rapid world growth, and the modernizing process, have had negative consequences of catastrophic proportions. This is evident in the destruction of the environment and the social crisis that has resulted from the rapid growth of cities and the trend toward urbanization. Social infrastructures have been unable to keep pace with these developments. Despite serious social consequences, the quest for growth has continued unabated. Governments and their leaders have been resistant to curbing scientific and economic activity in the interests of the environment and dwindling resources. Attaining figures that reflect high growth has remained a priority. High growth has come to symbolize economic power. No country wishes to remain in the low-growth league which is deemed a sign of economic and political impotence.

Pursuit of Growth

The frenetic pursuit of economic growth which has been so characteristic of recent decades is currently the subject of strong critique. Economists, environmentalists, and social ethicists are pointing out that the infatuation with high GDP figures, supposedly a measure of a country's economic welfare, belies true economic well-being. In response to this outcry, nations and their organizations are being confronted with new constraints. Many socio-economic interest groups are resisting the pressure to foster economic growth purely for its own sake. Sustainable growth is being held up as the new goal.

Role of Business Organizations

There is also much discussion regarding the power and role of business organizations. This has increased to such an extent that multinationals, in particular, eclipse the power of many nation states. Some claim that these organizations are the key change agents of the world and, as such, their influence in political, social, cultural, and economic spheres is pervasive. Seen in this light, organizations are under ever greater pressure to be more attuned to the environment in which they operate. As a sub-system of their world, they need to understand the rhythm and tempo of the larger system. Organizations must co-ordinate their own rhythms so that they can participate harmoniously within the greater system.

World Interdependence

Sensitivity to the world system also means that the organization's strategic planning perspective needs to be ever more macro. Doing business in Indonesia, for example, requires an understanding of the political, social, and cultural characteristics of Indonesia, South-East Asia and the Pacific Rim. It means comprehending the interconnectedness of countries and businesses within all of Asia as well as understanding the Asian-Muslim network and its socio-political implications. The complexity of Asia needs to be understood in relation to the rest of the world. Working with broad, interconnected perspectives is based on taking a systemic view. It requires scanning ever wider horizons and understanding the impact and implication of systems within systems. Only this type of approach can give businesses sufficient understanding of the environments in which they operate.

High Stakes

In the world in which we now move, the stakes are high. Due to the scale of political and business organizations' activities and the extent of their influence, there is much to gain but also a great deal to lose. If political leaders form shaky coalitions, their countries' security or economic well-being is severely compromised. If business organizations make poor investment decisions, they find that there is little shareholder tolerance or economic surplus to cushion their failures. If ethnic groups feel insecure, a skirmish soon escalates to civil war. This is the state of the twenty-first century world: seemingly minor ripples have major repercussions.

Co-creation

The mutual interdependence of the world is now commonly known and readily acknowledged. With the assistance of environmentalists and proponents of the new science, we have come to realize that we do not live in a fragmented world. We are not dependent on competition and collaboration for survival. 'Fourth Wave' thinking holds that the world is one and therefore we co-create. Environmentalists use nature as their reference point while the new scientists analyse social organizations.

In the political and social arena, we find acknowledgement of the world's interconnectedness. This is evidenced in the growing emphasis on reciprocity and collaboration between nations, among societies, and between business organizations. Partnerships, alliances, joint ventures, and collaborative enterprises are terms in current business jargon. The new watchword will be 'co-creation' as nations and organizations find new solutions through the conjoining of their competencies and skills.

Thus a new business metaphor is emerging. No longer is business a simple battle between two or more opposing troops. Business has become an elaborate dance, with and between many changing partners. As the music changes, the dance steps change and partners switch. Sometimes the tempo is fast and sometimes slow; sometimes the dance is long and sometimes short; sometimes the tone is high-pitched and sometimes it is deep.

Businesses select the dances in which they participate based not only on how well they know the music, or the steps that they know or want to learn, but on the availability of suitable partners. On the world business stage it has become increasingly difficult to dance alone. Knowing which dances to sit out is just as strategic as knowing when to be on the floor. Watching who else is sitting out can provide an outstanding opportunity to form alliances in anticipation of the next suitable dance. The current emphasis for business then is to put away the guns and learn how to dance. The game has changed from killing one another off to mutual survival. The new emphasis will be how, in conjunction with varying partners, to co-create new steps.

Social Change

The Western World is in a state of philosophical, scientific and technological flux. As bearer of modernity, it has led revolutions in technology and communications. Governments, social institutions, and business organizations are reorganizing and restructuring in order to maximize the advantages that flow from these revolutions.

The political and social principles on which the development of the West is based are also being re-evaluated. Politics and the role of government are under scrutiny. The meaning and practice of democracy is continually being challenged as the issue of human rights gains greater attention. The tension between the rights of the individual and concern for the common good has become central to the discussion on the need for greater public morality.

Disenchantment with an ultra-rational, scientific secular emphasis grows. Many people are seeking to re-enchant their world by substituting other-worldliness and mystery for the Enlightenment-driven worldliness and rationalized intelligibility. This is evident in the resurging interest in religion, the growth of Evangelism, interest in science fiction, and the popularity of movies like Steven Spielberg's Jurassic Park.

Social ethics, and in particular business ethics, is attracting increasing attention from all stakeholder vantage points. No longer can organizations pursue profits at the community's expense. They are now obliged to take responsibility for their own mess of pollution, effluent, or waste. While still expected to fulfill their role as redistributors of risk, stimulators of the economy, and providers of jobs, organizations no longer have a free hand in setting their own limits. Both government and societies have abandoned the *laissez-faire* concept so eagerly advocated by ardent free-market capitalists. Business organizations face increasing government legislation as well as critique and restraint from their surrounding societies. This trend is likely to escalate before some kind of equilibrium is established.

Communities are becoming increasingly conscious of their self-identity and their desire for self-determination. People are straining for self-empowerment and self-authorization, thereby shunning traditional hierarchical authority structures. Evidence of this exists at all levels as ethnic groups, religious groups, and cultures assert their rights to unique identities and value systems.

Western discourse is filled with talk about diversity and post-modernism. Diversity recognizes the multiplicity of cultures, religions, and interest groups. The term implies societal acceptance and tolerance of these divergent groups. Post-modernism implies a recognition of multiple, unique realities and truths. In a post-modern world there is no longer a defining normative reality and attendant sub-realities. As the modern physics shows, all are but multiple manifestations of one ultimate reality.

The implications of post-modernism have challenged the validity of fields such as sociology replacing them with disciplines such as Black Studies or Women's Studies. Sociology assumed that social groups could be objectively observed and their values, attitudes, and behaviours, interpreted and compared against a controlling norm. The concept of a controlling norm is no longer applicable in a post-modern society. Diversity and plurality comprise multiple realities each equally normal and normative.

Demography

Another major issue confronting all corners of the globe is demography and its political, social and economic consequences. Demographic trends reveal that the older and wealthier nations have an aging population, while the poorer and less developed countries continue to stagger under high birth rates, increasing life expectancy, and mass rural emigration to cities. Burgeoning shantytowns of unemployed people are evident in all high growth but less developed economies. The inability of the social infrastructure to respond has resulted in high crime rates, abject poverty, social unrest, and a loss of traditional values. The social cost is exorbitant and growing.

Wealthier countries are responding to demographic challenges by increasing dependence on technology. Automation and robotization have taken the place of blue-collar workers. New technologies are deployed to reduce production costs in order to remain competitive with low labour-cost countries. This strategy, combined with stringent immigration policies, exacerbates the refugee crisis of young, unem-ployed people seeking work in the wealthier nations. The pressure that these bottlenecks create is destined to mount.

To the non-Western world, the global and modernizing trends are being both economically embraced and culturally rejected. The export of Western values to the non-West is increasingly being resisted. This has fuelled a growing rise in fundamentalism.

While non-Western countries may embrace modern products and services, the meanings that they hold, or what the symbols represent, are different. A hamburger at McDonald's in New York has a different meaning to the consumer than a hamburger purchased in London, Moscow, or Tokyo. While Indonesians now purchase Levi jeans and sweaters from Benetton, they do not aspire to be like the Americans or the Italians. Their meaning-making systems and values remain Indonesian.

Contrary to the belief that globalization and modernization would have a culturally homogenizing effect, the opposite is proving true. People typically find it easier to define who they are by stating who they are not. Being confronted with American jeans and Italian sweaters clearly reminds and reinforces for Indonesians that they are neither Americans nor Italians, nor do they want to be.

The Concept of Limits

The post-Second World War years have been a time of unprecedented economic growth. Financed by the US Marshall Plan, Europe and Japan have rebuilt themselves from the ashes. Amazement at the speed with which this has been achieved is surpassed only by wonder at the technological and communication advances that occurred as nations rebuilt their industries and decimated infrastructures. America in turn gained enormous benefits from the economic growth that ensued as a consequence of the revitalization of Europe.

However, the enormity of the post-war boom had a serious psychological effect on the entire world. The preoccupation with continuous growth gave rise to a new, blatant, and arrogant disregard for limits. As we review our score sheet for the twentieth century, while we may take pride in many of our achievements, they have come at a great price. We have damaged our environment, both on the earth and in the surrounding atmosphere. Cultural conflict has reached new heights as insatiable greed and lust for power has cost nations and their institutions both credibility and the goodwill necessary for constructive dialogue. Business in capitalistic societies, supposedly guided by an 'invisible hand' that will self-correct, regulate deleterious behaviour, and serendipitously promote the interests of society, has lost all notion of limits.[2] Spurred on by the avaricious desire for greater economic power, many businesses have forgotten that they are part of a system, and as such have a specific yet limited role to play. As its power has grown, business has mistakenly assumed that it could ignore the greater whole, decide its own function, and set its own limits. The Adaptive Age will prove a powerful wake-up call.

From a social and religious viewpoint, our limitless rationalizing process has landed us in the inevitable 'Iron Cage' so aptly predicted by Max Weber at the beginning of this century. Because of the focus on an efficient, functionalist-rationalist society, the technical order rather than the moral order has come to prevail. The seduction of modernization has turned persons-in-community into individuals-in-society, who are consumed with the idolatry of the self.

The Adaptive Age will counter this disregard for limits. It will be a time when nations, politicians, institutions, and business organizations are forced to comprehend the notion of 'enough': enough growth, enough power, enough profits, and enough rationalization. Enlightened self-regulation will become an important feature of the Adaptive Age.

The Fallacy of Misplaced Concreteness

The *fallacy of misplaced concreteness* is a phrase coined by Daly and Cobb (1994) in their book entitled *For the Common Good*. This term describes the tendency to define all manner of phenomena or modes of existence in quantifiable and concrete terms. According to them the discipline that illustrates this principle to the extreme is economics. Daly and Cobb point out that economics, as a social science, leads (or rather misleads) to sweeping generalizations and conclusions. They describe it as a science based on enormous abstractions whereby it assigns concrete measurements to many 'soft' and qualitative issues that are neither concrete nor quantifiably definable. Examples of this distortion are the so-called 'economic costs' of a human life or the economic measure of the quality of life. These, they argue, cannot and should not be abstracted into a statistic or a formula. Daly and Cobb highlight how Westernization, with its modernizing trend, increasingly finds succour in numbers or formulae. This tendency to define and control the softer or subtler aspects of life that defy definite and certain measurements or parameters, is what I would refer to as looking for a technical fix for an adaptive problem. The proliferation of economic theories that pervade all political, social, and business arenas, is further evidence of our flight from the messiness of reality to the distant and dispassionate laboratories of technical solutions.

The fallacy of misplaced concreteness has so crept into our lives that we have edited out the possibility of leaving something hazy, indistinct, uncertain, and undefinable. Anything that is comprehended only through feeling or intuition is eliminated. Our Enlightenment inheritance has cornered us into finding definitions and measurements for all that we observe and experience. Everything now has a cost and a benefit which we use for comparison or justification. Regrettably this excessively rationalistic approach has helped us to avoid the real work that we need to do. The real work means facing and grappling with the fuzzy, uncertain, messy particulars of value-laden situations.

The new reality is that we are realizing that many current measurements of human well-being are fallacious and inappropriate. We also realize that what defies measurement must remain so, and must be understood in another way. Possibly the waxing of the *yin* will come to our aid.

The Changing Nature of Work

One very sobering, and for some, very sombering reality is that the 'social contract' regarding jobs has expired. No longer can people assume that, if they have completed their part by getting trained or educated, they will get a job. The new reality is that proportionate to the growth in the world population, there will be ever fewer jobs.

What was once a hopeful dream has turned for some into a tragic horror story. The vision that technological progress will free people to indulge in more leisure time and improve their quality of life has revealed a dark underbelly. Whereas in the past new sectors have emerged to absorb displaced labourers, the economic system's capacity for employing workers is fast approaching its limit. This applies particularly to the advanced nations and is already a feature in some of the advancing nations. This new reality is discussed at some length in Jeremy Rifkin's book *The End of Work* (1995).

The current business emphasis on the development of a twenty-first century techno-paradise where technological advance and production efficiencies reach ever greater heights provides a real threat to the future potential workforce. The history of so-called economic progress and industrialization tells us about the mechanization of farms and the loss of farmers; the mechanization of factories and the loss of blue-collar workers; and now the mechanization of service industries and the loss of service industry workers. As workers' operations become more mechanical and as computerized machines are able to take on ever more complex tasks, a growing portion of the workforce is being displaced by technology. The 'visible hand' of the government as an employer has 'withered away' for very different reasons than Karl Marx had in mind. The public sector has shrunk in most nations as it too has been under pressure to modernize and cut costs. Massive worker layoffs have occurred in all sectors and at all levels.

The growing percentage of the long-term unemployed provides some evidence of this new reality. It is also an indicator that re-training for newer skills is no longer the panacea. Soon, only highly educated knowledge workers will be in demand. A generation ago a bachelor's degree was considered a relatively high qualification. Nowadays, more and more jobs require a doctorate as the minimum entry qualification. The demand for average and even above-average skills will no longer exist. It is possible that in the not too distant future only rocket scientists will be employable as the rest of us succumb to an Orwellian future dominated by scientists and machines that makes '*1984*' seem like a benign pantomime.

In his book, Rifkin also discusses the failure of the 'trickle down' theory of technology. This theory holds that as technology displaces jobs this will result in cheaper goods. As a consequence, people will need to earn relatively less than before and will also experience greater purchasing power. In response they will purchase more, thereby sustaining growing levels of production in a continuous cycle of increased demand supporting increased supply. Rifkin claims that this theory does not work in practice. First, he argues, that when people have no jobs they have very little, if any purchasing power, and second, he observes that the extension of markets will not be able to keep pace with the rapid increases in production. Even now it is plainly evident that the markets of some emerging nations are under pressure to find new markets for their mass produced goods. An example is South Korea, which is actively investing in countries in Africa in the hopes of stimulating the local markets there.

Rifkin also asserts that America's shift from a thrift society under-pinned by the Protestant ethic to the present hedonistic consumption society, occurred as a direct response to the massive media and marketing pressures exerted on consumers by big businesses. This began during the sixties when the second major industrial shift from manufacturing to services took place and has gained momentum since then. He claims that this has also resulted in the buy-now-pay-later mentality that has fuelled the boom in consumer credit.

The current trend in re-engineering and downsizing means that those who have jobs are expected to work longer hours for relatively less pay in real terms, while those who have been laid off, realizing the unlikelihood of getting a job in the near future, have to deal with the psychological and emotional stresses of the loss of self-identity that is associated with not having a job. Rifkin provides ample statistical evidence to support his claims. He also refers to the future as signifying the end of the middle class and highlights the severe social ramifications of this growing phenomena in some of the 'economically mature' nations.

In response to the declining number of jobs, some countries have tried to increase the numbers employed by introducing shorter working hours and job sharing. There are also a growing number of organizations that have shifted from employing full-time to part-time workers in an attempt to reduce their fixed costs and to avail of the growing pool of people who are out of full-time work and are at home. The latter activity has been an attempt to address one side of the earnings equation, i.e., to reduce costs and to optimize the use of technology. The other side of the equation, however, notably the distribution of the share of businesses' cost-cutting and productivity gains, has not been addressed with the same creativity or determination. The development of employee share option schemes has been some attempt at redressing the employer-employee ownership and power imbalances.

The social consequences of the mounting numbers of unemployed include increased crime and delinquency among young adults, a growing gap between the have and the have-nots, and a rise in fundamentalism as the disenchanted decry the modernizing forces of capitalism and its influence.

The declining number of young people who are getting jobs have a different attitude to work to those of the previous generation. They reject the workaholism of their baby-boomer parents and are inclined to take a very functionalist and detached view of their jobs. For them it is quite clearly a means to an end, and issues such as commitment, loyalty, and putting the firm first, do not feature as primary issues in their mindset. A job is a job is a job. They will perform it perfunctorily and when it no longer suits them they will move on. This is a very different work ethos to that of the baby boomers and it requires a different corporate culture and management style in order to optimize this new worker-employer relationship.

The social implications of the new reality regarding a potentially near workerless world are profound, and the manner in which nations will address the consequences of their productivity advances will provide an important statement about their communal values. The changing nature of work is thus both a significant economic and social issue for the next millennium. The adaptive challenge to both organizations and individuals regarding the role of work and management of the workforce calls for a new type of sensitivity from organizational management. This means that a new style of business leadership is urgently needed.

The Clash of Cultures

Samuel P. Huntington's recent book, *The Clash of Civilizations and the Remaking of World Order* (1996), has placed the issue of culture on the top of the intellectual and political agenda for the next century. People in businesses, however, especially as a consequence of globalization, have been grappling with cross-cultural challenges for centuries. In fact, the history of trade and economics is all about the conflicts and negotiations between cultures as a consequence of finding new trading routes and doing trade. It is only recently, through the advances in international communication, that a broad picture of the criss-crossing interrelation-ships of the world's cultures is emerging and making itself available for some kind of analysis. Cross-cultural issues are now also the daily currency for many business transactions and awareness of the need for cultural sensitivity has been heightened.

The benefit of Huntington's book is that he holds up the bigger picture of our multi-cultural world and discusses the behavioural patterns and power frameworks revealed by the major cultures as they stand at the end of the twentieth century. Amongst others, he addresses the themes of the shifting balance of power between nations, the relationship between power and culture, conflicts generated by Western universalism, the responses to the re-awakening of Chinese power, and the future of the West as its own civilization. While many people do not agree with his prognoses of an imminent clash of civilizations, he provides an extremely well-researched systemic view of the major world cultures and sets out what he believes to be their agenda. Although one might question several of the answers he proposes to cross-cultural challenges and dilemmas, he raises some critical questions. One of his key themes is that, despite the so-called homogenizing effect of globalization and modernization, there is ample evidence that the world is becoming more heterogenous. He discusses some of the consequent political and social implications. He does not address the potential impact on businesses. I intend to fill this gap by discussing specifically the potential impact on business organizations in Chapter 3, 'Strategic Focus for the Twenty-First Century.'

These then are some of the key realities facing us on the cusp of the twenty-first century. While some of these realities are by no means new, many of them present us with difficult value decisions. Recognizing the value-tensions that arise as a consequence of these new and difficult realities, requires global and cultural awareness, sensitivity, and the ability to take a systemic view. An interrelated world, where it is said that a butterfly can move its wings over Chile thereby causing tidal rain and winds over the China seas, requires systems thinking. Taking a systemic view provides us with an opportunity of possibly understanding what can and cannot be understood. This is a necessary insight for leaders and strategic planners alike.

Systems Thinking

Orienting businesses to the Adaptive Age and the new realities facing the world requires taking a systemic view. Adaptive challenges, by their nature, are systemic issues, and dealing with systemic issues requires systemic thinking. Everything should be looked at in the context of the larger system. Taking a system's perspective requires understanding and analysing the organization as a sub-system of an ever-larger whole. Organizations are part of communities, which are part of societies, which are part of towns, cities, states and provinces; which in turn are part of regions, countries, nations, continents and so on.

It is common knowledge that to understand frogs we need to study the pond. We know this because it is not possible to reduce nature to fundamental entities or essences. As modern science reminds us, the essence is the whole. Attempting to reduce things to their essence is not possible in an inter-connected world where the part reflects the whole and the whole the part. To understand a living phenomena it must be understood in its entirety, both in and of itself, i.e. holistically, and as it relates to the larger system in which it is embedded. The latter understanding is often termed environmental or ecological understanding or sensitivity.

To grasp the properties of the parts requires observing the dynamics of the whole. The whole is primary. Once one understands the dynamics of the whole, one can derive, at least in principle, the properties and the interactions of the parts. For the business organization, at its widest or most macro level, the whole is the universe, and at its more proximate level, the whole is the society in which the organization operates. Deciding the level of analysis and synthesis most appropriate to understanding the dynamics of the organization within its surrounds is not easy. Practice, insight, and intuition all assist in honing these skills. In business organizations, assessing the level of analysis is one of the challenges facing those responsible for the strategic planning process. This will be discussed at length in the chapters on the 'New Leadership' (Chapter 4) and 'Leadership and Strategic Planning' (Chapter 6).

Systemic analysis then is a continuous review of the relationships within a system. The new science informs us that a systemic perspective demands recognizing that all living phenomena are connected in a myriad of non cause-and-effect, and non-linear networks. These networks are in perpetual flux and motion. At best, the future behaviour of these networks can be estimated with some probability, but not with certainty.

Systemic analysis also requires a sensitive understanding of functions, roles, structures, and behaviours of the component parts or sub-systems of the greater whole. The advantage of systems thinking is that it enhances one's ability to see relationships, and to see how interconnectedness creates both the dissonance and harmony necessary to generate the beat and rhythm of any system. Further, systems thinking focuses our study of phenomena on their adaptive capacities not just their behaviour. For example, while it may interest us to observe the actual competitive behaviour of another organization, we are really far more concerned with the reasons that underlie its actions and how this behaviour may provide an indicator of its capacity to survive and thrive. Systemic thinking helps one to redirect attention to the organization's adaptive challenges and its adaptive capacity to respond.

Systems thinking is about taking a multi-perspective approach. Due to the interrelatedness and interdependence of the world, problems are usually embedded in complicated and interactive webs that cannot be viewed or dealt with from one single perspective. Multiple and competing perspectives are necessary to unveil the true nature and dimensions of any phenomenon. This assists in unveiling the true underlying causes.

Systems thinking emphasizes processes. It encourages the organization, notably the strategic planners, to pay attention to the processes by which the organization achieves its goals. In natural systems, structure is the natural manifestation of a process and should be left to form itself. Organizations should take heed of this natural inclination of living systems. Too often they spend enormous amounts of energy and time structuring and restructuring in order to improve or enhance their processes. This is placing the cart before the horse. Processes are the creative force of the organization. As with natural systems, structures that facilitate processes will automatically form where the processes are healthy and congruent with the organization's purpose. Organizations, therefore, should place emphasis on understanding and honing processes allowing the structures to form themselves.

Systemic problems, being integral by nature, require integrated solutions. Within a business organization, systemic problems often signal a need to revisit and review the organization's mission and its core competencies. Only when the organization feels that its mission and core competencies are consonant with one another, can it really formulate realistic, integrated solutions. As I shall argue throughout this book, identifying adaptive challenges through insightful and proficient systemic analysis, is the fundamental requirement of the new leadership and the heart of the strategic planning activity.

The Macrocosm-Microcosm Principle

An integral part of systems theory is the macrocosm-microcosm principle. This principle holds that in a living organism the characteristics and force-fields that exist in the whole system are recapitulated in every part of the system. For example, the DNA that makes up the human body, is contained in every cell of the body. Scientists need only a scrap of skin to determine the genetic makeup of the whole body.

In human organizations, on the micro-level, small parts of the system may contain different emphases in values, attitudes and behaviours from the larger organization. To a significant extent the smaller system will have imported most of the values, attitudes and behaviours of the larger system. Integrated systems exist in both harmony and tension between and among component systems. If a sub-system is out of sync with the larger system, the small system will experience conflict and distress. In response it will need to fight for survival. This experience of distress is one of the critical symptoms that signals the existence of an adaptive challenge.

Systems that are subsets of larger systems, therefore, provide a great deal of information about the larger system. We research small systems so that we might make inferences about the larger population or society.

The macrocosm-microcosm principle is an important concept for strategic management. Continuous evaluation of the larger systems within which an organization operates, provides important information about whether or not the organization is in sync with its environment. Checking out the values, attitudes and behaviours of the larger system can serve as a reality check for an organization's own values, attitudes and behaviours. Systemic analysis of values, attitudes and behaviours is the remit of new leadership.

The New Leadership

Many believe that the twenty-first century cries out for a new type of leadership. This is leadership that is in tune with the new realities and the value issues that are at stake. It is leadership that refrains from providing easy answers that prove to be a handful of empty promises. It is leadership that seeks out the real issues and challenges us to face the difficult problems. It is leadership that recognizes adaptive work for which there are no easy, painless solutions. It is leadership that encourages us to learn in new ways, and to persevere even when times are difficult.

The new leadership holds steady and confronts us with reality, especially when it seems difficult to digest, discouraging us from devolving into technical work. The new leadership is able to mobilize resources, to tackle tough problems, and develop people's adaptive capacities. The new leadership helps people clarify their values in light of changing realities. It helps distinguish reality from fantasy and helps resolve conflicts between new values and cherished, old values. The new leadership emphasizes interdependence, and encourages individual and communal moral agency.

The new leadership takes a systemic approach to grasping situations and understanding problems. It understands the dynamism and intricacy of the interconnectedness of systems and is able to take a multi-perspective approach, even where some perspectives might be in apparent conflict with one another. The new leadership understands that what we see depends on the way that we look at it, and that therefore multiple, equally valid, realities exist. These realities are not to be suppressed or ignored but held in dynamic tension as part of the pulse of life.

The new leadership embraces the 'elaborate dance' metaphor and the new reality of the co-creation of new steps. It realizes that the 'competition as war metaphor' is both anachronistic and inappropriate for the Adaptive Age. The new business leadership sees the organization as a continuous dance of energy, co-creating steps with its partners, who are often the competition.

New leaders recognize that concepts and theories are only limited and approximate. New leaders knowingly relinquish the relentless pursuit for absolute or correct answers and change their emphasis to arriving at ever more subtle questions.

Only this type of leadership can help us avoid repeating the blunders of the last century. We need this leadership in our nations, our societies, our institutions, and our business organizations. As businesses play an increasingly significant role on a global scale, we need prudential business leaders with socio-political as well as economic sensitivity. Every organization can and should exercise this type of leadership. Inability to do so will undoubtedly place the future survival of the organization at severe risk.

In the Adaptive Age, those responsible for the strategic planning function of the organization will be responsible for instilling this new form of leadership. The concept of hierarchical leadership is no longer appropriate, therefore part of the leadership function will be to empower, encourage, and authorize others to exercise leadership. A key strategic activity, which is paramount in exercising leadership, is the ability to distinguish between adaptive and technical work.

Adaptive Work Versus Technical Work

It was Einstein who expressed the concern that the perfection of means and the confusion of ends seems to characterize our age. I have termed this same phenomenon our preoccupation with technical fixes as opposed to dealing with our adaptive challenges. Ends are about values, while means are about the procedures and techniques used to attain those ends. Adaptive work is about understanding the ends to which we are called or driven and working on the value challenges that these might represent. Technical work is the procedural work that is carried out once the adaptive work has been done. Technical work is about means to ends, and when it comes to means, we usually can readily make choices. As our technical abilities have increased, we have become artful at increasing the number and forms of alternative means to ends, thereby giving us more and more choices.

Making choices about our ends or values, however, is a far more difficult enterprise. Most often these values have been hard-earned through lived experiences and are therefore deeply cherished. Values such as loyalty, traditionalism, honesty, freedom, justice, and independence are not readily altered or reprioritized. Values are also inclined to be held as absolutes. Take the case of loyalty. Where loyalty is held to be a primary value, any challenge to the idea that there might be instances where, say, honesty should take precedence over loyalty, (for example where a family member has committed a crime), would imply being disloyal. Finding a middle ground, or being able to hold competing values in tension is exceedingly difficult.

In a complex, interrelated world, where new realities are continuously emerging, the pressure on people's value systems is immense. One way to side-step dealing with value tensions is to avoid doing adaptive work. This is achieved by diverting all attention and energy into technical fixes, i.e. paying excessive attention to means rather than dealing with clarifying ends.

Being able to distinguish adaptive work from technical work is one of the key skills required of new leaders. This will be explored in depth in Chapter 2, 'Adaptive versus Technical Work'. The distinction between adaptive and technical work and its implications for business will be taken up further in the next chapter.

The New Face of Strategic Planning

There is currently a resurgence of interest in strategic planning. During the early 1990s strategic planning seemed to have lost its prominence as the highly skilled management technique devoted to out-thinking competitors and galvanizing the energies of internal resources. The wane in strategic planning activities was for good reason. In many organizations strategic planning had become a functional exercise that had lost the spirit of creativity and challenge on which it was originally based. Instead, the planning activity had devolved into a list of technical problems seeking solutions. As Peter Senge says in his book *The Fifth Discipline,* many strategic plans reveal more about today's problems than tomorrow's opportunities (Senge 1990:210).

For many organizations the strategic planning exercise failed to innovatively guide the organization in creating its future. Those dedicated to the firm's strategic planning process became fixated on analysis and the development of technical solutions. For more and more organizations strategic planning took on the role of grandiose budgeting. Over time the intellectual agility required of a good strategic planning process was forgotten or bypassed.

Recently, however, thanks to the publicized effectiveness of scenario planning, the strategic planning activity has attracted renewed interest. The role of organizations' strategic planners is being revisited, and innovation and creativity is once more being infused into its function.

It is often said that the world in which organizations now participate is far more diverse and complex than in any previous time. This alone bespeaks the need for a group of people who are left free to consider and ponder upon the effects of a complex, changing world on the organization. As I have already emphasized, the strategic planners of today need to be a new breed. They require new skills, new sensitivities, and a new systemic mindset. Their role in the twenty-first century is to exercise leadership. This will be achieved by identifying adaptive challenges and helping the organization to work on the value-tensions that these represent.

Summary

The world is moving into a new phase termed the Adaptive Age. This 'new wave' has reached swelling point and is about to crash on many shores. Some organizations will be able to surf this wave with a degree of equanimity while others will be tossed and tumbled as its growing momentum unleashes irreversible forces.

The interrelatedness of the world in which we live is becoming more apparent. Scientific, technical, and political-social changes reveal to us that we need to take a systemic view if we have any hope of grappling with the growing complexities of daily living. Business organizations have their part to play in addressing the problems of a seemingly fragmented world. The role of businesses in both creating new world realities and formulating a response to those realities is now centre stage. The realm of business decisions can no longer confine itself purely to factors that influence the economic bottom-line. Social, cultural, religious, demographic, and political issues need to be understood as the critical inputs and outputs of business processes.

In order to adjust to this rapidly changing environment, business organizations need a new kind of leadership and new leaders. New leaders need to take a holistic, pluralistic, and multi-cultural approach when exercising leadership. The new leaders of the organization are likely to be those, at least partly, if not fully, occupied with the organization's revitalized strategic planning processes. This cadre of 'new reality' thinkers needs to challenge the organization to face its adaptive challenges. They need to be attuned to the multitude of new realities that are continuously being unveiled, and they need to ensure that the organization, threatened by changing values and the pace of change, does not take flight into preoccupation with technical fixes.

New business leadership, made manifest through the efforts of the strategic planning process, is the topic of this book.

Key Points Raised in this Chapter

▸   The new era, the Adaptive Age, is in the making.

▸   The Adaptive Age is characterized by renewed focus on values.

▸   New types of leaders are needed in the Adaptive Age.

▸   The Adaptive Age is also characterized by new 'Enlightenment' thinking.

▸   A move to systems thinking is increasingly evident.

▸   There are new realities in the Adaptive Age which are influencing a shift in values.

▸   There is a distinction between adaptive and technical work. The Adaptive Age is switching the focus from technical to adaptive work.

▸   There is revitalized interest in strategic planning sparked partly by increasing interest in scenario planning.

SUGGESTIONS

■   List the new realities facing the organization, either directly or indirectly.

■   Evaluate the value changes that these imply.

■   Assess whether any of these value changes are in conflict with the values espoused and practiced by the organization.

■   Consider the extent to which the strategic planning function tracks new realities and identifies the new values that these might signify.

Further Reading

Capra, F. (1991) *The Tao of Physics*, Shambala, Boston.
Capra, F. (1996) *The Web of Life*, Doubleday, New York.
Daly, H.E. and Cobb, J.E. (1994) *For the Common Good*, Beacon Press, Boston.
Drucker, P. (1989) *The New Realities*, Harper Business, New York.
Heifetz, R.A. (1994) *Leadership Without Easy Answers*. Harvard University Press, Cambridge, MA.
Huntington, S.P. (1996) *The Clash of Civilizations and the Remaking of World Order*, Simon & Schuster, New York.
Senge, P.M. (1990) *The Fifth Discipline*, Century Business, UK.
Thurow, L.C. (1996) *The Future of Capitalism*, William Morrow and Company, Inc. New York.

Notes

1 The modern period is considered to have begun with the turn of the Seventeenth century. (Copleston, Frederick SJ. History of Philosophy Volume IV. Image Books. New York. 1994.)

2 'He intends only his own gain, and he is, in this, as in many other cases, led by an invisible hand to promote an end which was no part of his intention. . . . By pursuing his own interest he frequently promotes that of society more effectively than when he really intends to promote it.' (Adam Smith, *The Wealth of Nations*.)

CHAPTER TWO

Adaptive versus Technical Work

Leadership and Adaptive Work

The notion of adaptive work as distinct from technical work has already been introduced. These concepts, as used throughout this book, are based on the insights of psychiatrist Ronald Heifetz and his work on leadership at the JF Kennedy School of Government. He suggests that the kind of leadership required by the two types of work are different.

Heifetz situates his discussion of leadership primarily around the importance of identifying the adaptive challenges that society and organizations need to face. He suggests that often adaptive challenges are inappropriately identified as the need for more effective technical work. The consequence of misdiagnosis is ineffective leadership or no real leadership at all. For Heifetz, real leadership is about dealing with difficult questions that challenge the very nature of our meaning and value systems. Leadership for adaptive work entails the co-creation of a solution through meaningful participation of all relevant stakeholders. It does not mean that solutions or visions are imposed on others by powerful and charismatic leaders.

Heifetz' insights are based on his work with highly experienced but 'burnt out' community leaders. Many of them have lost their jobs or been rendered impotent in their ability to effect change, often for so-called political reasons. While studying their experiences, Heifetz arrived at a new understanding of the issues and challenges facing those who endeavour to exercise leadership. His interpretation of the causes of failed leadership is different from more conventional analyses. The latter tend to focus on the ineptitude or inadequacy of the leader in either formulating or implementing an appropriate change programme. The leader is usually diagnosed as having failed by having the wrong temperament, selecting the wrong programme, lacking political sensibility, lacking appropriate technical or industry experience, or being insufficiently thorough in the actual implementation of change.

In contrast, Heifetz approach focuses on the leader's ability to grasp changing realities facing a community or organization and to understand the value-tensions that these represent. Exercising leadership is not about coming up with easy answers, but rather about getting the community or organization to face its value-tensions and to make practical progress on resolving these tensions. Based on many discussions and interviews, Heifetz' has concluded that burnout or assassination occurs essentially for two reasons: either the leader tries to force changes and ignores the underlying value-tensions or, due to changed circumstances, the community feels that its cherished values are under threat and the leader does not address the resulting distress. Resistance to the leaders' vision or change efforts usually leads to their expulsion or 'assassination'.

The real measure of leadership is the ability to mobilize people to work on difficult questions that radically challenge their lives and affect their ways of making meaning. Using this definition implies that exercising leadership entails gaining appropriate trust from one's constituents and empowering them to recognize and deploy their own moral agency without encouraging dependency.[1] Exercising leadership means getting stakeholders to put their own shoulders to the plough in order to effect the adaptive changes that their community requires. It does not mean devising a vision on their behalf and then persuading them to be supportive and/or compliant. Leadership is about getting people to do *their own* work in an environment where they are suitably focused, encouraged and supported. Exercising leadership is essentially about encouraging others to do the adaptive work that they need to do.

While Heifetz' work is aimed at the socio-political arena, I propose to import these concepts into the socio-economic domain. The patterns and paradigms evident in society are mirrored in the business organizations of those societies. While their scale may be different, the same questions, problems, and challenges that confront political and social leaders confront business leaders. In all realms, similar values are under challenge, and similar work avoidance behaviours occur. Identifying the adaptive challenge is largely about understanding this phenomenon and being attentive to which values are under challenge and which work avoidance patterns are occurring. Helping people to engage in adaptive work is the work of leadership and, as we will explore in further chapters, a critical activity of the strategic planning function.

The Adaptive Age and Adaptive Work

The Adaptive Age is in the ascent and is characterized by a renewed focus on ends. The Adaptive Age heralds renewed attention to adaptive work and will serve as a correction to modern society's excessive focus on rational, superficial, and supposedly value-free methods of attaining ends. Ends themselves are now coming into primary focus. As ends are about values, this means that the world is refocusing on the importance of values. In other words, it is becoming more value-driven. The inclusive word, 'world', implies that the majority of nations and societies are presently engaged in the struggle for value clarification, regardless of their economic position or status.

A cursory review illustrates this current preoccupation with values. South-East Asia is a vivid example. Many South-East Asian countries are facing the reality that their social contract regarding an abundance of jobs and a continually increasing standard of living is now over. The notion that Asian capitalism influenced by the Confucian ethic had its own built-in check-and-balance mechanisms appears to have been mythical optimism. Thailand, South Korea, Malaysia and Indonesia, are all facing severe economic upheaval. This has precipitated a rethinking of the value tensions and trade-offs involved in their radical modernizing pro-grammes. The current fate of these countries illustrates the costs of unchecked capitalism operating at full throttle, cloaked by corrupt protectionism, and supported by political nepotism. Rapid moderniza-tion under these conditions has meant the loss of traditional values and widespread social and economic distress. It will be interesting to observe whether the secularizing power of modernism and capitalism prevails in the face of the backlash by disenchanted traditionalists and fundamen-talists. Power struggles around core values are likely to dictate the political agendas of these South-East Asian countries for some time to come.

China, 'the awakening giant', has its own dialectical political and economic programme to deal with, while Hong Kong is re-evaluating what it means to be a Chinese nation. Even the usually self-assured, inscrutable Chinese are presently being forced to carry out self-appraisal and self-scrutiny. Despite the size and latent power of the Chinese nation it is not impervious to the value-tensions involved in globalization and modernization.

The states of the former USSR are facing a variety of self-identity crises culminating in social, political, and economic disarray. A critical question has become: Who are we and what distinguishes us from other states that used to be part of the Soviet Union? Retrieving their self-identity is tremendously important if they wish to obtain international recognition and regional independence.

The creation of the European community, intended to weld certain European nations together into a coherent and competitive economic unit, has not had the homogenizing effect that the Euro-technocrats hoped. If anything, members of the European Community are more, rather than less, conscious of who they are and who they do not want to be. Italians will remain Italian by nature, as will the Spanish, the Portuguese, and of course the French. The increased attention given to Scotland striving for independence is just one example of the many value-challenges facing a supposedly united, United Kingdom.

Across the globe, differences in culture, values, customs, and behaviour have become accentuated in recent years. Just as the peoples of Europe are enormously different, so are the peoples of the various parts of the United States. People from Oklahoma and Kentucky have many different values from people in Massachusetts and California. These value differences seem now to be taking on greater significance. Simply being an American used to provide a US citizen with sufficient public identity, even though most immigrant groups privately preserved their ethnic identities. This is no longer the case. In the public domain being a US citizen is not enough. People want to be recognized as an Italian, Irish, African, or Jewish American.

Africa has always placed great emphasis on its tribal differences. Regrettably this rich and beautiful continent remains embroiled in conflict and ethnic confusion. It is a continent torn apart by its value conflicts. Sadly, South Africa's problems have not been ameliorated by the new power sharing between black and white. Many people, including Nelson Mandela, do not seem to realize that the real adaptive work is only about to begin. This adaptive work means dealing directly and incisively with the value-tensions that exist. These tensions are far more complex than issues of black versus white. Despite the new regime, the deep work of integrating different values and perspectives is not getting done. If anything, there appears to be a growing sense of denial of the true realities facing the country. South Africans need to redefine their self-identity.

Defining, claiming, and appropriating one's self-identity is a weighty preoccupation for many nations at present. Asserting one's self-identity means emphasizing what makes one different from others and laying down one's boundaries or limits. Appropriating one's self-identity begins with clarifying one's core values and thereby claiming what one finds meaningful and how, in the light of this, one makes meaning. These core values and meaning-making endeavours are made evident to the rest of the world in one's beliefs, customs, and behaviours.

A quick overview of the world on the eve of the twentieth century highlights the pre-eminence of struggles with self-identity and the reclarification of values. Table 2.1 summarizes some of these global tensions.

Just as nations, states, and societies are re-establishing their identities and redefining their values, so must businesses. The challenge is great as operations and relationships increasingly cut across every strata of every nation of the world. Businesses shape and form the countries and societies within which they operate. They are also shaped and formed by those nation-states and communities in an ongoing interweaving, intermingling, and interconnecting, that has created a highly intricate web of relations. Businesses are truly in the thick of it all. Understanding the value tensions of the myriad communities with whom they relate, especially when each has its own nuances and self-identity struggles, is a formidable task. For future survival every business depends upon astute leadership skills and perspicacious strategic planning. The adaptive challenges facing businesses are many and increasingly complex.

TABLE 2.1   Examples of nations' value-tensions

Country	Value-Tension
Afghanistan	Extreme fundamentalism vs moderate fundamentalism.
Australia	British colony vs Asian country
Canada	French vs British Canadian
Germany	West vs East German
Ireland	Irish state vs British/Irish state
Israel	Jewish Israeli vs Palestinian Israeli
Japan	Modern Japanese vs traditional Japanese
New Zealand	Commonwealth country vs Polynesian country
South Africa	Black South African vs White South African
United Kingdom	U.K. subject vs English, Scottish, or Welsh subject

Business Organizations and the Importance of Values

Today more than ever, business organizations need to refine and redefine their identity and value systems. They are called upon to articulate what they stand for and the ends to which they strive. They need to be more attuned and attentive to the identity struggles of the communities with whom they relate: customers, suppliers, employees, investors, and partners.

The new realities outlined in the previous chapter all have a direct impact on these identity struggles. Business organizations will not be able to assume immunity to the powerful new social trends that have emerged and are emerging. These include re-awakened desires for meaningful identity, clarification of moral and communal values, and a return to tribalism.

Customers have more product and service choices than ever before. As they become more sophisticated buyers they are more discerning about what it is that really meets their needs. They are no longer satisfied tinkering with various means to ends. They want immediate evidence that they are on the path toward achieving those ends. The end of consumption now lies in engaging in meaningful experiences that reinforce self-identity. If this does not occur, customers switch or exit. We have only to observe the challenges facing McDonald's to see the effects of consumer disenchantment when the organization's product or service no longer proffers meaning.

Suppliers increasingly desire symbiotic relationships with their customers. This mutually advantageous relationship requires integrity, concern, and attention. Most organizations realize that this is the only way to remain in business for the longer haul and are thus actively working at sustaining these networks. Working together to solve problems, and forming a web of relationships that augment the innovation and distribution process, is recognized as a critical ingredient to the competitive advantage equation. No longer are suppliers and customers considered to be separate identities. Nowadays their values and identities need to converge so that together they can make and deliver a congruent product or service to the end customer. This means that suppliers and their customers need to know one another well. They need to understand one another's values and comprehend how they each make meaning.

For the customer, the supplier has increasingly become an extension of the self. This means that the supplier is expected to assist the customer in attaining self-fulfillment. Self-fulfillment is tied up with self-identity and meaning-making. For customers and consumers, life has become less frivolous. They want to see and feel their progress toward ends. For businesses, especially from both an operations and marketing point of view, this has enormous implications.

Employees have also become more sensitive and attuned to their values. They desire a balanced life where the demands of a personal life are recognized and valued. They want their jobs to be meaningful and to be part of a meaningful life. Despite the shortage of jobs, their tolerance for unrewarding work has lowered. Many people would rather quit and take their chances with potential unemployment than remain in untenable work situations. Workaholism is no longer an honourable ethic. On the contrary, it is now denounced as evidence of work mania and seen as evidence of an unbalanced life.

Investors too have been encouraged to become more community conscious and discerning regarding their investment decisions. Although the bottom-line still holds primacy, other values such as environmental concerns and corporate social responsibility have become important criteria that influence investment preferences. In response, investment funds are increasingly under pressure to spell out their core values and to openly commit to the values of their clients. This makes an already complex and difficult investment climate even more difficult to circumnavigate. Sensitivity to changing environmental and client values is paramount if the organization is to survive into the future with any equanimity.

Businesses are also more dependent on alliances and partnerships. It is recognized that a network of strategic alliances is an essential part of staying alive and being able to meet the speed of changes demanded by a rapidly changing and modernizing world.

Values and relationships are the life-blood of living organisms. Businesses are arguably the most pervasive and powerful living organisms in our economically driven world. In order to fulfil their systemic role they need to wrestle with the political and socio-economic currents that are forming the world. Business leadership must become value-sensitive and value-driven because changing world values represent their greatest adaptive challenge.

Adaptive Challenges Facing Businesses

While each business has its own specific adaptive challenges to deal with, there are some general value-tensions that are affecting all businesses.

Grappling with the implications of these broad challenges only gets a business to the starting block. It does not resolve the specific and nuanced response required to focus the business in light of its specific mission and strategic goals.

The new realities described in Chapter 1 provide some orienting ideas with respect to the adaptive challenges facing all institutions and organizations at this time. It will benefit organizations to engage in one or a number of workshops aimed at shaking out the implications of the new realities as they see them. Discussion should focus on what the new reality means, what values and meaning-making implications it has for stakeholders, and what value-tensions it presents to the organization. Here are some suggested topics:

Globalization

Consider what globalization means to the other members of the organization's network, e.g. suppliers, customers, distributors, employees, investors, and partners. Set out in detail the perceived impact of globalization on these network members. Focus not only on the physical and material challenges but consider the emotional and psychological hurdles that this might present. What value tensions might the organization anticipate? What ways of making-meaning will this challenge?

Think Globally, Act Locally

This is a popular aphorism, but what does it really mean? Thinking globally yet being able to respond locally seems to suggest being able to hold both the global and local picture in perspective. It confirms the macrocosm-microcosm principle discussed in Chapter 1. It implies the need for an ability to move back and forth between international trends (the macrocosm) while being attentive to particular manifestations of the trends in the local environment (the microcosm). This capacity to move back and forth between the big and the small picture and to interpret the implications at these various levels is a critical capability for all organizations.

Thinking globally and acting locally has become an operating principle for many organizations, especially those who claim to be environmentally sensitive and corporately responsible citizens. Organizations are advised to take time to think through what this means to them. What value-tensions does this present to its network of members and to its immediate stakeholders? Who will have to change and how?

Modernization

This is another popular phrase that dominates the media, but what exactly does it mean to the organization? What is it about this phrase that matters to the way the organization does business? On which critical criteria of modernization does the business have to focus?

- Is it the rapidity of change of products and services? Does this mean that innovation is the most important factor?

- Is it the speed of technological advance that is the key driver? Does this mean that research and development requires a boost?

- Is it the social mobility of potential customers and consumers that needs to be intensely monitored? Does this mean that market research and marketing should be the preoccupation?

- Is it the speed and rapidity of communication that is most important? Should public relations and advertising now get the greatest attention?

- Is it the secularizing affect of modernization that holds the key to consumer behaviour? Should the organization dispense with all references to traditional values and loyalties?

- Is a new secular, modern, mission statement required?

Or, should the organization simply focus on all of the factors just mentioned? We know that this is hardly possible. The organization will need to decide which aspect of modernization it upholds, and then devote attention to doing that well.

Again it is suggested that the organization spend time clarifying where it sits within the 'modernization paradigm' and how it intends to play that tune. Which value-tensions does this present to the network members and how does the organization intend to make meaning in a modernizing world. (Some argue that we now live in a post-modern world. This was alluded to in the first chapter. For the purposes of the discussion here, one could replace the idea of modernization with that of post-modernism and pose similar questions.)

Multi-Cultural Workforce

Never before have organizations had to contend with such a multi-cultural workforce. The tide of emigration and immigration around the world has meant that nearly all institutions and organizations employ people who come from all corners of the globe. This makes employee management more complex. It also means that presenting an integrated and coherent organization to other members in one's network is more difficult. How do customers, for example, understand the identity of an organization whose telephone operators are African American, whose truck drivers are Mexican, whose sales staff come from all corners of Asia, whose technical assistants hail from Hungary, Romania and Latvia, whose administrative staff are essentially a mixture of American, British, and German, and whose CEO comes from Texas? Only by articulating, consistently demonstrating, and always reinforcing the organization's value system will this organization be seen as a unity. Being seen as a unity is important. Customers want to deal with individual people, yet they want a united organization to stand behind those people.

Consider your organization. What uniting value binds together its workforce? Where are the value tensions? How do customers engaging with this organization make meaning by resonating with this value?

Mentality of the New Workforce

As we discussed in Chapter 1, the future workforce of young people, now in their twenties, is very different in mentality to that of their parents and grandparents. The notion of work has a different meaning to them. They see work most clearly as a means to an end. Finding satisfaction in work is limited to the distinct and narrow role that it plays in their life. Few see work as being an end in itself, performed for its own sake. Friends, family, sports, leisure activities and surfing the net, are the pleasures they seek. Work is there simply to make those pleasures possible.

Further, this young generation spurns supervision. They want to be given a task and the freedom to get on with it. Once it is completed they would like reinforcement, praise, and affirmation. This gives them the confidence to complete the next task. They are not particularly interested in why they are doing something, the how of doing it takes precedence. When they get stuck they want immediate attention and guidance as to how to surmount the problem. Once the required rule, formula or heuristic has been explained, they wish to be left alone again to proceed with their assignment.

This new breed of workers is functionally task driven. They have typically been brought up with the increasing range of computer gadgetry and video games. Learning how and which button to press has become associated with knowledge acquisition. They are not inhibited by the black box, and seldom curious as to what happens inside it. The main thing is that it works and that it helps them to do what they need to do. Once one task is complete they will perfunctorily move onto the next thing.

This seems a rather harsh and critical assessment of the future workforce. Undoubtedly, it is a generalization. Recognizing the limits of generalizations, however, it describes the experience of many people who supervise this new breed, commonly referred to as Generation-X. The mentality of a Generation-Xer is very different to that of preceding generations. For the parents of Generation-Xers work is seen to be almost the most important thing in life. It defines who one is and gives one social status and recognition. For many it is an end in itself and Maslow's hierarchy of needs particularly reinforces the work/self-actualization theme that devoted workers are supposed to move towards.

Managing Generation-Xers requires a very different management style. Recognizing their independence and self-sufficiency is paramount. Generation-Xers are also very value conscious and attentive to what gives them meaning. They aspire to be individuals yet follow the young herd mentality. Holding this reality up to them is a lost cause. Treating them as if they are special and that their values are unique and meaningful is the only way to gain their loyalty. The Generation-Xers are environmentally conscious and actively campaign for Human Rights. Attention to values is important if one wishes to gain any commitment.

I highly recommend a detailed review of the organization's current and future workforce requirements. This should include thoughtful attention to the influence of Generation-Xers on the organization and consideration of the implications for task allocation and management style.

Environmentalism

Environmentalism is an important topic. I do not intend to repeat the many important messages that have been espoused elsewhere. Suffice it to say that business organizations need to think about where on the environmental continuum they wish to place themselves. Do they wish to be leaders, laggards, or somewhere in between? How does environmentalism challenge their values? What value tensions does this trend evoke? Can attention to environmentalism enhance the meaning-making activities of members within the organization's business network?

Corporate Social Responsibility

Like environmentalism, corporate social responsibility (CSR) has become another management, marketing, and media fad. Being real about CSR is much more difficult than talking or writing about it. Systemically, by their nature, businesses need to exercise social responsibility if they wish to survive. I discuss this in far greater detail in Chapter 9, which discusses leadership and business ethics. There I argue that the purpose of business is not to be socially responsible. Rather, the systemic goal of business is to reallocate economic and financial risk. Social responsibility is part of the way that a business achieves this goal.

I would recommend, however, that businesses consider the value tensions that their understanding of corporate social responsibility presents and consider how this influences their relationships within their business network.

The Role of Women

Few would deny that the role of women in the world and the workplace has changed significantly. Some would argue that this change has been insufficient. I would argue that the role of women is going to assume even greater significance in the future. Purely from an economic standpoint, women now play a major role as bread-winners in their households. World-wide the growth in jobs for women is escalating, while that for men is declining. Women are also aspiring toward higher education. Many are now interested in getting advanced degrees and MBAs. While the importance of women in keeping the economic and financial wheels turning is still not adequately reflected in the boardroom or in the political arenas, womens' voices are becoming louder and clearer.

From a business perspective this has some profound implications. Organizations are advised to consider:

- how this will influence their future workforce;

- how this might shape their future target markets;

- the impact of womens' influence on changing consumer values;

- their attention to womens' issues in articulating their mission and values;

- the role that women play in the organization's own decision-making process.

What value-tensions does the organization foresee? What is the impact on the other relationships within the business network?

Technology

Claiming that we are in the midst of a technological revolution is a tedious and over-used cliche. The emphasis on revolution focuses on the bigger, faster, smarter machines that we use as our tools to help us along the way. In fact there is hardly an aspect of life now where we are content to participate without the use of tools as aids. This reliance on tools has fast become a total dependence!

Instead of being caught up in the competitive spiral for ever greater investment in new and smarter tools, organizations would be well-advised to consider how the impact of technology is changing meaning-making. For example, what does it mean to consumers that they now stand in long queues in front of conveyor belts while waiting to pay for their purchases? How do they feel about the fact that to the till operator they are just another customer whose goods need to be packed in paper or plastic? What does it mean to suppliers that orders are placed via terminals rather than with 'good ol' Joe', person-to-person over the phone? What does it mean to consumers that they can increasingly buy whatever they need over the internet? Going to the store is no longer considered a social activity but a chore. How do employees feel about sitting for hours in small cubby-holes in front of screens? What does it mean to children that games consist of mastering computer gadgetry rather than learning to communicate and negotiate with their friends? What does it mean to those who deliver goods that every second of their driving and stopping time is monitored by computer? What does it mean to investors that they can observe the firm's AGM by video?

This is a simplistic and minute sample of some very large questions. It serves as a reminder of how technology has changed the way we live, how we form relationships, and how we are made to feel worthwhile, or not, as the case may be. Undoubtedly advances in the science and medical laboratories have improved the quality of life for many people. Regrettably many of these advances, for example abortion, test-tube babies, and cloning, also challenge some very deep values. We have come to learn that nearly all technical advances are accompanied by negative side-effects which we try to minimize or overlook as long as possible.

What business people know above all else, is that everything has a price. All decisions imply trade-offs; deciding which trade-offs to make is the most difficult part about decision-making. Investment in technology is a special case in point. Understanding how the use of technology affects values such as care, self-worth, loyalty, fairness, justice, equal opportunity, good health, and a balanced life are the big, yet overlooked, trade-offs. The benefits of advanced technology (e.g. speed and efficiency) most often eclipse these important values. Being strategic about investment in technology requires understanding these trade-offs and managing them proactively.

Customers and Consumers

In the light of the new realities, and taking cognizance of the many changing facets of the world, e.g. multi-culturalism, pluralism, Generation-Xers, the role of women, the role of technology, the struggle for self-identity, and the return to being values-driven, organizations are challenged to anticipate the profile and nature of their future consumers. What will these people be like? What will their values and interests be? What will they deem to be a meaningful experience? What will drive their buyer or consumption behaviour? Where and how will they live? What will make them want to engage with the organization? How will the organization compensate for the fact that physical location is no longer an issue? To what extent does the business need people in its own organization? What role does the organization play in the larger system? What value will this role serve?

These are some of the myriad questions that organizations should be asking themselves. Asking the right questions is a significant start. Attempting to answer these questions is extremely difficult. Becoming fixated on clear and definite answers is ill-advised because it encourages the organization to become reductionistic and devolve into technical solutions. Anticipating or planning for a future that provides for many complexities suggests the use of the well-known technique of scenario planning. Scenario planning lends itself to looking at the future from a variety of perspectives, especially when paradigms or patterns are all that can be identified. Scenario planning and its usefulness in outlining macrocosms and microcosms will be discussed in Chapter 6, 'Leadership and Strategic Planning'.

New Realities Must Shape Organizational Values

Many business executives insist that they pay attention to the adaptive challenges facing the organization and that they are attentive to organizational values. They will go to great lengths to explain how well they treat their employees, suppliers, and customers. They will argue that they are a value-driven organization which has spent many hours in refining their company's mission statement. Some of the 'excellent companies' described by Peters and Waterman (1982) in their book, *In Search of Excellence,* could well fall into this category. Many of these organizations, IBM for example, have lost their 'excellent' status. Paying attention to values and being value-driven must be consistent with the changing realities facing the organization. This was clearly not the case for IBM. They lost sight of the fact that the new reality is that we have become a PC based world. Most PCs now do what mainframes used to do. 'Big' as better, more reliable, and smarter was no longer a value for many of their traditional customers. Value-driven as they claimed to be, IBM refused to adapt to this new reality. It cost them 'big'!

Adaptive versus Technical Work

Organizations need to be continuously attuned to their adaptive challenges and to be ready to do their adaptive work. Adaptive challenges involve recognizing new and changing realities and the value tensions that these create. Identifying value tensions and making progress on aligning values to new realities is adaptive work.

Technical work follows from adaptive work. Technical work entails devising routine methods and procedures, which are aided where appropriate by tools that assist in integrating the required changes. Technical work is often an implementation of adaptive work. If it is done instead of adaptive work it may amount to rearranging the chairs on the Titanic.

I turn now to the story of Hunt and Blake, a business organization that failed to recognize and meet its adaptive challenges. Instead it favoured technical work. This is a true story.

CASE STUDY: HUNT AND BLAKE

Hunt and Blake was a well-established timber and building products business. They had been in operation for over one hundred years and boasted a list of loyal customers. Their main market was the farms and small towns of rural areas in northern England. They had served these customers with care and concern for many years. Their strategy had been good friendly service, high inventory levels so that customers rarely had to wait for stocks, and a very lenient credit policy. They claimed to be a values-driven company, and made every effort to be a socially responsible corporation and a good employer. Their employees were loyal, content, and considered Hunt and Blake to be their life-time employers.

By the late 1980s, Hunt and Blake managed over 80 outlets, spread hundreds of miles apart. They purchased timber products directly from plantations and, once purchased, these products were hauled to other locations to be cut, treated, or processed. Most of Hunt and Blake's timber products required very basic carpentry skills in order to be installed. Their other building products were purchased direct ex-factory from three or four regular suppliers.

Hunt and Blake's turnover exceeded $400 million. Their board and senior management comprised family members, all descendants of the founding partners. Middle management was selected from the local community and the criteria for selection were based on the ability to communicate Hunt and Blake's friendly, family values.

During the early 1990s, Hunt and Blake began to face what, according to them, was unexpected competition. Competing outlets appeared in some of their major selling areas. All of these competing suppliers were owned by the same large timber company whose original market had been limited to supplying railways, mines, and other large construction projects. Little by little Hunt and Blake's customer base was eroded. Soon they began to lose their most loyal customers. Investigation revealed that the competition offered lower prices, a greater range of products, and more DIY assembly items. Over a period of three years, Hunt and Blake's turnover dropped slightly and then stagnated, despite several price increases. In contrast, the competitor's business appeared to be booming, as they opened new, bigger outlets in the larger towns.

Hunt and Blake's management team decided to engage consultants to help diagnose the problem and to advise them on how they might stem the tide of deserting clients. After several months of analysis, the consultants made three key strategic suggestions. These were:

- more modern, easy to assemble products be stocked for resale;

- lower levels of inventory be held, incorporating a wider range of items; and

- a more stringent credit policy be introduced to reduce accounts receivable from an average of 90 days outstanding to a more tolerable level of around 45 days.

The rationale for these suggestions was that Hunt and Blake was unable to be price competitive with such high inventory holding costs and the long delays in collecting cash from their customers. The consultants claimed that the competitive prices of the competition were the critical reason for the decrease in sales and loss of market share.

With the support of the board and senior level management Hunt and Blake strove to implement these changes. They invested in a new inventory management computer system and appointed a new director of purchasing. They hired a number of credit control staff to monitor the levels of accounts receivable and set new inventory holding levels. They revised their pricing structure, lowering the prices on some of the most successful product lines. Despite all of these efforts, the organization was unable to stem the loss of customers, which was followed soon by the resignation of disgruntled employees. After the fifth year of falling profits, the reluctant families sold their stockholdings to the competitors. Hunt and Blake, the faithful, honourable building supplier, was no longer in existence.

This story is a typical example of an organization and its consultants failing to realize that a company faces an adaptive challenge. Struggling managers and quick-fix consultants focus on symptoms rather than on underlying causes of problems. They seek relief in technical solutions to what is actually an adaptive problem.

The adaptive challenge for Hunt and Blake was that the values of the world were changing. Even farms and small country towns were progressing to a modern world. In a modern world, the traditional values of family and loyalty find it difficult to compete against the rationality of the market place. The company's adaptive challenge was to recognize the new reality and the ensuing value-tensions. Customers now wanted to shop in modern, efficient, price competitive stores, with a wide range of comparable products. The new reality included a world of increasing customer sophistication, where customers want to have choices, and where they can consciously exercise their buying power. Instead of loyalty, price and comparability have become the greatest purchasing discriminator. In the past, people may have appreciated wood products that required at least some basic carpentry skills to install. Modern people do not have the time, and/or no longer wish to make the time to develop their carpentry skills. The traditional approach to doing business (concerned, friendly, and familial), is also perceived as anachronistic in its ways, especially if it fails to clearly communicate that it has embraced modernity.

Hunt and Blake were facing an adaptive challenge of major proportions. The culture of the surrounding society had changed from one which held traditional values to one in which modernity dictated new marketplace values. As an organization in that society, they would be expected to reflect those same values. Their founding values, based on a traditional culture, were no longer the key values held by their customers. Their staff, chosen for their sympathy with the traditional values, were caught in the culture clash. They had identified with the organization's value system, and resisted new modern ideas and systems. Their values, attitudes, and behaviour remained embedded in the old ways. They feared that the company was becoming like their non-caring, money-grabbing competitors, but they also realized that modernity was an inevitable trend. Over time, many of them were modernizing their values too. Not knowing how to bridge the gulf between old and new values, the distress was too much. Many of them left the firm.

Hunt and Blake and their consultants did not begin by identifying the 'new reality' and the values at stake. What makes identifying the adaptive challenge so different from other techniques of analysis is the emphasis on values and meaning-making. This approach rests on the belief that the first work to do is to identify value-conflicts and tensions and to clarify the value changes that are needed. To proceed with technical work (e.g. introducing new systems without re-examining values), is, at best, premature. The value analysis may reveal that systems are not the critical issue anyway.

Hunt and Blake needed to orient the organization to the new values of the changing world. Management and staff should have been challenged to adapt their values to the new values of society. This required the exercise of a kind of leadership that the Hunt and Blake management team did not perform. Management and staff should have been included in discussions of the 'new world out there' and what it meant for their business. Everyone should have been engaged in discussions about how they might bring their values of family and friendly, long-standing commitment to the new world of modernity, price competitiveness, and efficiency. There should have been discussions on what they, as an organization with united goals, had to learn and what compromises they could and should make. Management and staff should have been encouraged to be innovative in coming up with a strategic solution, which would still give them unique meaning, purpose, and the essence of sustainable advantage. Without this emphasis on value analysis and meaning-making an organization is tinkering with superficial, short-lived quick-fixes.

Identifying the adaptive challenge is the heart of any work on strategic change and is prior to strategic analysis. It is critical to the achievement of an effective transition from the old to the new. Hunt and Blake resisted doing their adaptive work and fell into the trap of chasing technical solutions to solve adaptive problems. The demise was inevitable.

Indicators for Adaptive Work

As the story of Hunt and Blake indicates, a major task of organizations is to identify their adaptive challenge. Many people and organizations fail to do this well because they misperceive the nature of the threat. They then either downplay its significance, ignore it in the hope that it may go away, or treat it as the need for a technical solution.

Identifying the adaptive challenge is a difficult task. It requires investigating the combination of symptoms and diagnosing the ailment. The constellation of symptoms must be considered in the context of the world in which the firm operates. Knowing which combination of factors to attend to, and understanding in which context they signal an adaptive challenge, requires a sound knowledge of the business. Management must consider the organization's intended mission, how it intends to achieve that mission, and the values which it holds in common with its customers, suppliers, employees, and community. The starting point should always be a systemic analysis (discussed in detail in Chapter 5).

The need for adaptive work is usually signalled by a combination of factors, not one factor alone. What gives these factors their relevance rests on the extent to which they act as sensors to the firm's external environment. For example, sales revenues will always be a critical external sensor, but the combination of falling sales, plus the loss of customer loyalty, plus excessive hostility between organizational departments or divisions, is a clear signal that something is wrong with the system. Another example is the combination of a growing number of bottlenecks in the production or service process and the growing amount of overtime spent by staff in trying to mitigate their effects, often to no avail. This is a clear sign of a system in trouble. Problems of this nature require more than technical solutions to resolve them.

Another indication that a problem requires an adaptive rather than a technical solution is that the problem persists. People today are very good at solving technical problems. Part of growing up and learning to survive is finding ways and means of getting things done (or to avoid getting things done). People are resourceful. They can be incredibly innovative when it comes to circumventing problems that might discomfort them or impede their progress. Provided that members of an organization have adequate resources and sufficient autonomy, technical problems are usually resolved relatively quickly. People thrive on problem solving and generally prefer making themselves important through their ingenuity rather than their inability to resolve something. Therefore, when what appear to be technical problems are not getting resolved, there is usually something more at stake. Repeated or drawn out technical issues that never seem to be addressed properly, or appear to be an ongoing nightmare, are a clear signal of a system in distress. Regrettably, many management teams and consultants simply impose another technical solution over the old one in an attempt to quell the problem rather than resolve it.

Identifying the adaptive challenge also requires knowing when something needs to be changed rather than fixed. The strategies required to change something are significantly different from those required when something needs fixing. Change implies a development, a transformation, and a reordering of values and priorities. Change demands a new or different perspective, new or different attitudes, and new or different behaviours. It affects the entire organization to a greater or lesser degree and it requires a great deal of energy.

Fixing something is finite. It is rarely transformative and seldom affects the whole organization. We fix things, not people or living systems. The organization can fix its machines, fix its inventory levels, and fix its leaking delivery containers. It cannot fix its mission, its culture, its staff's attitudes, its inaccurate management information system, and its inappropriate computer systems. It must change them. Wherever the word and the concept 'fix' does not seem congruent with the problem being experienced, it suggests probing whether this is an adaptive rather than a technical challenge.

While there are no hard and fast rules for distinguishing between an adaptive and a technical challenge, there are some key indicators. A crisis or emergency usually signals the need for a technical response. Adaptive work might follow, but the first thing that must be done is avert the crisis or limit its consequences. If the organization is on the verge of bankruptcy, for example, every possible technical solution must be adopted to 'save the patient.' Only afterward is an underlying adaptive challenge considered.

Another indication of the need for a technical solution is a specific, short-lived problem. For example, if a plant is experiencing quality problems with its new hydraulic pump, this might be a purely technical problem, resulting from lack of expertise or inappropriate production equipment. Here a technical rather than adaptive response is appropriate.

A key signal that an organization is facing an adaptive problem is that the challenge comes from the outside. It arises as a consequence of a change in what it means to the customer, supplier, community, or competitor, to engage with the organization. Changes in the behaviour of any of these stakeholders may indicate that the organization no longer 'means' to them what it used to mean. This may occur because the organization is no longer delivering on its values or because stakeholder values have changed. For example, if customers find that using the organization's products makes them feel attractive, then the underlying values include feeling good, self-appreciation, and self-care. If they stop purchasing these goods, the questions to be asked include whether the products no longer provide this feeling (technical fix), or whether the values of feeling good and self-appreciation are still highly held by this customer group (adaptive challenge).

Since organizations are microcosms of the society in which they operate, to succeed they need to reflect some of the values and patterns of behaviour of that society. As in the case of Hunt and Blake, when the values of an organization and its stakeholders are out of sync, adaptive work is needed.

Another signal that an organization is facing an adaptive challenge is when competitors do new things in new ways. For example, the Body Shop introduced soaps and perfumes made from natural oils, sold in reusable plastic bottles. This was a clear sign of the growing change in values toward natural products and increasing concern for the environment. The old value of deriving status from the purchase of expensive perfumes, full of artificial ingredients, sold in non-biodegradable glass bottles, has been radically replaced by the value of consumer responsibility for the earth. Status is now bound up with being a concerned citizen rather than having an attractive and expensive smell.

Further signals of adaptive challenges include changing distribution of wealth amongst members of society, shifts in population trends, changing demographics in existent and potential target markets, changing consumer buying behaviour (e.g. shopping at night rather than during the day or shopping by computer rather than in person), altered channels of distribution (e.g. the sale of CDs at the convenience store), and changing methods of payment (e.g. customers no longer pay by cash or cheque, but prefer delayed terms of payment).

While adaptive work is usually precipitated by challenges that come from outside, there are some internal signals that indicate that an organization is experiencing some challenge which they have not yet identified or addressed. The following internal signals usually indicate adaptive rather than technical problems:

- a change occurs in the balance of power between functional areas and senior management in the organization;

- tried and tested organizational operating procedures are no longer effective;

- existing skills within the organization are rendered useless;

- excessive emotion surrounds technical problems that do not seem to get fixed;

- complexity grows in getting the organization to clearly identify and follow through on achieving its goals;

- congruence is missing between the mission of the organization and its market image;

- the management team feels a loss of control;

- repeated unethical behaviour occurs;

- severe conflict erupts between members of senior management.

Step One in Adaptive Work: Identifying the Adaptive Challenge

Having recognized the need for adaptive work, the organization's adaptive challenge must now be identified. As discussed in Chapter 1 and the beginning of this chapter, the organization should be continually recognizing and acknowledging its new realities. New realities typically signal or imply new or changed values. Responding appropriately requires changes in attitudes and behaviour so that adaptation is possible. It demands new perspectives, unveils new paradoxes, and reflects back new or different behavioural paradigms.

Identifying the nature of the adaptive challenge typically begins with perceiving that something is discordant between the organization's values and behaviour and that of the environment. A sense prevails that a discrepancy exists but its nature and form are not yet clear. There may be a number of signals indicating that the problem is likely to require adaptive work. These signals must be examined to see what they indicate about the new reality.

Identifying the adaptive challenge requires insightful investigation into the true causes. Regrettably many organizations, like Hunt and Blake, become distracted and fixate upon the symptoms. Disgruntled sales staff, for example, will quibble over the pay when really they are embarrassed to work for an organization that has a poor image in the local community.

Diagnosing this correctly means that the issue must be examined for the value that it contains. Perceptive probing might reveal that the organization has neglected its image with regard to community responsibility, its corporate mission no longer inspires confidence, or its customers find better product integrity elsewhere.

Accurately perceiving the true nature of the adaptive challenge is the most difficult part of the adaptive work. A diagnosis naturally dictates the cure; so too with identifying the adaptive challenge. Organizations are advised too take time and to engage the creative and systemic thinkers amongst their staff in identifying the true nature of the problem that they face.

Once an adaptive challenge has been identified, reality testing is required. This entails engaging employees, customers, suppliers, members of the community, and even competitors in discussions concerning the newly perceived reality. Reality testing is the attempt to grasp the problem fully by repeatedly clarifying the values and meanings that are being challenged. Rushing the reality testing process, a frequent tendency by those anxious to get on with the more comfortable technical work, will prove detrimental in the longer run. Time is needed to elicit any conflicting views or challenging perspectives. When those engaged in the process feel that the adaptive challenge has been clearly defined and articulated, adaptive action can begin.

Step Two of the Adaptive Work: Reorienting Values

Since the identification and articulation of the adaptive challenge involves clarification of the value issues at stake, the next stage of the adaptive work entails changing an organization's attitudes, beliefs and behaviour to make them consonant with the values of the new reality. This part of the adaptive work means addressing the conflicts between the values that people currently hold and the new values that are required. It includes coaxing, encouraging, challenging and motivating management and employees to clearly and unambivalently embrace the new reality. It implies developing appropriate responses so that the new reality can become an integral part of people's perception of the future. This is the type of adaptive work that should have been carried out within Hunt and Blake. Reorienting values should always take precedence over any other work.

Adaptive work includes distinguishing between illusion and reality, resolving internal conflicts, and placing the perceived difficulties of the new reality into perspective. It demands innovation and learning. Often the most difficult type of learning is the unlearning of old values, attitudes, and behaviours. Adaptive work requires transformative learning that affects the core of who one is, rather than just what one does. It implies finding new meaning in new ways of being. Adaptive work is the deepest and most powerful learning that there is.

One example of adaptive work is that which the recovering heart attack patient faces. Once the technical work in the form of appropriate medical care has been done, the patient has to face his or her new reality. This will entail a careful diet, attention to rest and exercise, cutting back on work, and generally reprioritizing elements of his or her lifestyle. New meaning has to be found in performing new activities or in doing old activities differently. This work is not easy, but it is essential. Ignoring the new reality will inevitably result in a relapse, or worse still, no second chance.

Mergers and acquisitions are prime examples of adaptive work in the business environment. Especially for the acquiree company, corporate life often becomes a whole new reality. Different corporate values may be expected or imposed. New philosophies regarding care for employees or customers may radically challenge existing ones. Different codes of ethics, reward systems, or management styles may conflict with deeply embedded and valued current modes of existence. Due to people's resistance to change, it is not surprising that so many acquisitions and mergers fail miserably to deliver on their promises.

Adaptive work is difficult because it radically challenges values and the manner of meaning-making. Our values affect the way that we screen reality and the way that we construe our own reality. Our value system is part of our 'software of the mind'.[2] It is part of our mental program that can only be altered through active intervention. This intervention occurs as a result of acknowledgement, choice and action on our part. What we see and what we perceive depends on what we care about. Due to this perceptual bias, we often only see what we expect to see, hence our need of those who challenge us and who raise varying points of view. The consequence of challenge is reflection. Reflection makes us re-examine and reconsider our view of reality. Adaptive work is about challenge, reflection, and action. All three activities are necessary, and appropriate action is the hardest task of all.

Why we have to do adaptive work

Aristotle raised the issue of whether we ever really live in the present. He highlighted the fact that we actually live between the future and the past. The future is always arriving and the present is almost immediately the past. This implies that we don't really exist in the present! The present is a continuous response and integration of the future as it arrives. Adaptive work is about living in the present, a present that is continuously embracing and absorbing the future. Inability to do this threatens survival.

Adaptive work, however, is not only about survival. It is certainly no less than survival, but holds promise of a great deal more. Adapting is not just about coping, accepting the status quo, or submitting in silent resignation. It is also about creating the future.

There is a saying that you can either make the future, take the future, or, if you sit somewhere in between, you will never know what hit you. Some organizations, notably Coca-Cola, Microsoft and Toyota, are key change agents which create the future to which the rest of us respond and adapt. Watching the makers of the future, it behoves us to develop our own response. Our actions also play their part in framing what the future will look like. An example of 'future-making' comes from the world of computers. Until fairly recently there were two 'worlds' in software, the Mac-world and the DOS-world. Microsoft, the developer of DOS-based products, has taken the initiative, and by outplaying Mac has now made it a Windows world. Microsoft, plus its collaborators, has thus 'made' our software future, for a while at least. Apple, the Mac developer, has not yet defined a response that encourages confidence in its future. Some say that Apple may be considered one of those 'in between' organizations. Organizations that vacillate between trying to embrace the future, while simultaneously clinging to traditional values and behaviours, are unlikely to survive. Like Hunt and Blake, they will lose sustained vision, meaning and purpose resulting in a loss of shareholder, customer, and employee credibility. Their demise is inevitable and due to their propensity for ostrich-like behaviour, they truly will never know what hit them.

'Taking the future', on the other hand, does not signify inaction. It entails the explicit recognition that the future is being made all around us and that we need to change our values, attitudes, and ways of doing things if we are to thrive. We are called to play our part, although the fundamental parameters may be set by others. Adaptive work thus involves proactively responding to the new future. It is about creating, forming, and negotiating one's own future within the larger framework of the world. Adaptive work is not only about surviving, but surviving well. It is about thriving and about having and making choices.

Organizations that do not develop a robust capacity for doing adaptive work will not thrive. In the longer term, like the dinosaur, they are likely to die. Some organizations only face their adaptive challenges when they have reached a critical condition. New chief executives are brought in to provide the intensive care. Regrettably, the treatment is often drastic but the disease is not cured, as hundreds of thousands of laid-off employees will testify. Eager new CEOs, turnaround teams, and management consultants tend to overemphasize the technical problems rather than reorienting the organization toward its adaptive work. As a consequence of their intervention, the organization might move from the acute to the chronic stage of ill-health, but the need for adaptive work will remain. The story of Apple Computers provides an excellent example of adaptive problems that will not go away.

Resistance and Disequilibrium

People resist change. A perceived discrepancy between what is and what will be, causes discomfort; so with organizations. Discomfort occurs within the organization in response to a sense of disequilibrium. In an effort to dispel this feeling, it is common for people to deny the need for change and to engage in activities that serve to resist change. Resistance may be conscious or not conscious and may result in overt or covert behaviours. The degree of denial and resistance reveals the extent of the disequilibrium being experienced. It also provides an indication of the organization's experience with change and its capacity for adaptation. Organizations that radically resist change are usually not at the vanguard of competitive activity.

Organizations typically have three ways of dealing with disequilibrium. They either ignore it, adopt work avoidance techniques, or embrace the changes by doing the necessary adaptive work. Japan Inc.

provides a good example of an organization which has rapidly and effectively responded to adaptive challenges. They have been so effective at this, that their core competence has become doing adaptive work. Japanese organizations excel at taking a very macro approach to their systemic analysis, getting to grips with the new realities, and researching the underlying value issues at stake. A well-known example is their leadership in the small, fuel-economic car market, which they created very shortly after the first oil crisis in 1979. American car manufacturers insisted that Americans would not swap their big, swanky Chevy's for smaller, less swanky, and more cost-efficient vehicles. Wrong! The Japanese grasped immediately that values would change. As we have seen, since the beginning of the eighties economy has become a far more important value to most consumers than swankiness. Since then the Japanese ability to adapt to new realities has increased in speed and potency. Western organizations often boast about how the Japanese are indebted to the West for teaching them so much. In fact, we have a lot to learn from them!

There are also organizations that tend to ignore disequilibrium in the hope that it may prove to be a temporary discomfort. IBM, prior to the arrival of Louis Gerstener, stubbornly believed that the disequilibrium they were experiencing was both temporary and insignificant. Despite falling profits, loss of market share, and repeated criticisms from their customers and shareholders, IBM adamantly insisted that their ship was not for turning.

Other organizations, rather than do the adaptive work that is required, adopt work avoidance techniques. This usually takes the form of fixating on technical solutions and being preoccupied with technical work.

Technical Work

Technical work is work that focuses on doing, rather than being. Technical work, which emphasizes what we do, should follow from who we are. Technical work should thus be consonant with adaptive work. Focusing on technical work when one should be doing adaptive work is similar to rationing the number of trees that may be cut, rather than educating the community to find alternatives to wood.

Technical solutions lend themselves to routine problems. Once problems have become routine they are part of the way of doing things and no longer require adaptive work. Confusing technical work with adaptive work is akin to routinely treating a smokers' chronic bronchitis with antibiotics, but never helping them to stop smoking. It provides temporary relief followed by even greater distress as the bacteria develop resistance and the lungs break down. Continued insistence on a technical solution will not make the larger problem go away and will result in a life and death situation. The same situation occurs in organizations that persist with technical work when adaptive work is required.

The Importance of Technical Work

Technical work is naturally a vital part of business. Technical work itself is not a bad thing. The concern is that technical work must be appropriate to the problems that are being addressed. Once the adaptive work has been done, and the strategies and tactics for adaptation have been developed, then the organization's competence in technical work will come into play. The technical work that follows the adaptive work will be the final follow-through of the strategic response to the adaptive challenge. Efficacy of technical work lies in the appropriateness of its timing and its congruence with the adaptive work required.

Examples of technical work used as substitutes for adaptive work abound. These include:

- repeated reorganizations and restructurings;

- the creation of new positions with elaborate titles e.g., 'Co-ordinator of Multi-Disciplinary Work Initiatives';

- frequent board-room reshuffles;

- appointment of high profile directors to the board;

- aggressive merger and acquisition activity;

- proliferation of new programmes and new products;

- long and frequent meetings;

- excessive attention to co-ordination of activities;

- attention towards minority groups given excessive emphasis and media hype;

- frequent periods of downsizing;

- price cutting and regular manipulation of prices;

- manipulation of reward systems;

- excessive emphasis on procedures rather than processes;

- revision of accounting policies and balance sheet window dressing;

- high investment in technology relative to the technology component of the organization's business strategy;

- continuous refinancing, or revising of the organization's capital structure;

- repeated redefinition of the target markets being served;

- undue emphasis on personnel policies and procedures;

- implementation of new layers of management.

Some kinds of technical work are more easily identified than others. Every type of organization in every type of industry has typical kinds of technical work. Banks upgrade their cash machines, accountants revise their audit manuals, software companies update their software, and retailers revise their purchasing and inventory policies. It may be an idea to review your own organization and to consider the typical technical work that gets done. Having done this you might consider how often your organization elects to perform technical rather than adaptive work.

The Failure of Business Leadership

Business leaders often come by that title as a consequence of notable business achievements. Notable business achievements are high growth, exceptional profitability, positively publicized merger and acquisition activity, and remarkable turnarounds. Regrettably, however, few business leaders are able to sustain long-term success. The book, *In Search of Excellence*, by Tom Peters and Robert Waterman, is a prime example of how many businesses are accoladed for excellence founded on strategic short-term success and excessive attention to technical solutions. A significant number of the '*excellent*' companies mentioned in their book failed to keep in tune with the new realities, resisted their adaptive challenges, chose instead technical mode, and were saddled with the old style of leadership. Old style leaders tend to repeat behaviour that has been successful in the past without responding to the new realities. They fail to understand the nature of adaptive rather than technical work and do not give the work back to the people. Even though the eight attributes that Peters and Waterman describe as characterizing excellent companies remain apt 15 years after their book was written, there is a critical dimension missing: the key orienting activity of leadership. This orienting activity includes monitoring the new and changing realities and presenting those challenges to their organizations as the primary strategic work. Deploying technical solutions to address adaptive problems will only work in the short term. The organization will disappear long before the adaptive work does!

ATTRIBUTES OF EXCELLENT COMPANIES

- A bias for action

- Close to the customer

- Autonomy and entrepreneurship

- Productivity through people

- Hands-on, values driven

- Stick to the knitting

- Simple form, lean staff

- Simultaneous loose-tight properties

Adapted from Peters, T.J. and Waterman, R.H. (1982) *In Search of Excellence*, Harper & Row, New York.

Howard Schultz, the CEO and rising star of Starbucks, a Seattle-based coffee retailer and chain of coffee stores, insists that it is only values that matter. In his new book, *Pour your Heart into It*, he discusses the importance that he places on integrity, passion and instinct. He claims that values, relationships, and loyalty are undervalued commodities in many American companies. Schultz discusses what it has meant since the organization has gone public. According to him, it has been the humbling realization that every quarter, every month, and every day, he could become a servant to the stock market. He has learned how artificial the stock price is, and asserts that it neither reflects a true value of the company nor of its management. He has decided to make decisions that he believes are right for the company and not the stock price. He is intent on holding up the reality of the importance of values.

Being oriented to values is more than being values-driven. the former pays attention to the meaning-making that underlies values. It is about knowing what ends those values serve. Being values-driven means having some explicit values to which the organization can orient. This does not mean that they are good values or the right values. Being values-driven is necessary but not sufficient. Schultz, contrary to the 'excellent' companies, appears to understand this important distinction.

Summary

The defining work of leadership is identifying the adaptive challenge and holding up this reality to the organization. The adaptive challenge usually implies value-tensions that occur between new realities and the organization's present values. Exercising leadership means orienting the organization to the new values and mobilizing them to shift and adapt.

Identifying the adaptive challenge is strategic work and is prior to the development of strategies. The strategic planning function should be engaged in recognizing new realities and interpreting the adaptive challenge. The adaptive capacity of the organization is enhanced if it is continuously confronted with new realities which serve as its focus of orientation.

There is a need for technical work; however, in most cases adaptive work should be prior to technical work. Organizations that fixate on technical work in preference to performing their adaptive work will struggle to survive in a rapidly changing world which is refocused on values.

Key Points Raised in this Chapter

▶ New realities usually imply shifts in values. A change in values presents an adaptive challenge to the organization.

▶ Leadership is the ability to identify adaptive challenges.

▶ Adaptive work entails orienting people to the adaptive challenges so that they can respond to changing realities.

▶ Performing technical work when there is a need for adaptive work is detrimental to the health of the organization.

▶ Leadership is the activity of mobilizing others to do their own adaptive work.

▶ Strategic work is about understanding changing values.

▸   Strategic analysis is about evaluating stakeholder values.

▸   Indicators exist for adaptive work.

▸   There is a time for technical work.

SUGGESTIONS

■   List the major adaptive challenges faced by the organization over the past three years. Assess whether these challenges were addressed with adaptive work or whether the organization chose to respond with technical solutions.

■   Review the process that the organization uses in order to do its adaptive work. Have these processes been effective? If not why not?

■   List the types of technical work that the organization is regularly engaged in.

■   List the overt and covert ways in which the organization deals with distress. Compare this to the list of typical technical work that the organization performs.

■   List the current points of distress within the organization. Could these be indicators of distress for value-tensions that have not been addressed?

Further Reading

Daloz, L. *et al.* (1994) *Common Fire*, Beacon Press. Boston, MA.
Heifetz, R.A. (1994) *Leadership Without Easy Answers*, Harvard University Press, Cambridge, MA.
Hofstede, G. (1997) *Cultures and Organizations: Software of the Mind*, McGraw-Hill, USA.

Notes

1 These themes are discussed in detail in *Common Fire*, by Daloz *et al.*

2 A phrase coined from Geert Hofstede's book, *Cultures and Organizations*. Here he refers to cultures as mental programming, and includes symbols, heroes, rituals, and values as constituting the concept of culture (page 7).

CHAPTER THREE

Strategic Focus for the Twenty-First Century

Setting an Agenda for the Next Millennium

Organizations should long ago have begun working on their agenda for the next millennium. Developing this agenda requires them to be both proactive and reactive. Having spent the opening chapters discussing the reactive issues to which organizations must respond, I turn now to the proactive aspect of agenda setting.

Being proactive means deciding first on what, how, and with whom the organization is going to co-create its future. To do this effectively it is necessary to understand the explicit and implicit forces that are ushering in the new age. This new age, which I have dubbed the Adaptive Age, is marked by a renewed focus on values.

Changing values creates value-tensions. These usually precipitate organizational adaptive challenges. Business leaders within organizations need to take a systemic perspective in order to unpack what these adaptive challenges mean for the organization and what kind of adaptive work they imply. Business leaders must decide how they might exercise leadership and what the new strategic focus should be. This type of strategic activity presupposes the need for at least one or more people who are permanently responsible for the future strategic direction of the organization. The people who typically spend time thinking about the organization's strategic direction are commonly referred to as the strategic planners. Sometimes the strategic planning activity is undertaken by a group of people permanently engaged in the strategic planning process. In other cases, people are called together from time to time to form a strategic planning working committee. Once the work is done this group is disbanded and its members continue with their usual business functions. Either way, it is essential that the organization include people dedicated to monitoring the organization's adaptive challenges. I would recommend, however, that the organization appoint a group of people permanently committed to and continuously engaged in the organization's strategic work.

Strategic Agenda

The first work of the strategic planning activity includes drawing up a strategic agenda. I would propose that the strategic agenda includes at least the following strategic aspects:

1 Decide on the nature and form of the strategic planning activity. The nature will set the objectives and the form will set out how and by whom these will be achieved.

2 Consider the macro-environment, the specific implications of globalization, and the impact of a multi-cultural world.

3 Prepare for the new face of capitalism.

4 Evaluate the implications of new 'life' and 'business' root metaphors.

5 Identify all significant stakeholders and determine their values. These values need to be continuously monitored and revisited in depth over time. Consider any current and future value-tensions that exist or that may develop.

6 Evaluate present alliances and consider the need and potential benefits of new ones.

7 Establish or refine the process for seeking out strategic growth opportunities and identifying strategic growth threats.

The sub-agendas that describe in detail how each major agenda item will be achieved will naturally depend on the type and size of the organization. The components of the strategic agenda will now be developed one-by-one.

Nature and Form of the Strategic Planning Activity

A revitalized interest in strategic planning makes sense in light of the rapidly changing, complex environment in which organizations have to compete. It also makes sense in view of the multiple nuances that affect every aspect of business today. For example, the idea of segmenting a market and then targeting its supposedly most profitable portion, is simplistic in the extreme. Understanding consumer markets nowadays requires a range of both 'hard' and 'soft' skills that need to be attuned to the macro and micro-cultural environment. The ability to move backwards and forwards between the larger and the more immediate picture requires a certain amount of expertise and time. While many people may have the expertise, the time element is usually the limiting factor. To do this task well there must be time for detailed awareness, composed reflection, adequate assessment, and deliberated responses. Few people in line positions can take this amount of time away from running the business. It is also true that people engaged in operations are often too close to see changes in their competitive environment. Having people who can take the time to do this, provided they do not disappear into an ivory tower, can be extremely beneficial. I advocate that an organization employ a dedicated strategic planner, or where appropriate, a skilled planning team.

Defining the Strategic Planning Activity

Here are some guidelines for defining and/or refining the strategic planning activity. The strategic planning activity itself will be discussed in greater depth in Chapter 6.

Step 1

Decide on who is responsible for the strategic planning leadership of the organization. Consider the trade-offs between a dedicated person/team and part-time members.

Step 2

Decide on the nature of the strategic function itself. What does the organization need it to do so that the organization can meet its adaptive challenges? How best might this be achieved?

Step 3

Decide on the systemic approach required so that the organization can evaluate and understand the values of its stakeholders and identify stakeholder tensions that exist or may arise. (Details of how to carry out a systemic analysis are discussed in the next chapter).

Step 4

Evaluate alternative strategic planning methods and approaches that might be adopted, (e.g. forecasting, contingency or scenario planning methods). Formulate an approach that appears to meet the organization's short- to medium-term requirements.

Step 5

Strategize on an appropriate reporting and feedback method between those engaged in strategic planning and other members of the organization. Be sensitive to the need for strategic planners, line management, and staff functions to work well together. Remember that in networks there are no hierarchies.

Relevance

The nature and form of the strategic planning activity sets the nature and tone of the organization. Its objectives, the personalities of those involved, and the manner in which it shapes and is shaped by the activities of the organization serve as a clear statement about the organization's values. The nature of the strategic planning process and the way in which strategic ideas are communicated and influence the business, clearly indicates to those inside and outside of the company how carefully and seriously the company understands its role within the larger system, i.e. the community or nation.

The strategic planning activity is one of the most sensitive, if not *the* most sensitive process within an organization. Everything about this activity requires thoughtfulness and integrity. After all, the strategic planning process is the organization's claim not only to what it is, but what it would like to become.

The Macro-Environment, Globalization, and A Multi-Cultural World

This is a big heading to swallow all in one gulp. How can any one person, or even a team of people, get their arms around the complexity and mounting implications of a rapidly changing, interconnected world. Our global, multi-cultural world is now consciously engaging in, and working with, the connections that are adding to the complexity and speed of change. The new science tells us that living networks continuously move and perpetually change. This provides us with some explanation of what we actually see happening in the world today. The characteristics phenomena of living organisms have not changed over the centuries. The change lies in our awareness. Growing awareness of who we are and how we are constituted gives us greater power to participate more proactively and creatively in shaping our future. It is this self-awareness that the strategic planner/s need to foster.

The Role of westernization

A superficial, Occidental-oriented glance at the world would appear to indicate that all countries and their markets are converging towards greater westernization. This includes evidence of a strong penchant for capitalism. Peering through these western-tinted lenses has led many western nations and western-based business organizations to believe that they are in the driving seat. They erroneously believe that western culture dominates and that globalization will be led by the West. Wrong! This non-reflective hasty assessment of world trends is greatly misleading. Undoubtedly many countries are striving to modernize their political, social, and economic systems. And, undoubtedly, they have looked westward for their cues as to how the West has done it. Furthermore, on the surface, many countries may appear to be importing the western, modernizing machine lock-stock-and-barrel. A closer, and less western-centric perspective reveals, however, that most countries are taking an eclectic approach to importing modernization. While they wish to modernize, they wish to do it their own way and to colour it with their own brand.

Oriental countries are well known for their ability to syncretize philosophies and cultural systems. Their approach to modernization is no less syncretic than normal. They will modernize with an eastern twist and their capitalistic systems, once these settle down, will undoubtedly operate in eastern style. While the characteristics of their own cultural stamp on capitalism is not that clear when it comes to Africa and the Latin American countries, their desire to modernize their own way is starting to show through.

Political scientist, Samuel Huntington, in his book, *The Clash of Civilizations and the Remaking of World Order*, argues that cultural identity now drives global politics. His central theme is that culture and cultural identities shape the patterns of cohesion, disintegration, and conflict in the post-Cold War world (Huntington 1996:20). He also claims that westernization is in decline, and that its continuing universalist pretensions are bringing it into conflict with other nations. He suggests that in the post-Cold War world, the most important distinctions between people are cultural, rather than ideological, political, or economic. The most basic question that both people and nations are attempting to answer is: Who are we? They are answering that question by referring to the things that mean the most to them. Huntington argues that their values, shaped by their tribes, ethnic groups, religion, language, history, customs and institutions, are what is most important to them.

Huntington's book offers a detailed historical, political, and cultural review of the major civilizations of the world. He identifies what he calls civilization faultlines, which he believes will result in the future clash of civilizations. He discusses the waning influence of the West, which is contrary to most westerners' grandiose beliefs. He proposes strategies for the west to better preserve its own strengths and culture in light of the growing influence of other civilizations.

While Huntington is not without his critics, his well-researched thesis provides some very thought-provoking questions. What he has done is to place the issue of culture centre stage in the western political arena. He does not, however, discuss his thesis' implications for businesses. Since politics and business radically influence one another it behoves business managers to reflect on the issues that he raises. Managing businesses that operate on an international basis, and even the smallest of businesses is exposed to the effects of internationalization, we need to become far more culturally sensitive. This is one of the vital tasks of those responsible for the firm's strategic planning.

The popular old practice of 'environmental scanning' does not suffice for an adequate understanding of global cultural complexities. The very term smacks of a quick check of the horizon to identify menacing clouds. It also alludes to something up in the air, away from the earth, thus rendering environmental issues distant from what is going on in the day to day life of the corporation. The new term that I propose is 'systemic analysis'. This term orients organizations toward understanding that they are part of an infinite number of systems. This requires them to understand the nature of systems and to define the systems that are most significant to them.

A more detailed discussion of systems and systemic analysis will continue in the next chapter, while the need for 'deep' reviews of cultural issues and the development of cross-cultural empathy will be elaborated upon in Chapter 6.

Relevance

The better the organization is able to grasp and work with the knowledge that it is a microcosm of the whole, the more powerfully it will be able to manage its global, multi-cultural connections. Once strategic planners realize that there is nothing occurring 'out there' to which the organization should respond, but that everything is connected 'right here', the more effective will be their analyses and the more potent their strategic advice. By educating and attuning the rest of the organization to this phenomenon, management will become more effective in *identifying change signals and value-tensions.*

Working systemically, management will start to see that what supposedly is changing out there, is really happening here under their eyes, undoubtedly culturally contextualized and nuanced. It could have been seen, maybe even anticipated and worked with to strategic advantage, if management had been appropriately attuned and aware at the right time. In sum, the organization is a virtual mini world, that must live and improvise in real time as it bounces, vibrates, resonates, and participates in time to the beat of the rest of the world. Businesses are shaped by what is happening and shape what happens. Knowing and working with this phenomenon enhances the organization's capacity to adapt.

Understanding that all roads to modernization do not lead to New York, London, or Rome, but to myriad countries, capitals, and cities, demands great cultural and ethnic sensitivity to a multi-cultural world. This capacity will guide the organization in nuancing its strategy globally and locally. It will enable management to shape its marketing strategy to be ethnically appealing, it will assist operations in making the appropriate production trade-offs, and it will enhance management's capability for dealing with a multi-cultural workforce.

The New Face of Capitalism

As an economic system, capitalism has undoubtedly beaten other economic systems hands down. Once the coercive forces that insisted on their existence were disempowered, communism and socialism have been discarded with haste and a certain amount of disgust. With few exceptions, every modernizing country is modelling its economic system along capitalistic lines. Capitalism as an economic system transcends class and social status, bringing new dreams and new hopes to the disenfranchised and dispossessed. Capitalism holds the allure of 'anything is possible' and 'anything goes' and is seen as the door to uninhibited opportunities of wealth and freedom.

Inspired by the inflated promises of capitalism, some struggling political regimes are trying to have their cake and eat it. Economically they stimulate, support, and personally benefit from the unbridled freedom of market forces. Through nepotism, cronyism, and protectionism they still hold significant central power over the economy. This political-economic dualism does not work as evidenced by the plight of the economies in Malaysia, South Korea, and Indonesia. Will the next explosion be in China?

In the more modern economic nations the honeymoon with *laissez-faire* capitalism as an economic system is over. For many the dreams of new freedom and equal opportunity have been dashed. The economically advanced nations are under pressure to find a more socially and politically congruent form of capitalism. Political rights and economic rights need to be synchronized. There is little point in pretending political democracy and human rights if those who cannot win power in the market place are disempowered and disenfranchised.

The Inevitable Iron Cage

The problem of the secularizing influence of wealth was foreseen by the Protestant reformer, John Wesley. Despite his exhortation to Christians to gain all they can, save all they can, and grow rich he realized that this would result in a decay of religious values. Riches, and the pride, anger, and love of the world it brings with it, are the inevitable results of the industriousness and frugality that Methodism promotes.

Sociologist, Max Weber, concluded his seminal work, *The Protestant Ethic and the Spirit of Capitalism*, on a similar note. He anticipated that the pursuit of wealth, stripped of the religious and ethical meaning that Protestantism tried to give it, would result in a preoccupation with external goods. The pursuit of wealth would no longer lie on the 'saint's shoulders like a light cloak, freely thrown aside at any moment' but would become an 'iron cage'.

According to Weber, people need a set of ideas which legitimize their orientation to the world and provide meaning to goals. He called this 'rationalization' and suggested that we try to master reality by means of increasingly precise and abstract ideas. We also try to reach particular practical ends by increasingly precise calculation of adequate means. Rationalization is thus a means-and-ends schema for mastering everything, especially the non-rational or the inexplicable. On a practical level it provides norms, sanctions, and motivations for living in the world. The motive for rationalization derives from the need to overcome the irrational and the meaningless in life and to establish some sense of meaning and order.

For Weber, the Protestant spirit of *inner worldly asceticism* produced a culture whose central values were

- to seek mastery over the world;

- to seek mastery over other people who were seen to be prone to sinfulness, wickedness, sensuality and laziness;

- to seek mastery over the self by controlling impulses that would lead to immoral or excessive behaviour.

Weber claimed that this set of cultural values emerged uniquely from the later forms of Calvinism in the late 1500s and early 1600s. This religious culture, he argued, provided the seedbed for the formation of the spirit of modern capitalism. While Weber acknowledged that other material, technological, economic, and political conditions were needed to make modern capitalism a possibility, he believed that the key ingredient was the cultural and religious values that legitimized capitalism to society. It would be interesting to know how Weber would evaluate the growth of capitalism in non-Protestant countries, especially Asia.

Weber also discussed the scientific character of modern western culture and the prestige that was attached to science. He questioned the universal significance and value of science and remarked that its claim to be the only possible form of a reasoned view of the world has brought culture into ever greater senselessness. According to Weber, the grandiose claims of science has not culminated in the emancipation promised by the Enlightenment, but rather in 'senseless hustle in the service of worthless, self-contradictory, antagonistic ends.'

The Iron Cage – A Signpost to Hell?

In the dusk of the twentieth century, we are now facing the anticipated *and* unanticipated consequences of the rationalization process Weber described. Many claim that America in particular, has become a secularized, consumerist society, devoid of meaning and on the brink of nihilism. Despite our insistence on freedom and individual rights, it would appear that we did not choose in freedom to be where we are today. Our striving to make sense of the world has extended itself to conquer and master the unknown. It has inspired ever further rationalization in order to dominate and explain away the nonrational, leading to ever greater, and more complex spirals of disenchantment and demystification of the world.

This determined and dogged attempt to demystify the world and rationalize the nonrational has come at a price. Increased mastery of the world has led to greater and greater abstraction from the real, the concrete, and the unexplainable elements that are inherent in the lives of humankind. Weber saw this as the inevitable price of modernity. Modernization brings with it the erosion of meaning, the endless conflict of polytheistic values, and the threat of the iron cage of bureaucracy. Rationalization makes the world orderly and reliable, but it cannot make the world meaningful.

Western society is the leading example of modern capitalism which has taken the notion of rationalization to its extreme. The market system, as the organizing principle of capitalism, dictates the prevailing social order. This social order is both the embodiment and the expression of freedom. Those with wealth have the power. Creation of wealth is the supreme motivating force of a modernizing, secular society.

Weber was pessimistic about the future of the capitalist spirit. He believed that the original religiously inspired spirit of capitalism has fled the iron cage. Abstraction and excessive reliance on science, rather than the humanities, has resulted in the fallacy of misplaced concreteness. Demystifying and disenchanting the world through methodologies dependent on empirical data and scientifically observable facts and validation procedures, denies the reality of the world. In reality, the world is, and always will be cloaked in mystery.

This phenomenon of abstraction and reliance on science, as Weber predicted, has led to increasing secularization of western society and a focus on individualism. According to many religious, social, and political critics, the result is a gaping hole in moral life; a trend which has been both stimulated and reinforced by the practice of vigorous rationalistic capitalism. Capitalism that was originally devised as a means to an end has become an end in itself. For moral, cultural, social, and political critics, and even enlightened economists, present day religious, social, and economic life in most strongly capitalistic countries bears ample evidence of the iron cage syndrome.

Capitalism with a Human Face

In many of the developed countries a distinct disenchantment with capitalism exists. Adam Smith's 'invisible hand' that would supposedly act as a corrective to excessive self-interest and self-serving capitalism, has, many claim, remained invisible. Governments have been chastised for not adequately playing their part in keeping a prudent balance between allowing freedom in the market place and protecting the weak, and the disadvantaged.

In some circles there is a growing cry for capitalism with a human face. This form of capitalism which pays attention to the growing disparities between rich and poor, is one tempered by concern for society and the public good. In these circles one hears clamours for Corporate Social Responsibility, employee profit sharing, and investment in community projects. Inspired by this growing trend some confident corporate managements shun the powers of the stock markets by investing 'dividend money' in improving the environment and sponsoring various welfare programmes.

The prominent MIT economist, Lester Thurow, in his book, *The Future of Capitalism*, critiques the current state of capitalism, (the US in particular), and highlights the need for a powerful integrating ideology; something which he claims is lacking in both democracy and capitalism. As he points out, neither democracy nor capitalism have any focal point, common goal or common good. They both stress the individual and not the group. Workers are encouraged to maximize their own incomes, firms are expected to maximize their own profits, and voters to vote for their own self-interest (Thurow 1996:159). As he sees it, in the US version of capitalism there are no duties and obligations. Only market transactions exist.

Thurow uses the metaphor of 'punctuated equilibrium' to discuss his perspective on the current state of the world. A period of 'punctuated equilibrium', a term taken from biology, is a time when the environment suddenly changes. The dominant species dies out and is replaced. During this period evolution takes a quantum leap; everything is in flux, disequilibrium becomes the norm, and uncertainty reigns. During this period, he explains, a new game with new rules requiring new strategies will emerge. Some of today's players may be able to adapt and some won't.

This viewpoint is similar to that of William Hutton, who critiques 'Conservative capitalism' in his book, *The State We're In*. He claims that rampant capitalism has led to a fracturing of British society, increased income inequality, and a general abandonment of society to the market. He castigates governments who believe that free markets are the solution to economic difficulties. Hutton claims that the capitalist market system has bound society together by an amorality which is built on exclusions.

Roger Terry, in his book, *Economic Insanity*, also claims that the economy dictates our morals – what is good for the economy is supposedly good for us. He states that the problems of capitalism are systemic in nature, i.e. the system is at fault and tinkering with the system will not alleviate its problems. He believes we must devise a new system.

The list of critics of the capitalist system seems to grow daily. Even the master of self-interest, investment guru George Soros, has reportedly criticized the self-interest perspective of the market place. Even he anticipates substantial changes in the future.

Will the growing discontent with capitalism usher in a capitalism with a more human face? Some questions which organizations might pose include:

- How might the face of capitalism change? Could there be a new version of socialist-capitalism?

- Will a more public morality impose some constraints on free market forces?

- Will the visible hand of the government play an increasingly significant role in the redistribution of wealth?

- Will there be a new impetus in encouraging the creation of new wealth?

- Will new legislation be imposed that levies a 'social tax' on for-profit organizations?

- Will accountants come up with new ways of accounting for externalities?

The End of the Middle Class

Lester Thurow, amongst others, also foreshadows the end of the middle classes. He claims that western capitalism in its current form, is eroding the very class that spawned its development in the first place. As Robert Heilbroner puts it, in *21st Century Capitalism*, capitalism destroys the authority of so many institutions that in the end it even turns on its own. The bourgeois who 'invented' capitalism are thus having their own capitalist foundations rent assunder as capitalism vitiates the very assumptions on which it is based.

Thurow and others provide evidence of the growing disparities between rich and poor and illustrate that there are essentially two classes left: the rich and the poor. The former middle classes have, by and large, become poor. They are the ones who have shouldered the burden of making the rich richer and of subsidizing the poor. It is the middle classes who are paying the price of political ambivalence and stop-go policies. It is the middle classes who are losing middle management positions and jobs. It is the middle classes who are taking pay cuts and who are working longer hours. It is the middle class who are being ousted at the time of re-engineering programmes or as a result of mergers and acquisitions.

From a business perspective the idea of a dwindling middle class is startling. For most organizations, these are the people who consistently fulfil their role as active consumers. These are the people who support new products and read and respond to marketing campaigns. These are the people who are the sophisticated buyers that encourage organizations to innovate and differentiate. These are the people who take time to use the products of the market place to best effect. These are also the people who provide many organizations with their management teams. These are the professional people who serve as doctors, lawyers and accountants, who sit on school boards, who support charities, and who maintain neighbourhoods. It is the middle classes, according to social philosophers from Aristotle to Max Weber, who are the backbone to any polis or society. Without the middle classes we are back to the Dark Ages.

Growth of the Non-Profit Sector

Another visible phenomenon is the growth of the non-profit sector. Interestingly, the growing number of non-profit organizations is not just evident in America and Europe, but in Asia, Africa, and South America. According to Peter Drucker, non-profit organizations have a great deal to teach businesses (Drucker 1992). Their activity in the market place is forging new bonds of community; is encouraging new commitment to active citzenship and social responsibility; and is promoting public values. People who work for non-profits usually are committed to a mission and have a passion. Non-profits do not base their strategy on money but use the mission as their guiding focus. There is usually a well-defined actionable mission statement, and there is high motivation and productivity of knowledge workers. The governance of non-profits is usually better than for-profits as board members believe in the mission, are engaged, and meddle. They keep a wary and concerned eye on the activities of their organization. Their allegiance is to the mission, the members of the organization, and its role in society.

For-profit business organizations need to ask themselves what the growth of non-profits and their mission and management style might mean to their businesses. Some critical questions include:

- What role are not-for profit organizations fulfilling that for-profit businesses might fulfil?

- How might they partner with these organizations to strategic effect?

- Will non-profit organizations take business away from for-profit organizations? If so, how and why?

- Will consumers of the future prefer to deal with not-for-profit businesses and, if so, how might for-profit organizations mitigate against this?

These important questions should stimulate investigation into the causes of the growth of the non-profit sector and the needs that they are satisfying.

Relevance

Organizations should be deeply concerned with the forces that are changing the face of capitalism. They need to consider its effects on customers, employees, investors, and the larger community. Some factors to consider include:

1   Does the organization want to be a leader or a follower in shaping the future economic system and the profile of an ideal 'capitalistic' enterprise?

2   How might the organization indicate to its stakeholders that it is keeping abreast of the changes in stakeholder values?

3   Are there any new and different strategic partnerships that might be formed?

4   What new legislation affecting market practices might come into effect?

5   How might the organization deal proactively with new pressure groups?

6   How is erosion of the middle classes affecting the profile of customer and consumer markets? How will this affect products and services?

7   What value-tensions might new trends create for investors who support the old system?

8   Are there any new performance benchmarks that might be set which reflect a more balanced view of corporate performance?

9   What value-tensions might these new trends create within the organization itself?

10   How might the organization contribute towards re-enchanting the world?

New Life and Business Root Metaphors

In Chapter 1, I discussed the emergence of new root metaphors. Root metaphors or integrating symbols represent the ideas, feelings, and images that groups use to characterize or describe themselves. Different cultures tend to associate themselves with different types of metaphors. Some delineate more masculine and others more feminine features. There are some root metaphors that seem to transcend culture. An example is the idea of the world and the human person being characterized as machines.

We no longer live in a 'machine world' where the machine metaphor is adequate to describe our actions and responses. We have also recently dispelled the notion that the world is a construct made of building blocks that can logically and rationally be deconstructed and reconstructed based on our mastery of a hierarchy of rules. We are learning that our cause-and-effect analysis no longer unlocks the door to many of the universe's secrets. We realize that this approach at best gives us but a smattering of knowledge of what is at stake.

We have also been awakened to the fact that the idea of 'certainty' is a human construct. Nature is teaching us that nothing is absolutely certain or predictable. All of life coexists within a network of probabilities and possibilities which we can potentially influence through increased self-awareness. The only certainty to which we can cling is that nothing is absolutely certain, (except that we will leave this world as we know it). We have been told for aeons by sages, prophets, and philosophers, that our attention should be turned towards our attitudes and intentions. Even the supposedly value-neutral, empirically-driven scientists are telling us the same thing.

This new awareness alerts us to the fact that moral injunctions are also strategic ones. Live in the present, be attentive to the here and now, and focus on the quality of relationships – these now assume more than moral meaning. It reminds us that living a good life requires being self-aware and strategic. Not only for individuals, but for the organization: living a good life means conjoining moral and strategic perspectives.

New Business Metaphors

The life of business is also now being described by new metaphors (see Table 3.1). The old metaphors of war and game, citadel and fortress are no longer appropriate. Business organizations are now seen as a network of relationships that can best be described as a 'hub' or 'node' within a complex web of universal relationships. The concept of 'standalone' can no longer be used as a working metaphor as it is too far removed from reality to be meaningful.

Business as War

The often used metaphors of 'war' or 'game' are particularly inappropriate for business in the Adaptive Age. The war metaphor implies that the world of business is 'a killing field'. It assumes that business is a never-ending battle that always culminates in winners and losers. In a war, the idea of win-win or sharing the spoils does not readily come to mind.

War language includes words like 'death', 'destroy', 'beat',and 'out-manoeuvre'. This type of language is hardly life giving! The war and battle metaphor is bound up with notions of dominance, damage, and destruction. War language deliberately emphasizes desperate measures where everything is at stake.

TABLE 3.1 Root metaphors

Old	New
Machine	Organism
Hierarchy	Network
Citadel/fortress	Hub/node
War/battle	Dance
Sport/game	Jamming

Preparing for war calls for desperate measures. In that context attention is focused on the opposition's weaknesses. One's own weaknesses are concealed as much as possible or are understated. Preparation for engagement includes acting with bravado and practising the battle cry. Long hours are spent to buttress the war machinery and prepare the troops. Supposedly inept soldiers, who fail to take on the enemy adequately, are readily disgraced and given their walking papers. Attention to individual feelings and needs are ignored. Discipline and self-sacrifice in the interests of future glory are demanded in the greater interest of surviving each battle. Each battle is considered to be a strategic milepost in winning the war. The Geneva convention does not apply – prisoners are not taken. Kill or be killed consumes the business war mentality.

People who live preparing to make war live a tense and anxious life. Many employees would undoubtedly describe their experience at work as being in a continuous state of war. Each day is experienced as a battle. This kind of atmosphere hardly encourages creativity or generosity. People who live in a perpetual state of war fear the loss of their lives. This might be experienced as a fear of a loss in status, fear of authority, fear of power, or fear for their jobs. These many fears, combined with long hours of sloging in the trenches, belong to the age of the 'Technical Fix'. In this instance, if the battle is being lost, the focus is on changing the weapons by developing new and more powerful ones. Unfortunately the enemy is doing the same.

In the age of the Technical Fix, all challenges are treated as a call to arms. Technical work treats a challenge as something to be overcome, to be suppressed, made to surrender, or dominated. Technical work is aimed at finding a winning solution that will effectively 'destroy' the problem. The idea of holding something in creative tension does not exist when carrying out technical work. Technical work denotes mastery and domination.

Business as a Game

The business as a 'game' metaphor is also no longer appropriate. Business is not a game. It is serious. It is not played from time to time. It is not dependent on the weather or the disposition of the players. It is a continuous and ongoing event. There is also no independent umpire to mediate the close line calls.

Games are intended to have distinct winners and losers. No one really values a draw. Most often a draw is viewed with disappointment by both spectators and players. By contrast those who win are looked upon as heroes, masters, or super stars. Fear of losing this superior status motivates them to win some more, with ever more dedication and defiance. The game soon becomes a blood sport, and thereafter takes on the characteristics of a war. Think of the recent behaviour of famous boxers, ice skaters, not to mention soccer hooligans.

Preparing for a game usually means 'dressing up', donning a different outfit, and selecting one's 'weapon'. This indicates that something different, even special, is about to happen. While wearing the 'game' outfit, players are expected to assume competitive positions, to perform different manoeuvres, and to attend to different rules. Game tactics focus on exaggerating one's own strong points while protecting and concealing weaknesses. Strategies focus on anticipating the other team's moves, blocking and blindsiding them where possible.

Real life seems to be suspended for the duration of the game. Once the game is over, 'normal' life resumes as do daily life behaviours and tactics. Many game players never get off the 'playing field' and for them, however, life itself becomes a desperate game. In these instances, the game soon assumes the life-and-death proportions of a series of battles.

The game metaphor is nowadays inappropriate for business. Business organizations do not operate in suspended time, but operate within real, normal time. Some, regrettably, do not try to do so. They are the exception rather than the rule.

Businesses may play to the whistle, but that strategy is usually short-lived as they have to deal with the consequences of their short-termism. Trying to set different rules for the business 'game' which are not consonant with the political, social, cultural, and environmental arenas of the world is also proving to be a dead-end strategy.

A new metaphor that is replacing the 'game' is that of 'jamming.' This describes how jazz players come together and make music through improvisation and playing off one another. Sometimes music is made by a soloist, followed by one or more musicians as they participate in creating the evolving melody. No particular tune has been planned in advance; the melody and harmony simply emerges.

Business as an Elaborate Dance

In the Adaptive Age a useful new metaphor for business is that of a 'dance.' This is no ordinary dance. It is an elaborate and sophisticated dance. It demands being in tune with both the external and internal environment. It is a competitive dance, where participants aspire to be the best and to look their best. Participants focus on their own strengths and their contribution to the overall performance. They are concerned with what they might 'bring to the party', and how well it might fit in with what others might bring. Participants are seeking harmony. This includes the expectation of a certain amount of appropriate dissonance.

The language associated with dance is 'rhythm', 'being in tune', 'moving well', 'getting the beat', and 'being a good partner'.A dance is both serious and fun. It is invigorating, challenging, and life giving. A dance is disciplined and creative. It requires strength and agility. It benefits from the integration of both the masculine and the feminine.

Good dancers execute their steps to perfection; they also experiment with new ones. A dance is real-time and creative. It invites participants to use the beat and tempo in new and interesting ways. A creative dance, in particular, calls for rapid responses and improvisation. It means taking risks and making mistakes and sometimes sitting out a tune. It also sparks the challenge of trying again.

A dance is purposeful and requires commitment. Few people abandon a dance midway. Even those tired and footsore are energized by the motion and movement that is co-created by all elements (dancers, spectators, and the band), present at the dance. Usually dancers will rather switch to a slower pace than quit the dance floor. Participation, honour, prestige, and responsibility for the success of the dance are some of the factors at stake.

People who attend dances try to make the best of themselves. They take care and attention to what they wear, who they go with, and how they behave. They realize that the success of the dance is highly dependent on their participation. Participation imparts contribution. Knowing that they need to participate means that they understand that they will have to both give and take.

Dance participants need to be sensitive to others, both on and off the dance floor. They realize that dancing alone is not much fun. Good dancing takes place where there are good relationships. Partners are not only eager to improve and show off their own strengths, talents, and skills, but they are prepared to assist others do the same. They realize that the dance floor is infinite in size, and that the number of combinations of dance routines exceeds the imagination. No one needs to be banished or 'killed off'; there is ample space and opportunity for all. Those who quit the dance do so either through lack of commitment, competence, perseverance, endurance or a combination of these factors. Many leave in search of other dance floors and other dances. The exits and entrances are part of the natural ebb and flow of life.

Dance participants are those attentive to and optimistic about their dance. Their energies are positively engaged. Many are eager to find new partners with whom they can enhance their performance and with whom it is fun and challenging to co-create new steps.

There are no rules, no umpires, and no weapons required for this dance. The harmony and dissonance, rhythm and beat are sufficient to set its boundaries. As the music changes, the steps become more intricate and complex. Those that cannot keep to the rhythm, or who cannot co-create suitable steps, sit out or leave.

Dancing calls for cognitive, intuitive, and physical skills. It requires being in the present as well as anticipating and strategizing about the next steps. It requires good people skills and attention to relationships. It means knowing one's own strengths and weaknesses and who will be suitable and helpful partners. It also means knowing when to quit.

This then is the new business metaphor – business as an elaborate dance. In her book, *When Giants Learn to Dance*, Rosabeth Moss Kanter also uses the dance metaphor. She claims that businesses need to be capable of faster, more nimble action. They need to engage in creative manoeuvring. They require more flexibility and agility and they should engage in more and closer partnerships. She also discusses the change from adversary to ally as companies pool, ally, and link their knowledge and resources across increasingly blurred boundaries.

Business is no longer viewed as an 'I win – you lose' scenario. It is a potential win-win situation where all parties are expected to do some winning, at different times perhaps, but each in their own way. In the globalizing business world, where the complexity of relationships has reached new levels, comparison between organizations is becoming more and more difficult. Being a good dancer, who can sustain the rhythm and beat and even create new steps, eliminates the need for reductionistic comparisons. The dance metaphor signifies positive life energy and hope. It does not signify despair, loss and destruction. It does not instil anxiety and fear. Rather it unleashes the creative and energetic life forces of those invited to participate. All who want to join the dance floor are free to do so at their own risk. The demands of the dance will dictate who can sustain the pace of adaptation and change.

The 'dance' metaphor serves as a far more evocative and inspiring root metaphor than that of 'machine', 'war', 'battle', or 'game'. The dance of business also remains deeply in touch with and embedded in the realities of normal, everyday life.

It is not only giants, but all creatures who need to learn how to dance.

Relevance

Changes in root metaphors usually signal significant social paradigm shifts. This means that new viewing points have been reached which open the windows to new understandings. New root metaphors imply new values, new ways of making meaning, and new value tensions. The symbolism of the new metaphor provides the key to shifts in meaning and values. For example, viewing people as living organisms rather than machines, has enormous implications for every possible dimension of social life. Organisms live and die. They need to breathe and be nourished so that they may survive and prosper. They are unique, complex, and mysterious. They are both strong and weak. They are powerful communicators yet remain, in part, unfathomable. They cannot be programmed or fixed. They can be motivated, inspired, stimulated, and challenged. In most cases they will respond. There is little absolutely predictable or mechanistic about humans. They are driven by values and love, not by oil and electricity. Sometimes they cannot be turned on, and sometimes they refuse to be turned off. What an enormous shift in a root metaphor!

Recognizing these new life metaphors stimulates new perspectives and new ways of thinking. The use of imagery, symbols and rituals to describe the world in which we live, tells us an enormous amount about who we are and what we are about.

Being attentive to changing metaphors is part of the sage-like and prophetic element of the strategic planning process. Engaging in creative imagery and language can be a powerful way of describing the root values of the world in which the organization participates, and of the values and interests of its stakeholders. Consistently engaging in describing the world through images and metaphors will enable strategic management not only to understand the implications of new metaphors, but to identify them as the shift is taking place. This places the organization in a very powerful strategic position. Strategic planners are encouraged to abandon analytical jargon-speak and to be articulate, colourful and creative in describing the many vistas of the organization's world.

Stakeholder Values and Value-Tensions

A very important agenda item for the strategic planning team is the identification of organization stakeholders. The concept of stakeholders is an old one. It simply means identifying all those people or groups of people who have a stake in the organization and its performance. The stake may not be material; it may be, for example, emotional. The stake may not be explicit; it may be implicit. It may be indirect rather than direct. Whatever the stake is, large or small, and however it is held, is significant. What is important is knowing the type and number of stakeholders, the classification of their interests, (material, emotional, direct, or indirect, etc.) and the power of their influence.

Some suggestions

1   Identify all stakeholder groups, regardless of size and sphere of influence.

2   Classify their interests and determine their explicit and implicit power within the organization.

3   Identify and assess those stakeholder groups who have allegiance to, or, are in partnership with one another. Assess which groups' interests might be diametrically opposed.

4   Define the organization's values and compare these with the values of each of the stakeholder groups.

5   Determine the new realities facing the organization and clarify the value-challenges that these represent.

6   Distinguish the value-tensions that each group is experiencing. How might this change in the future?

7   Consider which stakeholder group has what to learn.

Relevance

Understanding the makeup and interests of one's stakeholder groups is important to any organization. The stakeholder groups describe the organization. They are the parts that comprise the whole. Evaluating stakeholder positions sets out the multiplicity of consonant and competing interests that holds the organization in tension. It clarifies why the organization behaves the way it does. It identifies who establishes the ground rules and who are the players on the periphery. It provides an indicator as to the organization's limitations and what its potential is likely to be. It defines the hierarchy of values and interests which classify the organization's culture. In short, it provides a portrait and a narrative of the organization as a network.

From this picture, management and those responsible for strategic planning can assess the organization's adaptive capacity, its points of resistance, and its blind spots. Knowing who has what to learn is powerful strategic information. Being armed with this vision and understanding of the organization's dynamics provides a critical starting point for any transformative change process.

New Alliances and Partnerships

A remarkable trend of the 1990s is the range and variety of strategic alliances made between so-called competing organizations. With little exception, organizations that intend to compete on an international basis and who wish to survive in the longer term form strategic alliances across a variety of fronts. Much has been written on this subject and suffice it to say that strategic alliances and partnerships are undoubtedly an ongoing agenda item.

I would like to provoke consideration of new types and forms of alliances. By new types, I mean alliance and partnerships across traditional divides, e.g. for-profit and non-profit organizations, corporations and partnerships, networks of corporations with networks of individuals. By new forms, I would like to suggest non-traditional partnerships in the form of federations, funding of competitors' mutually owned subsidiaries, the mutual sponsorship of venture capital funds, and so on.

An interesting example of new liaisons is that of Eastern Railway, an operator of trains from London's Liverpool Street station. Last year it began an experiment with its commuters. Commuters can have free travel and the chance to make a profit on the way to work if they act as part-time guards from the 'end of the line' stations east of London. The unusual recruitment drive offers £5.25 per hour and commuters could save up to £3500 per year on fares (*Financial Times* 1997). In order to qualify, commuters have to undergo a training programme. This is certainly a creative approach to forming new stakeholder partnerships.

The ability to form stable and trustworthy relationships that fulfil distinct objectives has now become a business necessity. The flexibility and agility with which these partnerships can be assembled and disassembled will be a future telling point. The dance floor requires many partners and many steps. When the music changes, new, competent partners need to be found who can respond to the beat. If one waits too long, the dance will be half over before one gets to the dance floor. If one spends too much time on the sidelines negotiating the dancing principles, one might miss all the appropriate dances. Foresight, agility, and response time are the necessary skills for participating in the dance. Doing the steps well is an increasingly smaller part, albeit a significant one, of the entire routine. The dance itself is as important as are the other dancers on the dance floor.

Some suggestions

1   List all the direct and indirect stakeholders in the organization.

2   List the activities which the organization has in common with these stakeholders, including key competitors.

3   Identify similarities and differences.

4   Consider how the stakeholders currently perform their activities.

5   Consider whether there is any way that the organization and the stakeholders could form an alliance that will be to the parties' mutual benefit.

Relevance

The world is an intricate living web of networks. Networks exist within networks. All organisms, living institutions, and organizations are networks in and of themselves, and they are linked to an infinite variety of other networks. Networks survive based on their links and relationships. Forming and managing relationships is the key to survival and well-being. As the network is in constant motion and change, being able to respond appropriately is part of the network dance and ritual. The new competition is about the ability to form more creative, responsive, and resilient networks than other organizations. It is no longer the notion of being a lone citadel on a hill fighting off the rest of the world with arcane weapons developed in foreboding and forbidden dungeons. Competitive power lies in the competence and responsiveness of creative relationships working in harmony, not in taking the stance of the lone warrior or isolated and impregnable fortress. Developing the organization's capacity to form shrewd and potent alliances is the task of the strategic planning team.

Search for Strategic Growth Opportunities and Threats

A critical aspect of the strategic agenda is to devise a method for identifying strategic growth opportunities and strategic growth threats. Strategic growth opportunities are opportunities for profitable investment. They arise whenever a 'market' holds the promise of growth in either volume or profits. (The definition of a market is usually firm specific, hence I will use the generic term 'market' here.) These might be existing or new markets to the organization. Opportunities might also arise out of the emergence of new markets from existing markets where, for example, consumer values and needs have changed or consumer behaviour has changed.

Strategic growth threats are threats to both the organization's existing markets and to markets in which investment is under consideration. In some markets, where there is only a short time horizon for profitable investment, both a strategic growth opportunity and threat may exist. Managing this window of opportunity requires exiting the market at the right time. This calls for strategic timing and marketing agility.

Strategic growth opportunities and threats need to be identified well in advance. Once the opportunity or threat has been identified, it takes time to make the investment and to mobilize the necessary resources. It is also likely that other organizations will have identified similar opportunities, and their entrance to the market may impede one's own. Not getting there first may significantly affect the level of expected profits and thereby detract from the opportunity. Getting there first, however, does not take priority over getting it wrong. As we all know, strategy is about timing, timing, timing.

The role of strategic planning in identifying strategic growth opportunities and threats will be discussed in detail in Chapters 6 and 7. Suffice it to say, that being in tune with the ever-changing new realities is the *sine qua non* for any strategic planning process.

Relevance

The greatest pressure facing all business organizations is the pressure to grow. If organizations do not grow, in the longer term they will die. Growth is therefore a necessary, but not sufficient, engagement of all businesses. Investment in growth needs to be strategically sound and profitable. It should be aimed at identifying a pipeline rather than just one-off opportunities.

The need to grow arises out of the commoditization of all products and services as they reach market maturity. This means that as the total volume of a product or service increases, supplier dependency on volume and market share, combined with growing consumer sophistication, forces prices down. This makes all goods and services less profitable in the longer term (see Figure 3.1). All organizations thus need to find new markets and to innovate new products and services.

Identifying profitable investment opportunities is the life-blood of the organization. It enables the organization to invest, raise money, gain stakeholder confidence, and grow. Sometimes these opportunities are identified in combination with a partner or alliance, and sometimes they are executed with the assistance of partners. However it is achieved, the need to continue searching out new opportunities is paramount. This is the primary task of the strategic planning function.

Summary

Organizations should be developing a strategic agenda that is in tune with new realities and addresses the value changes that these imply. It is recommended that organizations engage in systems thinking when evaluating the macro-environment, the effects of globalization, and the move to an increasingly multi-cultural world.

Key change signals exist in the economic arena. A main one is that unchecked capitalism is no longer acceptable to many of its former

FIGURE 3.1 Commoditization of products and services

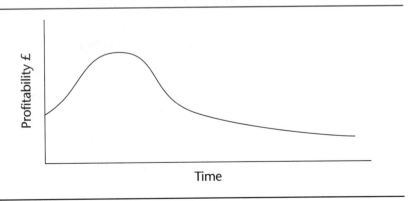

proponents. In the more mature capitalistic economies there is public recognition that unchecked capitalism does not always benefit the larger system. Changes in the way that capitalism is practised are being called for and the rise of non-profit organizations could prove a market challenge to for-profit companies in the future.

The Adaptive Age is also ushering in new root metaphors. Business is no longer viewed as either a 'war' or a 'game'. A new metaphor which is gaining popularity is that of 'dance'. Changing root metaphors invariably signal social paradigm shifts and changes in values. The switch from a 'war' to a 'dance' mataphor had profound implications for the leadership and strategic planning functions of businesses.

Business organizations are being challenged to do new things in new ways. This includes forming new and innovative alliances. The ability to form flexible yet appropriate alliances will be critical to the development of future competitive strategies.

Part of business' strategic agenda is the identification of strategic growth opportunites and threats. Organizations are dependent on this for future growth and profitability. This strategic task is increasingly more complex which supports the view that organizations require dedicated resources for the strategic planning activity.

Key Points Raised in this Chapter

▸   The organization should have developed a strategic agenda that includes recognition of the new realities.

▸   The organization should have resources dedicated to the strategic planning function.

▸   There are global changes occurring that signal changes in value-systems.

▸   There is pressure on the capitalistic system to change.

▸   There are guidelines for evaluating stakeholder powers and interests.

▸   New root metaphors signal changes in mental frameworks and value systems.

▸   Organizations need to be innovative in creating new alliances.

▸   Organizations need to identify strategic growth opportunities and threats.

SUGGESTIONS

- Review the organization's current strategic agenda and ensure that it includes new realities and the value-tensions that these present to different stakeholders.

- Test out new realities and value-shifts with members of stakeholder groups.

- Hold workshops where members of the organization can discuss the value tensions that they experience.

- List the strategic growth opportunities and threats that the organization has identified. Ensure that political, social, religious, economic, environmental, technical, and demographic issues have been taken into account.

Further Reading

Drucker, P.F. (1989) *The New Realities*, HarperBusiness, New York.

Heilbroner, R. (1993) *21st Century Capitalism*, W.W. Norton & Company, New York.

Koa, J. (1997) *Jamming: The Art and Discipline of Business Creativity*, HarperBusiness, New York.

CHAPTER FOUR

The New Leadership

The Hunger for Leadership

Leadership has been the preoccupation of the 1990s. The plethora of books, articles and training programmes that claim to reveal the prized insights and skills associated with leadership defies the imagination. Surprisingly, the demand for literature, workshops, and courses on leadership still exceeds supply. Why is this so?

Perhaps the idea of leadership promises some kind of deliverance to the alienated, relieving them of confusion and disenchantment. Surely it inspires the ambitious, filling them with hopes of power and influence. The very fact that leadership has attracted so much attention over the past decade is an important indication that the world is experiencing a lack of leadership in almost every sphere of life – a view held by the disillusioned and opportunistic alike. Warren Bennis, in his book, *On Becoming a Leader*, published in 1989 and presumably written one or two years earlier, begins his first chapter by asking, 'Where have all the leaders gone?' (Bennis 1989:14). He quotes a *Time Magazine* cover story, dated November 1987, that proclaimed that 'The nation calls for leadership and there is no one at home'. Judging by the state of our world today nothing much has changed.

Why does this clamour continue? I believe it is because we need to find a new model of leadership. The old model no longer works. We need especially to give up our cherished belief that leaders 'take charge'. This popular notion belongs to a previous era. We need to embrace a new type of leadership. The new leadership will not be provided by a 'take charge' elite, but will emerge from the capacity that lies within each and every person. It will be a leadership that does not presume to have all the answers, but one that seeks to empower others to work on their own problems. It will be a leadership that skilfully provokes and accompanies people and organizations as they undertake their difficult work.

In the twilight years of the twentieth century, nations, societies, ethnic groups, and business organizations are expressing a profound sense of alienation, confusion, and disenchantment. Many blame this on lack of leadership and claim to feel 'leaderless'. Finding leaders who have a new approach to new realities is considered the panacea for all ills. The expectation remains that leaders should provide palatable answers to life's challenges during these perplexing, ambiguous, and changing times.

The kinds of challenges, problems, confusions, and tensions experienced by many people these days are summarized below. As the table shows, disorienting issues are always value-laden. They are issues that radically challenge human values. The problems that stem from these disorienting issues can only be addressed if we deal directly with the core values that are being challenged. Technical fixes that address the symptoms may provide a temporary distraction but do not come to grips with the deeper systemic issues. New leaders need to tackle systemic issues if they intend to enhance the adaptive capacities of their constituents. Working directly with the distress and disorientation that result when values are under threat is the only way to cope with the challenges that the future invariably presents.

COMMON DISORIENTING FACTORS DURING PERPLEXING, AMBIGUOUS AND CHANGING TIMES

- Balancing personal/work/family life.

- Tension between individual rights and communal obligations.

- Changed expectations regarding jobs and job security.

- Changed expectations regarding the nature of work.

- Impact of technology on life in general.

- Impact of technology on the nature of work and where it is performed.

- Speed of information flow.

- Redistribution of power to new holders of power.

- Gender arrangements.

- Legitimization of multiple voices.

- Increasing number of interest groups fighting for power.

> - Effects of large scale immigration.
>
> - Growing disparity between rich and poor.
>
> - Increased exposure to and interaction with multiple cultures.
>
> - Ethical questions generated by biotechnology.

Leadership in the Political and Social Arena

Few political leaders today seem to inspire deep-seated confidence in their ability to lead their countries into the twenty-first century. Many leaders tend to force their visions and views of the world onto their communities. Additionally they try to solve problems that they do not fully comprehend, nor for which they have any cogent, well-thought-through answers.

Leadership in the Business Arena

Business organizations are also facing a crisis of leadership. The upheaval in the business arena over the past decade has had a profoundly negative effect on the socio-economic situations of many nations. The USA, UK, Germany, France, Japan, Thailand, South Korea, and China are all struggling with these issues. The work lives of the present and future generations have been profoundly altered. Corruption and fraud, bank-ruptcies, downsizings, retrenchments, restructurings, re-engineerings, and merging and breaking up of large businesses, are all evidence of the chaos that is accompanying socio-economic changes. Big business, as the most prominent and powerful vehicle of capitalism, is being blamed for all and sundry social and political ills. Big business is the target of a great deal of anger from a significant portion of the people who experience hurt and suffering as a consequence of economic restructuring. The social responsibility of business is actively being debated. From a leadership point of view, it will be interesting to see whether business leaders will exercise leadership in responding to their critics.

In light of the current state of affairs it is no wonder that there is a clamour for a new kind of leadership. This leadership needs to *be* different, not just *do* things differently. The critical question is: How should the new leadership be different and how can we recognize this difference? The leadership practices of the past will no longer do. We need a new kind of leadership. The 'old' leadership style promised to have all the answers and instead delivered broken promises, confused policies, and technical, quick fix solutions.

Why the World Needs Leadership

I often begin my workshops or classes on leadership by asking participants why we need leaders. Invariably this results in at least a few seconds of astounded silence. Initially my question is considered too simplistic and obvious to warrant serious attention. When I press participants a little further, it emerges that the question is not really that simple nor is the answer that obvious. Slowly the discussion gathers momentum. Some say that we need leaders to lead us, but continue to be very vague about what kind of leading they are talking about. Most agree that leaders present us with a vision that inspires hope, and claim that both the vision and hope have a beneficial, unifying effect on society. Others say that leaders help to keep order and stability, provide guidance during difficult times, and uphold communal and institutional morality.

During these class discussions, participants also insist that leaders have integrity, insight and empathy, and that leaders provide answers to problems and help people deal with complexity and adversity. Many examples of leaders and their leadership qualities are cited. Some hail from the political sphere, like Franklin D. Roosevelt, Mahatma Gandhi, and Nelson Mandela, while others are well-known social leaders, like Mother Teresa, or Dorothy Sayer. What is notable is that names of business leaders, with the possible exception of Bill Gates, almost never arise.

Despite the fact that business plays such a leading role in both the political and social arenas, class participants, most of whom work in businesses, appear to dismiss the names of business executives when discussing leadership issues. In a time when there is a blatant need for the exercise of leadership by business people, it is a frightening reality that leadership is not apparent in this quarter.

After the discussion on why the world needs leaders has played itself out, I usually challenge the class or workshop participants on their notion of leaders and the definition of leadership that they have presented. For example, I might ask if Hitler could be considered a leader who had a compelling vision. He gave many Germans hope and unified a large percentage of the population. Was this leadership, and if so, is this the leadership that the world needs? What about Yasser Arafat, Colonel Gaddafi, Gerry Adams, who are well-known leaders? Are these the kind of leaders upon whom the world should depend? A critical question arises as to what kind of leadership we now turn to for our future visions and hopes.

In response to my challenges class participants begin to inject moral qualifiers into their definitions of acceptable leaders. 'Ah, no', they insist, 'Leaders must be moral. They must have the well being of their citizens at heart. They must act for the benefit of the common good'. I then respond by enquiring about who should be the ultimate moral arbiter. Who will decide on the appropriate moral requirements? Who should decide which of society's myriad interest groups should be considered first? Who should have the responsibility of defining the parameters of well-being? To which of society's challenges and ills should leaders give priority? Should it be trade competitiveness, defence, or welfare? And so the questions go on.

The purpose of my challenging the participants in this way is to illustrate the personal, subjective, relative, and value-laden nature of leadership. People who are dubbed leaders by some are certainly not considered leaders by others. There is no absolute context or value-free definition of leadership. Believing this to be the case is a large and dangerous fallacy which many books and programmes regrettably tend to promote. Undoubtedly, there are some people who many of us will see as being outstanding people, for example Mahatma Gandhi. These people exercise leadership in very significant ways. However, the idea of leadership as an objective, definable laundry list of character traits and behaviours has long since lost credibility.

I am also eager to get away from the notion of a leader as a paragon of virtue who shoulders the responsibilities and carries the burden of society's challenges and ills. All-time paragons of virtue do not exist. Even Gandhi treated his family despicably; Nelson Mandela trained to be a guerilla fighter and gave orders to place bombs that could kill civilians, Franklin D. Roosevelt and John F. Kennedy were clearly not invested in the idea of marital fidelity, and so the list goes on. Leaders are human. It is from within our fallible humanity that we exercise leadership. No human being is above humanity and woe to every nation or group who has placed their leaders in that position.

With this very human perspective in mind, throughout this book I will argue that a more wholesome, modest and sensible approach to the notion of leadership is that leadership is an activity that can be exercised by anyone. We should not aspire to finding or creating broad-shouldered leaders on whom we can become dependent. Rather, we should foster a society with institutions and organizations in which everyone is both encouraged and given the opportunity to exercise leadership. Sustainable learning organizations are only possible when the exercise of leadership is given back to the people.

What this book promotes is the exercise of leadership throughout organizations, where the leading light and tone is set by the executive team and those responsible for strategic planning. It should be their explicit mandate to inspire and nourish a learning environment where meeting adaptive challenges and exercise of leadership is an ongoing process.

Before considering what it means to exercise leadership, it is important to discuss the difference between leadership and authority.

Leadership versus Authority

Leadership is often confused with authority. Frequently those in authority are applauded and glorified as great leaders, especially when they appear to be warding off unwelcomed change or the looming threat of ambiguity and uncertainty. This confusion is especially prevalent in the business arena where senior managers are frequently referred to as the organizations' leaders. The title of 'leader' is usually accorded them by virtue of their power and status, rather than their ability to guide the business through transformative changes.

The functions of authority differ from those of leadership. Authority figures are expected to provide direction and protection. They are expected to chart the course and hold the boundaries. Those in authority are also expected to control conflict, to uphold and maintain norms, and generally to provide orienting functions regarding group status and physical place. People in authority are expected to solve routine problems, to alleviate distress and to ward off danger. They are expected to have the answers and to shoulder the responsibility for solving difficult problems.

Power is conferred on persons in authority in exchange for the others' diminished personal responsibility for dealing with complex and difficult issues. The drawback of having strong, competent authorities is that people tend to abandon their own personal agency and give all the power and responsibility for decision-making to the authorities. Because of such excessive dependence and submission to authority figures many people forget that they in fact have power and agency. Indeed, to serve them in exchange for the conferral of power, they authorize the authorities. Due to excessive dependence on authority, there is also a tendency to misunderstand the purpose of leadership, and how and why it is different to that of authority.

While the role of authority is necessary and important, it is not sufficient. We need leadership as well as authority. Leadership can be exercised from a position of authority, however, for leaders having formal authority this not only provides opportunities, but adds some tensions and constraints. Leading from a position of formal authority is very different from being in a position of informal authority, as exercising leadership means recognizing changing realities and mobilizing people to do adaptive work. This creates tension, distress, and disorder, something that authorities are supposed to quell.

Leaders are supposed to challenge the status quo. They are expected to encourage adaptive change and to inject a sense of urgency. They are supposed to provide a holding environment while people struggle with the disequilibrium and distress that the new realities are causing. Unlike authorities leaders do not provide answers but give the adaptive work back to the people. They remind constituents of their own agency and their own personal investment in the solutions they are seeking from others.

Leaders operating from a position of informal authority have greater room for manouevre. They are not expected to keep order and create disorder at the same time. They are also less caught up in the confusion between adaptive work and the need for regular, effective routine technical solutions, to meet pressing daily problems.

Being in the role of formal authority and seeking to exercise leadership can thus create many conflicts for the leader and confuse his or her constituents. Discussion of the leader's role in positions of formal and informal authority will be taken up in more detail in Chapter 5, 'Exercising Leadership'.

Misunderstanding of the nature of leadership often arises as a consequence of the confusion between authority and leadership (see Table 4.1). Because people in authority are expected to alleviate the distress of others, to show the way, and take sole responsibility for all mistakes in the process, people seek authority rather than leadership. They want those in authority to take away their burdens rather than challenging them to do their part in resolving the issues. Many leaders have been 'assassinated' for exercising leadership, in favour of those who simply wield power and authority. This is the reason for leaders 'not being home' as the November 1987 *Time Magazine* article calls it.

Authority versus Leadership Issues

People look to authority figures to provide remedies for their problems, thereby relying on those in authority to alleviate their distress. This tendency frequently results in an inappropriate dependency on authority figures to provide answers to problems where in fact they may have none.

TABLE 4.1   Leadership versus Authority

Leadership	Authority
Hold up changing realities	Provide direction
Identify the adaptive challenge	Chart the course
Mobilize for adaptive work	Solve technical problems
Give the work back	Provide answers
Heighten distress and urgency	Alleviate distress
Provide a holding environment	Provide protection
Challenge the status quo	Uphold and maintain norms
Generate creative tension	Control conflict
Set new boundaries	Hold existing boundaries
Support dissenting voices	Clarify group authority and status

Expecting easy answers has landed us in the technical quick-fix world that is causing us so much difficulty at present. In the complex world in which we live no one person can claim absolutely to have the right answer. The answers to today's problems have to be collectively co-created by all stakeholders. Recognizing and helping to resolve the numerous trade-offs involved in a complex solution is part of exercising leadership.

Authority figures are given power in exchange for shouldering the burden and responsibility of the problems of others. This results in people acting with less personal agency in matters that directly affect their lives and their future choices. They forget that they are the principals, and that those in authority are merely their appointed agents whom they have empowered, and whom they can disempower. Instead, many disempower themselves as they overlook the fact that they can retract the power that they have conferred. The authority figure should be the service provider, not those who have conferred their power.

Confusing authority with leadership also results in an inclination to value stability and order over uncertainty and change. The comfort of stability and order are pursued rather than the challenge of creativity and chaos. Destabilization and disarray are essential to the emergence of new solutions. Leadership must help people resist the comfort of maintaining order and withstand the anxiety of allowing the disorder that brings new answers into being.

While good leadership helps people with the anxieties of change, it does not allow people to become emotionally distant. People often handle the distress of problems by dumping responsibility for the solution on the authorities. Leadership must prevent emotional 'outsourcing' because pain motivates the change process.

Over-dependence on authority encourages people to shut down their own emotions, to distance themselves from issues, and to be externally rather than internally motivated.

In organizations that place excessive emphasis on authority, power becomes the currency for getting anything done. Power, rather than influence, becomes the mechanism by which people are mobilized. This may be done explicitly by issuing commands to carry out some action. More subtly, power is wielded by keeping people in fear of losing their own power or even their jobs. Authoritarian environments are unhealthy and are impediments to creating a learning organization that enhances people's adaptive capacities.

Now, more than ever, we need people who can exercise leadership rather than assert authority. We need leaders who can induce learning through challenge and creativity. We have perfected the hierarchical model where those higher up the ladder are conferred with power and authority. Now we need leaders who give away their power and who actively engage in getting others to reassert the power that they have given away.

Exercising Leadership with Authority

It is possible to exercise leadership from a position of authority, but it requires enormous skill in moving back and forwards between the two different roles. A classic example is that of Mikail Gorbachev, prime minister and ex-leader of the Soviet Union's Communist Party. Gorbachev tried to perform both these roles simultaneously and ended up suffering the consequences. Although he recognized the new realities, namely that communism is no longer a feasible political, social, or economic option, he was unable to sustain holding up the new reality while trying to keep order under the old regime. He lost control, could no longer set and hold boundaries, and lost grip of events as they accelerated at a pace for which he was unprepared. At the same time his attempts at exercising leadership, laudable as his intentions seemed, were continuously vitiated by a return to playing the authority. It might be argued that had he not been an authority, his attempts at exercising leadership might have been more consistent, thereby rendering more effective results. Instead he lost his authority and his leadership was undermined. In effect he was 'assassinated'. He was forcibly removed from office and has lost his voice. Fortunately history completed what he began.

Exercising Leadership Without Authority

Exercising leadership while not being in a position of authority has many advantages. In this instance the person is not expected to play two almost conflicting roles. If we think about great leaders in our time, Gandhi, Luther King, and Mandela, they have all been without formal authority. What they did have, however, was informal authority. This means that their constituents recognized them as being people who understood changing realities and who could inspire new visions. These leaders could challenge the status quo and they could provoke challenge and create disorder. They did not promise their followers easy times, but rather pressed forward with the urgency of a shared goal. This goal was the shaping of a new reality which heralded new core values. These values were peace, freedom, equality, equal opportunity, and justice – a direct challenge to the old reality. If these leaders had been in positions of formal authority they may have not been able to achieve what they did so efficaciously.

Recognizing that the ability to exercise leadership is more difficult when one is in a position of authority is an important insight. For those in authority, a way of managing both roles is to partner with those who have informal authority, and to support those with dissenting voices. South Africa's De Klerk managed to do this and is rightly recognized as not only a competent authority figure but as a person who exercised leadership in a remarkable way.

Formal versus Informal Authority

- Formal authority is explicitly conferred power in exchange for service.

- Informal authority is implicitly conferred power to represent, resolve, or affect the choice of action by a group.

New versus Conventional Notions of Leadership

Many discussions that surround leadership still focus on the charisma, personality, traits, and actions of leaders. The plethora of books that have swamped the market recently still tend to promote the idea that leaders are exceptional people with unusual strengths and capabilities. Books with this message advocate that once leaders have mastered certain ways of being, they can lead most followers almost anywhere. This view of leadership smacks not only of the 'old' hierarchical way of thinking, but denies the enormous potential for leadership that lies within everyone, not just a chosen few, given the appropriate environment and circumstance. A significant portion of leadership material is also elitist in style. These materials have a language and manner that suggest that they can only be consumed appropriately by special people. These special people supposedly have the temperament, persuasive powers, communications skills, and intelligence, to take on the enormous burden and responsibility of leadership. The message of these books is 'only the eligible should apply'.

In old-style leadership, where the emphasis is on authority rather than leadership, the leader decides on the organization's vision, motivates others to co-operate, and monitors and controls behaviour. For this type of leadership, 'how to take control', or 'how to lead' books and programmes, may have been appropriate. For the new reality of the twenty-first century world, however, this no longer fits the way the world works; nor, in the main, is this style of leadership acceptable. We need to stop searching for special individuals with so-called leadership potential and aim at developing the leadership potential in everyone.

Conventional Leadership Books

From the conventional view of leadership, many business executives or CEOs are hailed as leaders for heading organizations that have achieved large revenue growth or above average profits. Books and anecdotes abound as to how these supposedly visionary people have led their corporations to success. The fact is that over the past few years we have been living in times of reasonable economic growth, so growing a company has not been extremely difficult. The human consequences of the enormous downsizings, retrenchments, and restructurings involved in these supposed success stories is also not factored into the equation and is carefully omitted from these heroes' score sheets. In other words, current profits may be the result of adaptive challenges faced by previous management, and true profits that include the economic costs of restructurings, downsizings, etc. are not really taken into account. Society, rather than business, carries the latter cost.

The second disturbing characteristic of ersatz leaders, is that, for many, their successes have resulted from short-term strategies, most of which are technical fixes rather than real adaptive solutions. Few of these leaders are really concerned with their legacy once they leave the organization. Sadly, their true commitment to the organization is often affected by the price and timing of their share options. An interesting question is how their organizations will perceive the achievements of these people in three or five years time. Indeed, will the organization even exist in three to five years time! The discussion of the fortunes of the 'excellent companies' in Chapter 2 hopefully provided an opportunity for salutary reflection on situations of so-called successful leadership.

Instead of hailing the successes and achievements of high-profile executives when times are good, the measure of true leadership should be how the organization deals with adaptation and change during difficult times. Further, leaders should be measured by their enduring legacies, rather than a short, centre-stage debut during their prime. And surely followers, especially the organization's employees and suppliers, should be given greater opportunity to pronounce on the efficacy of their leaders.

Leadership acclaim is often doled out or withheld by anxious shareholders, closeted academics, myopic stockbrokers, or the media hungry for a tantalizing story. Regrettably, the people directly affected seldom get a say. I have consulted with many organizations where the publically acclaimed CEO has few fans back home. The record shows that in many cases, the greater the public accolades for a supposedly extraordinary business leader, the quicker his or her demise. One need only recall the fanfare and hype during the heyday of Robert Maxwell of Maxwell Holdings, Asil Nadir of Polly Peck, Michael Milkin of Drexel Burnham Lambert, Michael Saunders of Guinness, John Scully of Apple, and a host of other angels of the business world. Great leadership can only be evaluated in the long run by diverse criteria of success (see Table 4.2 over).

Essential Ingredients for Exercising Leadership

Although the personality and trait theories of leadership has been all but discarded, certain common tendencies do emerge among those who exercise leadership.

In Tune with the New Realities

The prime function of new business leadership is to orient the organization to new realities and to hold up the value-challenges that are being created. New leaders exercise both insight and foresight in

TABLE 4.2   Changing Notions of Leadership

Conventional	New
Have formal authority	Have either formal or informal authority
Focus on personality	Focus on the activity
Exert power	Exert influence
Are assertive	Are attentive
Dominate	Integrate/partner
Analyse	Synthesize
Favour expansion	Favour conservation
Focus on technical skills	Focus on adaptive skills
Allocate resources	Mobilize resources
Are reductionistic	Aim to be holistic
Provide answers	Provoke questions
Hierarchical status	Key link in network
Reserved for a few people	Everyone can exercise leadership

reading the changing environment and translating its effects on the mission, values, and core competencies of the business. The new realities are understood to set the agenda of the adaptive work that needs to be carried out.

Max De Pree, ex-chairman of Herman Miller, describes in his two well-known books, *Leadership is an Art*, and *Leadership Jazz*, an approach to leadership that resonates with this attention to the new realities. In his book, *Leadership is an Art*, written some eight years ago now, his advice for leadership is deeply consonant with the systemic and interrelatedness concepts of the new sciences. He claims that the first step of the leader is to define reality (De Pree 1989:11). According to him, leaders should also liberate people to do what is most required of them: to change, grow, and strive for their potential. They can only do this if they are aligned to the changing realities of the world and are in touch with the consequences.

Vision

With rare exception, people agree that leaders need to have vision. Where disagreement occurs is in discussions regarding whose vision this should be and how this vision should be formulated. Many say that leaders search out or create new visions. In the more recent literature, it is asserted that vision needs to be co-created. Here a vision emerges from the joint efforts of all stakeholders as they grapple with their new realities. I prefer this latter approach. I do not believe that credible, realistic visions, which people will buy into, can be the rosy coloured picture or hubristic manifesto of one leader and her close colleagues. As Kouzes and Posner (1995) argue in their book, *The Leadership Challenge*, I believe that vision needs to be one that is co-created by the leader and her constituents on an ongoing basis. People will only follow if the espoused vision resonates with their values and ways of making meaning. Peter Senge, in *The Fifth Discipline*, also asserts that shared visions emerge from personal visions and that it does not work just to establish a strategic or official vision. A shared vision is needed in order to create a common identity. Senge also suggests that the role of the leader, rather than espousing a vision for others, is to hold the tension between the group's visions and the world's reality, thereby facilitating others to work toward closing this gap (Senge 1990:226).

New Ideas and Perspectives

Exercising leadership means injecting new ideas, and most of all, new perspectives into an organization. Usually these ideas and perspectives are in tune with the collective yearnings of individuals in the organization, thus making way for new possibilities and opportunities. The outdated notion of leadership, where leaders lead and followers follow, flows from the now redundant mechanistic view of the world. The new leadership places emphasis on flow and opportunity, where it is understood that everyone in the organization contributes to the diversity, ambiguity, and uncertainty of life as it moves in a continuous, pulsating motion.

Trust and Integrity

Leaders are also expected to be trustworthy, to demonstrate integrity and to have good interpersonal and communication skills. They are typically willing to challenge corporate inertia. Contrary to conventional belief that these attributes belong only to special people, all people who are deeply in touch with who they are, and who feel confident and empowered, have the capacity to exercise leadership. The 'paragon of virtue model' is no longer appropriate. It is out of the depth and fullness of our humanity and out of the combination of our strengths and weaknesses that we can truly be in touch with others. This makes for context-sensitive leadership where systemic issues are understood and values and roles are taken into consideration.

Continuous Renewal

In *Leadership Jazz*, De Pree expands on the importance of fostering people's growth processes by claiming that we should be in awe of human potential. Human potential, he argues, should be embraced as vital, creative energy and revered as a great mystery. In the same book he talks about leaders balancing the force of change and continuity. 'Change without continuity', he says, 'is chaos. While continuity without change, is sloth (De Pree 1992:74)'. He believes that leaders are responsible for continuous renewal; they should inject ambiguity, risk, and uncertainty into people's lives, and they should pave the way for change. This is achieved through encouraging participation in all directions, not just hierarchically, and showing by example how people can be enablers of one another.

Embrace Diversity

De Pree claims that leaders should endorse the concept of persons, and recognize and understand that the diversity in corporate life comprises a multiplicity of people's gifts, talents, and skills. He introduces the idea of 'roving leadership' whereby he asserts that in different situations, different people should assume the mantle of leadership. He promotes roving leadership, advocating that based on the diversity of skills, talents, and understanding of a particular situation, different people should be given the freedom, space, and encouragement to exercise their leadership skills. This approach seems congruent with systems thinking and the interrelatedness that is part of the new realities.

Deal with Dissonance and Harmony

De Pree also asserts that three of the key elements of people working together are how to deal with change, how to deal with conflict, and how to reach our potential (De Pree 1989:59). He believes that leaders should encourage contrary opinions as an important source of vitality. He sums up the role of leader as being akin to that of leader of a jazz band. This, he holds, is servant leadership which is focused on drawing the best out of others. By holding together the tension of the unpredictability of the music and players' unique gifts, the lead jazz musician coaxes out a melodious harmony. For De Pree, this is the role of a leader.

Empower and Liberate Others

Kouzes and Posner, in their book, *The Leadership Challenge*, describe how they believe leaders get extraordinary things done. According to them, leaders take on challenging opportunities and turn these into success stories. They also believe that leadership is for everyone and that opportunities for leadership are available to all of us every day. They see leadership as a process when ordinary people bring out the best in themselves, and they argue that organizations need to liberate the leader in everyone. This they claim is what makes extraordinary things happen.

Steve Jaworski, in his book, *Synchronicity: The Inner Path of Leadership*, also claims that to exercise leadership is to release human possibilities; it is the capacity to inspire people, and to get them centred and focussed.

These more recent leadership books, then, are noticeably moving away from the conventional notions of leadership and the confusions that surround leadership and authority. Leadership is no longer a privileged occupation for the eligible few, but is an opportunity available to everyone (see box below).

INGREDIENTS FOR EXERCISING LEADERSHIP

- Be in tune with the new realities

- Have vision

- Inject new ideas and perspectives

- Exude trust and integrity

- Be attentive to and capable of dealing with dissonance

- Empower and liberate others

Leadership: The New Definition

In this book the notion of leadership has a very different emphasis to the more conventional themes. It also builds on many of the innovative ideas of writers like Max De Pree, Peter Senge, James Kouzes and Barry Posner, and especially the work of Ron Heifetz. Here leadership is identified as an *activity* that initiates an *adaptive process*. This activity may be exercised by anyone, not only by a designated leader or someone with formal authority. Those who exercise leadership, however, must know how to use their formal or informal authority as positive tools to their advantage. The definition of leadership that will be used to discuss leadership and its place in strategic planning can be described as follows:

> Leadership is achieved by distinguishing adaptive challenges from technical challenges, mobilizing people to tackle the tough problems that this inevitably raises, and holding steady until the adaptive work has been done. Identifying the adaptive challenge and the adaptive work requires systems thinking enacted in detailed systemic analyses.

Shape of the New Leadership

New leadership differs from the old in critical ways. It places emphasis on exercising leadership rather than on being a leader. The shift of focus is to the *activity* and away from the person. This does not mean that people exercising leadership are not doing something different from their normal work or routine activities. It also does not mean that people's capacities do not differ and that some people do not have a greater capacity for exercising leadership than others. A significant purpose of this book is to dwell on how all of us might improve our capacities for exercising leadership, even though there will always be people who assume the role of leaders more often than most. What we are concerned with here is the *activity* of exercising leadership rather than a leadership personality.

Deciding to exercise leadership needs to be a conscious decision. Leadership requires commitment and time, plus a great deal of sensitivity and tenacity. Those who decide to exercise leadership also need to be aware of the potential ramifications of their actions. Exercising leadership is a high-risk business. If leaders do not carefully monitor the consequences of their actions and interpret these accurately, highly negative results may ensue. In extreme cases, as we know, leaders are assassinated. This regrettably common occurrence discourages many people from exercising leadership even when they are uniquely placed to do so.

Exercising leadership requires a different mindset to the conventional leadership approach. It is this mindset that distinguishes what I refer to as 'new leaders' and the 'new leadership' from conventional notions of leadership.

The New Leadership Mindset

The fundamental difference between the old and new leadership mindset is that the latter treats being and doing as an integrated activity. As the wise Chinese philosopher, Lao Tzu said, ' The way to do is to be'. Being is doing and doing is being. The new leadership is one that attunes itself to the nature and rhythms of life. This is reflected in a leadership style that is consonant with the inherent paradigms of living systems, i.e. new leaders understand what it means to be a human being and consciously effect their leadership by meeting people where they are.

The new leadership understands that there are multiple, equally valid realities, held by diverse groups from different cultures and diverse walks of life. These realities are understood to be part of the fabric of a diverse, vibrant, and creative world. History has shown that ignoring the fact that diverse groups construe their reality differently is a serious omission. Coercing different groups with different backgrounds and values to adhere to one master reality is not only short sighted, but has potentially disastrous consequences. The history of conflict between men and women, blacks and whites, Jews and Palestinians, Serbs and Croatians and the countries of the former USSR bears witness to this fact. Diverse realities continue to drive conflicts in Turkey, Malaysia, and Indonesia.

The new leadership refrains from providing easy answers or generating quick fix solutions. The new leadership takes seriously the continuously changing nature of realities which emerge in a world that is in perpetual change and motion. New leaders are able to understand and interpret the tensions that arise as a consequence of challenges to value systems that come from changing realities. A major skill of the new leadership is the ability to take a systemic perspective, to distinguish adaptive from technical challenges, and to act on this difference. The new leadership redirects the adaptive challenges back to the people who need to do the adapting. This is where the adaptive challenges and the adaptive work belong.

The new leadership has the skill to mobilise the necessary resources to tackle tough problems, and guides the co-creation of suitable responses by those who have to live with the consequences. The new leadership is able to hold steady in the face of challenge from, and conflict with, those who do not wish to acknowledge or embrace the new realities. This ensures that resistance to change, or dissent, is not hastily dispelled by engaging in quick fix remedies. Part of holding steady includes being able to provide a holding environment for those distressed by the consequences of the new realities. This means being able to moderate the heat to temperatures that people can withstand without their abandoning their adaptive work or seeking to assassinate or disempower the leader.

The new leadership excels in strategic partnering and recognizes that all participants in the system are potential partners. The construct of adversary is no longer apposite. Those who hold opposing views or engage in competitive activities are now viewed as complements rather than antagonists. This disposition allows for a completely different strategic and negotiating mindset. It frees up energy otherwise used for 'beating' or 'outmanoeuvring' the opposition, thus providing the freedom and space for more creative solutions.

Positioning the organization in the Adaptive Age and preparing for the twenty-first century calls for a new and different notion of leadership. The idea of 'born leaders' is both simplistic, out-of-date, and somewhat patriarchal. While some people have a greater flair for exercising leadership frequently or consistently, exercising leadership requires skills that potentially can be acquired by anyone. The new leadership believes this and actively fosters leadership in everyone, thus providing a critical ingredient for the development of a learning organization (see box below).

THE NEW LEADERSHIP MINDSET

- Being and doing is treated as an integrated activity.

- Recognizes the existence of multiple realities and that their existence provides grist for the mill.

- Continuously orients to new, changing world realities.

- Uses systemic thinking.

- Attends to the adaptive challenges and the adaptive work that needs to be done.

- Focuses on mobilizing resources.

- Understands the need to moderate the heat and hold steady in the face of resistance and distress.

- Works with the dance metaphor and is attentive to the creation of new alliances and partnerships.

Leadership and the New Science of Living Systems

New Leaders understand Human Nature and Culture

New leaders have a good understanding of their world, its values, culture and traditions, and the beat and rhythm of daily life. New leaders are deeply immersed in their culture, often representing a clear embodiment of its values. When necessary they are also able to take a few steps back to view their culture, as others might view it, from a distance.

New leaders have a feel for the strengths and weaknesses of their cultures, and recognize the culture's capacity for change. They are also sensitive to the psychological barriers that need to be surmounted in order to bring about change. New leaders monitor, embrace, and clarify the emerging paradigms presented by the new realities. New leaders understand human nature.

New leaders are in sync with the changing context of their environment, demonstrating adaptability and flexibility without vitiating the core values that they hold or which define their culture. New business leaders are perpetually testing that their realities are congruent with the new realties while aligning their organizational cultures to these new realities.

The ability to better understand human nature and the cultural web in which it is woven has been greatly enhanced by the findings of the new sciences. While new leaders may respond to their implicit understanding of humans as dynamic, living organisms, they can now gain even greater insights from the explicit knowledge available through new scientific understanding of what it means to be a living organism. Since living organism is the metaphor that has replaced the idea of humans as machines, it is important to dwell on the findings of the new sciences regarding the nature of living organisms.

Understanding Humans as Living System Networks

One of the profound new realities pervading all disciplines is the new scientific understanding of living organisms. This new understanding presents us with a developing theory of the interconnectedness of all living systems in an intricate and highly integrated system of networks. Within these networks three kinds of living systems exist, namely, organisms, parts of organisms, and communities of organisms. The configuration of networks which constitute these various organisms comprise multiple networks nested within other networks, forming one large interconnected web of living organisms. The network structure is not hierarchical, but rather reaches out in all directions, displaying multiple levels and multiple connections.

In a networked system the nature of the whole is always different to the mere sum of the parts. The essential properties of the network are the properties of the whole, which do not belong to any of the parts. These *systemic properties* arise as a consequence of the *organizing relations* of the various parts. For example the systemic properties of the totality of a (living) business organization stand apart from and exceed those of the functional divisions or departments.

The network's *configuration* of ordered relationships (i.e. the pattern of the network), provides the characteristics of a particular class of organisms or systems. If the network is dissected, taken apart, or damaged the systemic properties are destroyed. This means that the way in which living organisms organize themselves is a fundamental characteristic of the way that they 'do' and 'be'.

At different levels of networks different levels of complexity exist. *Complexity* denotes the systemic properties that exist at a particular level. At the more micro-level the pattern of relationships is less complex than at the more macro-levels. The properties of the parts of the network can only be understood within the context of the larger whole. Any part of a network is itself a networked pattern of relationships. No matter at what level one views the system, a network of relationships exists. 'Stand-alone component pieces', or 'building blocks' do not exist. These terms belong to an outdated Newtonian mechanistic view of the world and are no longer relevant to the understanding of living systems.

Self-Organization in Living Systems

The new science also reveals that the living organisms that make up the integrated network of life are *self-organizing*. Each organism's configuration of relationships is mapped by a pattern that is particular to that organism. This pattern prescribes the qualities rather than the quantities of the relationships within the networks. Scientists have discovered that living systems are open to the flow of energy and matter that passes through them from the environment, yet closed to how they organize and maintain themselves. This means that while they are dependent on continual flows of energy and resources from the outside, the way in which they self-organize is unique to them, being part of their 'genetic' code held within their self-organizing pattern. This means that external energy and information informs the organism of the need to adapt, while the inherent pattern determines how this will take shape (see Table 4.3).

TABLE 4.3   Key Properties of Organizations as Living Systems

Properties of Living Systems		Properties of Organizations
Systemic Properties	– properties that belong to the whole of the network	synergy and going concern value
Organising Relations	– create the systemic properties	inter-divisional/dept functions and relations
Configuration	– pattern of the network which provides characteristics particular to the organism; prescribes the quality of relationships	process and structure issues
Complexity	– denotes systemic properties that exist at a particular network level	organization structure
Self-organising	– achieved by inherent response pattern that prescribes how the organization will adapt	leadership and strategic planning function focusing values and core competencies to new realities
Feedback	– loops that are part of the organization's structure informing it of the results of its adaptive processes	formal and informal communication flows and MIS

Feedback as a Critical Function of Living Systems

As the living organism relates or engages with its environment, it receives continuous *feedback* through multiple feedback loops which are part of its structure. This continual feedback enables it to adapt and adjust its behaviour so as to optimize its relationship with the environment. This concept of feedback is intimately connected with the network pattern, enabling organisms to continuously organize and regulate themselves in response to their context and environment.

Putting together all of these findings, the new science holds that in a living system the product of its operation (i.e. its output), is its own organization. In other words, doing is being. Being and doing in living systems are inseparable, as for them being, is embodying their mode of organization, i.e. it is the doing. An illustrative example might be that of a flower. The flower's nature is to be a flower. That is its being. How it achieves this is by doing all the things that make it a flower. As a living organism it has inbuilt properties that prescribe the type of flower that it will be, its size, colour, smell, and so on. As a flower it is continuously engaged in being a flower. All its organic activities are centered around attaining its potential as the flower it was destined to be. Every doing activity is being.

Further, the pattern inherent within a living organism is the configuration of relationships among the system's components which determines the system's essential characteristics. Its pattern is therefore both the internal and external alliances and partnerships that make the organism function. These internal and external relationships make up the stakeholder network in a business organization which together describe what this organization is about.

The structure of the system is the physical embodiment of its pattern of organization. From an organizational viewpoint, the structure of the system prescribes the shape of the network and determines the links between various relationships. We might draw a parallel with the links between the marketing, selling, operations, and customer feedback functions.

The life process of the system is the activity of continually embodying the system's pattern of organization through stages of growth, development, and evolution. In business terminology we talk about the organization or product life cycle that goes through innovation, growth, maturity, and decline.

Implications for Business Organizations

These principles of living organisms have tremendous implications for business organizations. The product (i.e. the output) of the organization's operation is to continuously self-organize in response to the energy and information that flows to the organization from the environment. This explains why businesses are preoccupied with re-organizing in order to enhance their effectiveness. The actual configuration of relationships within a business organization, (e.g. how various functions interrelate or how information flows), determines how an organization actually executes its strategy and does its business.

The life process of the organization can be seen as the organization's adaptive work in order to continuously achieve its mission. It does this by attuning its core competencies to new realities and responding to changing market and customer circumstances. Organizations' structures also continuously change in order to facilitate and enhance their ability to execute strategy and deliver a distinctive product or service. Self-organization should flow from the effects of the environment and the demands made by the organization's stage in its life process. Self-organization needs to be recognized as the inherent adaptive capacity of a living organism in response to its (recognized) changing realities. The same applies to business organizations. Simply focusing on restructuring or re-organizing without understanding the systemic nature of these effects, rarely delivers worthwhile results.

When business organizations stray from the inherent principles of living systems, or if they focus only on one aspect and fail to sustain a balance among them, they get into serious difficulties.

A Closer Look at Self-Organization

The principle of self-organization in living systems is so critical to leadership and strategic planning, that it merits some further attention. Self-organization within a living system takes many forms.

First, a key characteristic of a living network is that it continually reproduces itself. It achieves this through the continuous maintenance, renewal, and replacement of its cells in continual cycles while still maintaining the overall pattern of its organization.

Another continual change that takes place is developmental change where new structures are created. Developmental change occurs in two ways. Either it occurs in response to environmental influences or it results from the system's internal dynamics that foster self-generated changes. As it continues to act with its environment, a system will undergo a series of structural changes, thereby creating a path or pattern of change. These developmental changes alter the system's behaviour affecting the nature and shape of self-generated structural changes, which in turn also affect the change path.

At any point on its pathway of change, the network's current structure is a record of previous structural changes. Each structural change influences the organism's future behaviour and future change path. These structural changes, some of which are self-initiated, novel internal system creations, result in the organism's development and evolution. The propensity and ability to achieve these developmental changes appear to be an inherent dynamic force within the system's pattern or configuration. In other words living systems are continuously adapting, changing, and restructuring. They are always becoming, moving from potential to actuality. This would appear to confirm the Aristotelian teleological view of the world! This has also profound implications from an ethical standpoint.

It has been discovered that in a living system the need to develop and be creative is part of its life force and energy. If only business organizations could take cognizance of the fact that they are living systems imbued with an inherent creative, energetic life force, which is waiting to be tapped and harnessed, instead of trying to suppress, limit, or control its expressive energy and power.

Development and Evolution

The findings of the new science reveal that the development and behaviour of a living organism is determined by its pattern and structure. The pattern prescribes the propensity for change, while the structure determines the range and type of change that might take place. In other words the configuration of relationships is what drives the change process and gives them their potentiality, while the structure of the organization is what aids or inhibits the potential which lies within the change process.

Another finding is that in response to environmental changes or challenges, organisms or systems evolve through symbiosis. The symbiosis of formerly independent organisms result in the formation of new composite entities. This has proved to be a powerful evolutionary force. Studies of the evolution of species reveal that the process of symbiosis results in an ever more intricate arrangement, co-operation, and co-evolution between living organisms. This diversity accounts for the resilience of life to changing circumstances and to environmental catastrophes. Living systems are resilient and have an inherent capacity for survival and creativity. They thrive on novelty. Nothing, it seems, can curb the creative spirit of life.

The Effect of the New Science on Business Organizations

In essence then, the new science tells us that integrated networks are the patterns of life and relationships are the essence of the living world. Organisms survive through a dynamic tension between the stability of structure and fluidity of change. Creativity is one of the key properties of living systems and diversity enhances adaptive capacities and adds resilience. Are these findings not in tune with the changing nature of business organizations? (see Table 4.4 over).

Leadership Implications of the New Science

The way in which a culture construes reality typically provides the basis on which it organizes its societies and businesses. If reality is perceived as predetermined and certain, where control and conformance is upheld as the norm, then society will set rigid controlling norms; it will implement hierarchical authority and status systems, and its groups and institutions will shun creativity as obstructive deviance. If, on the other hand, reality is understood to comprise the creative, fluid activity of highly interdependent relationships, where new bonds are being created all the time, and the potential for new behaviour is almost limitless, society will adopt a far more open, accepting, reciprocal, and flexible style when organizing its societies and institutions.

In light of this the perception of reality emerging from the new science has profound implications for not only science, philosophy, and politics, but also business organizations. As we gain a better understanding of the nature of living organisms of which we are a part, we should align our social and business structures accordingly. Congruence between our true natures and the way that we organize ourselves will undoubtedly lead to a more harmonious existence.

Furthermore, it is increasingly evident that we cannot address our business and economic problems in isolation. Politicians and business

TABLE 4.4 Findings of the New Science and Developments in Business

Principles of the New Science	Business Organization Response
Being and doing inseparable	Search for organizational congruence between mission, values, and activities
Interconnectedness of all living systems	Developing integrated networks both internally and externally
Configuration of networks	Dissolving hierarchy, create network structures
Systemic property of the whole different and more than the parts	Identify systemic properties of the organization as a whole and develop networks to optimize
Principle of self-organization	Let the process determine the structure
Behaviour is pattern and structure determined	Focus on enhancing relationships and develop a structure that places an emphasis on relationships Place emphasis on people's adaptive capacities rather than capabilities
Open, unconstrained, feedback loops	Develop unconstrained feedback loops channeled by attention to new realities and core competencies
Symbiosis	Develop partnerships and encourage co-creation and co-evolution
Capacity for creativity and novelty	Encourage unconstrained novelty creativity and focused on the new realities

executives expound at great length on the complexity of the problems that confront them. As we are discovering, and the new science is confirming, we cannot overestimate the interconnectedness of our pluralistic visions of reality or our seemingly isolated actions. At no level of operation or individuation can we consider ourselves to be an independent part or an isolated component. Regrettably, many leaders, in political, social, and business life fail to acknowledge this interrelatedness sufficiently.

We are realizing that the business paradigms that we apply to define problems and solutions require ever greater regard for the other relationships within the networks. Strategies based on 'us-and-them' are being replaced with 'we'. The new organizational mindset is geared to thinking laterally rather than horizontally.

In order to exercise leadership that is congruent to the findings of the nature of living systems we need to heed the following:

- Paying attention to relationships is primary.

- Linear cause-and-effect analysis has minimal relevance.

- Self-organization is a key principle.

- Feedback needs to be continuous and free-floating (i.e. it should not be contained or controlled).

- Motion and change are good.

- Adaptive capacities are far more important than skills and capabilities.

- Processes and optimizing links between relationships should determine the organization's structure and not vice versa.

- Creativity and deviance is healthy.

- Multiple perspectives and uncertainties are necessary and valuable.

Furthermore, the old idea of developing hierarchical structures based on a classification of building blocks no longer reflects the new reality. The predominant structure is networks.

Many of these new concepts and ideas seem counter to the traditional view of leadership and the role and function of strategic planners. Leaders are supposed to have power, and power derives from hierarchy. For new leaders the focus is no longer on power but on influence. Leaders and strategic planners are also usually expected to inject a level of certainty, be experts in analysis, and extract the essence of strategic issues or situations. They normally explicate visions, set goals and targets, decide on performance measurements, assess the skills needed to perform important functions, prescribe the areas of creativity, and downplay the impacts of diversity. This is all changing.

Summary

The Adaptive Age calls for a new kind of leadership. This is leadership that does not provide easy answers. Instead this leadership helps people to enhance their own adaptive capacity. The focus of the new leadership is on the activity rather than the person. New leaders are in sync with realities and help people deal with the challenges that these represent.

New leaders have a new mindset. New leaders understand the need to exercise leadership and to make creative and constructive interventions when appropriate. Exercising leadership requires understanding humans as living systems that have the capacity to self-organize and to learn through ongoing feedback from the system of which they are a part. New leaders understand that multiple realities exist and they take care to ensure that multiple realities are recognized and are not dismissed. New leaders place value on both the group and the individual.

Key Points Raised in this Chapter

▸   There is a lack of leadership in the business arena.

▸   The ability to exercise leadership comes from the depth of our humanity.

▸   Leadership and authority are different.

▸   New versus conventional notions of leadership.

▸   The primary task when exercising leadership is orienting the organization to the new realities.

▸   The ingredients for exercising leadership.

▸   Leadership as an activity that initiates an adaptive process.

▸   The need for a new leadership mindset.

▸   The importance of self-organization in living systems as being the capacity to adapt to new realities.

SUGGESTIONS

■   Review the activities of the leaders within the organization. Are they engaged in adaptive work or is most of their work technical work?

■   Consider whether it is possible for people in the organization to be in positions of authority and to exercise leadership.

■   Revisit the feedback process that occurs within the organization. What are its constraints?

- List the number of organizational restructurings that have taken place over the recent period. Have these improved the motivation and the performance of employees?

- List the people in the organization who have informal authority. Do the people in formal authority give them support or do they consider them to be a threat?

Further Reading

Heifetz, R.A. (1994) *Leadership without Easy Answers*, Harvard University Press, Cambridge, MA.

Wheatley, M.J. (1992) *Leadership and the New Science: Learning about Organizations from an Orderly Universe*, Berrett-Koehler Publishers, Inc, San Francisco.

CHAPTER FIVE

Exercising Leadership

A Reconceptualization of Leadership

In light of the many discontinuities and changing realities in the state of the world, it seems an appropriate time to reconceptualize leadership. It is not that we need more leaders, but rather that we need more exercise of leadership by persons in positions of influence and responsibility. We also need to empower and encourage those who are not formally recognized as leaders to use their informal authority to exercise leadership within their respective domains.

As the world becomes more interrelated and more complex we need to remind ourselves that we can never do for others what they must do for themselves. People need to be encouraged to gain confidence in their own competencies, especially their innate ability to be creative and to adapt. Exercising leadership, to use Plato's allegory, is akin to encouraging others to come out of the cave and to deal with the true, rather than the shadow, realities. As Plato pointed out, those who escape from the cave require great skill to persuade others to do the same. Such is the power of fixation to the known, no matter how limited and gloomy the known might be. The skill of mobilizing others to move to new ground, where they will experience the initial discomfort of new vistas, is called exercising leadership. It is based on at least the following foundational principles.

The Foundational Principles of Leadership

Five key influences form the foundational principles for exercising leadership. The first was introduced by Nicolaus Copernicus (1473–1543), who removed the earth from the centre of the universe. This insight made us realize that we were not the centre of the cosmos and the world did not revolve around us. On the contrary, his discovery challenged us to face the reality that our earth is a minuscule, insignificant part of an infinite system, the scope and complexity of which is, even to this day, beyond our conception. We are mere particles in space and *we* do the revolving.

The second major influence was that of Charles Darwin (1809–1882), who put forward his well-known hypothesis on evolution and natural selection. Darwin's insights have heightened our understanding of how things evolve and how survival depends on the ability to adapt. His insights have helped us to understand that the change process is by its nature an evolutionary process that manifests itself in incremental movement. From a leadership perspective this highlights the importance of adaptation and encourages patience and understanding of the importance of timing.

The third influence was Sigmund Freud (1856–1939). Freud gave us the notion of the unconscious. He highlighted the enormous influence it has over the way we construe reality, respond to challenges, carry our personal baggage, and interpret our environment. Freud has taught us that human behaviour is affected by unconscious as well as conscious processes and that our background, history, and culture significantly affect our behaviour, responses, and capacity to adapt.

The fourth influence was Albert Einstein (1879–1955), who introduced the theory of relativity which replaced absolute notions of time and space. What this has taught us is that all things are relative. An issue, aspect, act, or measurement can only be understood, assessed, or compared in relation to something else. The world of absolutes is gone.

The fifth influence is that of the new sciences. This places before us a developing theory on the interrelated networks and systemic properties of living systems. For human beings, who are arguably this world's prime example of complex living systems, these new findings help us to better understand ourselves. Awareness of these new findings should enable us to act more congruently to our true natures. This makes no small contribution toward enhancing our quality of life.

To know that the stance from which we see the world significantly influences our point of view, to understand that things evolve, to recognize the potency of unconscious processes, to acknowledge that all things are relative, and to adopt the notion that all living systems are integrated via networked relationships provides key foundational principles for new leaders. To apply these principles with attention and sensitivity is the hallmark of a new leader and the *sine qua non* of exercising effective leadership.

FOUNDATIONAL PRINCIPLES OF LEADERSHIP

1   We are not the centre of the universe – we are a tiny part in an infinite system.

2   As living creatures we are in a continuous process of evolution and we must adapt in order to survive.

3   We must be attentive to the power of the unconscious in influencing human behaviour.

4   All things are relative.

5   Living systems comprise interrelated networks linked by a complex of relationships that are in perpetual change and motion.

The Definition of Leadership

For the purposes of our discussion leadership is identified as an activity that initiates an adaptive process. The emphasis is on the activity of exercising leadership. I now turn to what exercising leadership means and how this is achieved.

> **Leadership is achieved by distinguishing adaptive challenges from technical challenges, mobilizing people to tackle the tough problems that this inevitably raises, and holding steady until the adaptive work has been done. Identifying the adaptive challenge and the adaptive work requires systems thinking enacted in detailed systemic analyses.**

Exercising Leadership begins with recognizing New Realities

Being able to exercise appropriate and effective leadership requires being attuned to the new realities. This is a continuous process as new realities reflect the perpetual motion of life. Those who are able to exercise leadership typically understand the new realities that affect their world. The first step is to acknowledge these new realities by discussion with other members of the organization. This serves to both communicate and test that these realities exist and that they are perceived correctly.

In the first three chapters we discussed some of the new realities that face most business organizations. We have also highlighted the need for a strategic agenda that places the ongoing recognition of new realities high on its list. I have advocated that dedicated resources be devoted to the monitoring of new realities and that these should be included within the strategic planning function.

Understanding New Realities requires Systems Thinking

In order to understand the nature of new realities and the value-tensions that they are likely to represent to different organizational stakeholders, a systemic perspective on the environment must be taken. This entails looking at the world as a series of interrelated systems and understanding how the macrocosm is reflected in the microcosm, and vice versa. With a systemic perspective, the features and characteristics of the greater world or system are reflected in the smaller systems that are part of, or subsumed by, the macro system. For example, when the wider world is experiencing 'chaos' at the macro level, countries often will be internally chaotic, communities will be struggling to hold onto established norms, and family life will be experiencing upheaval. Similarly, if we were to focus on the microcosm, say at the level of families within a society, undoubtedly we will find that this micro-system is importing and reflecting the disorder and disequilibrium of the larger system.

The prime purpose of systems thinking and systemic analyses is to identify and understand the relationships within a system or network and to grasp the meaning-making, values, and roles of these relationships from the perspective of the larger whole. Systems thinking requires one to be observant as to how relationships evolve, dissolve, and how and why new ones form. It also focuses on the roles that different relationships play and how they function within the operation of the entire system. Since systems thinking is so fundamental to the new organizational mindset it should be beneficial to discuss this in some detail.

A Detailed Review of Systems Thinking

It was not without profound understanding of the nature of things that Moses and scores of other Occidental and Eastern prophets went up to the top of a mountain or higher pinnacle to 'see' their God or to gain prophetic insights. 'Stepping back' or 'going to a higher viewing point' always provides a different perspective. By seeing the whole, we can better understand how the parts fit together and how the different parts are needed to constitute the whole. When we see the whole picture we experience the 'aha' feeling. That 'aha' feeling means that we have attained another level of understanding. Systems thinking is intended to take us to this higher level of understanding.

According to Peter Senge of MIT, systems thinking is *The* 'Fifth Discipline'. It is the discipline that fuses together the other four, namely personal mastery, mental models, building a shared vision, and team learning. Systems thinking, according to Senge, is the art of seeing the forest and the trees. It encourages seeing patterns rather than forces and events and facilitates organizing complexity into a coherent story.

Systems thinking is about seeing the bigger picture. It is akin to standing on the mountain and surveying the terrain. One takes in the contours of the land, observes and marks the hills and valleys, the fertile land, and the waste land. It is about looking far and near and about seeing the pattern of things as they lie. All leaders, including business leaders and strategic planners should engage in systems thinking. This should become a habitual way of seeing the world.

The criteria for systems thinking begins with understanding that all living systems are integrated wholes linked together by a network of relationships.[1] To understand systemically is to understand the nature of relationships. For a systems thinker, understanding the network of relationships and investigating the nature of those relationships is primary. The systems thinker understands that to perceive reality is to perceive a certain network of relationships. The systems thinker grasps that different people from different cultures and different walks of life have had different experiences and are themselves living organisms comprised of a variety of different networks. Different people also perceive their reality as a range of diverse networks of relationships. Understanding the implications of this diversity of networks helps us to understand why multiple realities exist. To be sensitive to multiple realities is vital in a cross-cultural world which is actively engaged in globalization. Cross-cultural empathy will provide enormous payoffs in dealing with employees, business partners, customers, and competitors. Sensitivity to the various networks of realities that different stakeholder groups hold is at the core of Adaptive Age thinking.

Advantages of Systems Thinking

Once one grasps the power of systems thinking it becomes second nature to take a systemic perspective. Such a perspective leads to seeing parts of the world always in relationship to the greater whole. This mindset is helpful in a number of ways.

Macro analysis

Systemic thinking leads to a more insightful and effective organizational macro analysis. When doing environmental analysis, for example, instead of drawing standalone boxes with a series of arrows going backwards and forwards, one will now draw networks that incorporate multiple strands of relatedness (see Figure 5.1). This will visually bring to light the interconnectedness of the external environment in a far more meaningful way than the box and straight line method. As networks flow in many directions, drawing webs helps show the true nature of the criss-crossed network of relationships. The complex ambiguities and contradictions that exist in the real world are exposed. A network diagram can also reveal where there is challenge and concurrence, competition and collaboration, and agreement and disagreement among those who make up the network. This is critical strategic information which is more easily captured by taking the systemic approach.

FIGURE 5.1 Environmental analysis – old and new

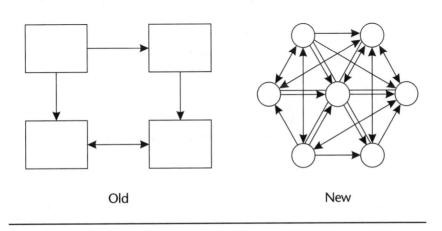

Old   New

In relationship

Systemic thinking allows for a better understanding of what it means to be in relationship. Initially the systemic exercise hones one's ability to actually identify relationships. It also helps to uncover what is driving each relationship and shows how the relationship manifests itself in reality.

We know that a critical attraction of relationships is that they give meaning. They are formed in order to satisfy the meaning-making needs of the participants. What is of strategic interest to business organizations is to understand which meaning-making needs and values are being met by which parties in the system.

The meaning-making needs among the parties to a relationship may not be the same. For example, customers may engage with the organization so as to fulfil their needs for a healthy lifestyle, economical living, status, avant garde behaviour, and so on. The organization, on the other hand, may make meaning by enhancing public health, increasing social mobility, or improving societal communications.

Sometimes the relationship is established for a mutual satisfaction of needs, for example, safety, security, loyalty, or the reinforcement of common identities. Mutually satisfying relationships are inclined to perdure and come to an end only when a radical reality shift occurs.

Needs themselves change, however, so relationships are in a continual state of flux. Business organizations fail to realize this adequately. They often assume that once they have identified the needs of their stakeholders 'for once and for all', all they have to do is satisfy them. Proactively monitoring meaning-making and value changes is executed by too few organizations. Apple Computers and McDonald's are examples that readily come to mind. Business management tends to forget that relationships are dynamic and open and that parties' expectations of the relationship are continuously adapting to changes in the environment and emerging new realities. Even relationships where both parties are meeting the same needs, are on the move. For relationships to be sustainable, therefore, there must be evidence of continuing reciprocity through co-creation and co-evolution.

The need to form relationships takes place not only at the individual level, but at the organizational, institutional and national level, too. In general, due to the affective dimension of relationships, people, institutions and organizations are reluctant to end them. This very obvious reality is underestimated by most business organizations. Customers are rarely anxious to switch. Attention to their changing values and needs goes a long way toward sustaining the relationship indefinitely.

Systemic thinking can also lead to identifying new potential relationships that had previously not been considered. This occurs particularly in the meaning-making and values identification stage, when common meanings and values are discovered underlying apparently different external cultural behaviours. Jewish and Irish systems or organizations exemplify this point. According to their external behaviour, these two groups would normally be considered poles apart. From a meaning-making and values point of view, however, they have many important similarities. Both are fiercely loyal to their families and their diasporean connections. They exhibit an intriguing combination of liberal and conservative values, believe strongly in their God and the importance of faith, respect the Sabbath more than most, prefer to mingle with their own, tenaciously invest in the education of their children, enjoy buying in small quantities, and live mindful of the 'inevitable' rainy day.

This example suggests that organizations should look at values rather than needs. Values are prior to, and drive, needs. Values relate to ends rather than means. In the Adaptive Age the focus must be on values and ends. People are tired of the excessive focus on means. They are insisting that these become more consonant with the ends that they wish to attain. Organizations must continuously monitor the ends that their stakeholders seek. This will help them to determine what drives the relationship with the organization and will enable them to understand their needs more astutely.

Shareholder groups and the organization

As a consequence of systemic thinking, the organization gains a better understanding of why stakeholder groups engage with the organization. By understanding the meaning-making needs that it fulfils, and the values that underlie those meanings, the organization learns what role it plays within the system(s) in which it participates. For example, to a typical client an insurance organization plays the obvious role of provider of financial security. A bank may play the role of provider of mobility; an important role that fulfils a critical need for some people in a modern world. For others, it may play the role of provider of prestige. For organizations, the bank may be the provider of credibility or flexibility. A supermarket chain, on the other hand, most often plays the role of household partner. The combined goal of the customer and the supermarket is to achieve convenient and economically efficient household management. To employees, suppliers, investors, competitors, and the social community, the organization fulfils other roles. These might include creator of jobs, provider of security, reinforcer of identity, and representative of scientific advance.

A specific example that illustrates this point is IBM and the role that it used to play for its customers. Ten to fifteen years ago there was a well-known adage, 'I can't get fired for buying an IBM'. Everyone knew what it meant. The safe and secure option in the otherwise treacherous, unchartered world of information technology was to buy IBM equipment. Having invested in IBM products and services, customers firmly believed that IBM would care for them almost better than they could for themselves. IBM would sort out problems, organize upgrades, carry out maintenance, and generally ensure that acceptable standards of technology and information flow would be sustained. IBM would be the reliable, expert partner, on which the organization could totally depend. IBM was viewed as *the* industry provider of both job and information security – no insignificant role!

By contrast, in recent years, in many organizations the contrary is true. One could now conceivably be fired if one invested in the inappropriate IBM equipment; such is the extent to which their previously enviable image has been tarnished. The fact that IBM has managed to turnaround and not lose the backbone of its customer base is not so much attributable to new management at IBM, but is testimony to the power of meaning, values and relationships. Customers who have important values invested in their suppliers are exceedingly reluctant to place their loyalty elsewhere. The psychological exit costs appear too high. Despite the current amount of marketing investment and hype, organizations still do not truly understand or cultivate customer relationships to the full. This is a theme to which I shall return repeatedly.

In general, an organization typically plays a multiplicity of roles which it has to manage in dynamic tension. These various roles call for attention to the value needs of the different stakeholders in the organization. Roles tend to be stereotypical. This means that they have certain expectations associated with them. If the organization fails to meet the expectations of the role into which it has been cast it is likely to surprise and disappoint a significant portion of its stakeholders. Clarifying its role within the larger system, and communicating stakeholder expectations that it intends to satisfy, is one of the most difficult organizational leadership tasks. The difficulty stems from the fact that most organizations do not really understand their role from a systemic perspective.

A further complication is that some of the organization's roles and values may seem to be in conflict. An obvious example of such a conflict is the role of provider of job security versus the role of provider of shareholder wealth. These apparent conflicts need to be managed. Role tension, however, is natural and healthy. It reflects an alive, creative, and dynamic organism that is continuously balancing and juxtaposing relationships.

Understanding the types and the nature of role tensions is part of exercising leadership. Managing those tensions systemically is part of the strategic planning function.

Understanding covert processes

Systemic thinking heightens one's ability to be observant of and attentive to the more subtle or covert processes that make up system dynamics. This arises as a consequence of being attuned to people and organizational meaning-making behaviour. Seldom do people behave in a strange or seemingly irrational fashion without a reason. Sometimes the reasons are obvious and require little interpretation. At other times, however, more covert processes might be at work.

An example that comes to mind is a recent experience at a conference that I attended. The conference was in fact on Leadership and Covert Processes. It was lead by an African American male and a Puerto Rican female. Both are trained psychologists and have gained credibility in certain circles for their skills in leadership workshops. The conference was attended by approximately 150 people, of which less than half a dozen were people of colour. Within the first day (it was a weekend event) the conference proceedings were in disarray. While participants ostensibly followed instructions by forming groups and attending sessions, very soon mayhem reigned. People misread instructions, argued over the agenda, ignored time limits, complained about the food, and challenged group facilitators at every opportunity. Throughout the weekend, conference participants seemed disgruntled and dissatisfied. Quite unexpectedly at the time, however, the conference ended on an upbeat note.

The covert dynamics were uncovered in the final session in a very candid discussion between participants and conference staff. During this discussion what became abundantly clear to the entire group is that we had enacted the conference theme – leadership and covert processes. While no one could be accused of intentionally having subverted the proceedings, in collusion our covert process had been to prove that two people of colour, especially one of whom was female, were incapable of holding together a predominantly white group. We showed them up as being incompetent and our actions were aimed at rendering them incompetent, so that we could prove our point. For example, they pointed out instances where their express directions were not followed by 150 people!

The closing workshop discussion began by taking a macro-systemic view. A detailed and expert analysis, lead by the conference leaders, revealed the authority and leadership issues that existed within the group. During the discussions the group's covert processes, aimed at de-authorizing the leaders, were deftly exposed and we were confronted with our own subconscious biases and predispositions that had so forcefully played themselves out. This was an enormous eye-opener to all of us. Prior to the conference we would all have adamantly insisted that we did not harbour any racial or gender biases. Yet, there it was, blatantly uncovered as part of our partisan subconscious. We had deliberately, yet covertly, challenged the leadership and authority of the conference leaders. By not being aware of, let alone open and direct about our feelings of prejudice and no confidence, as a group we had colluded in not giving the conference leaders an opportunity to assert their authority or control. We had spent the weekend sabotaging them so as to be able to assert that they had no authority or competence in the first place. I am sure that many people who have been in positions of authority and/or leadership have had similar experiences. When this occurs, not detecting what is going on renders one very vulnerable to potentially negative group dynamics. Many leaders have met their demise by not grasping in time the complexities of covert behaviours. Our conference discussions provided some compelling insights of how systemic analyses can be of great assistance in unpacking covert behaviours.

Exercising leadership requires one to understand not only overt but covert behaviour. This becomes especially important when new realities present significant value tensions and people resist doing their adaptive work. Understanding the nature of their resistance and the underlying reasons for that resistance is the first step toward dealing with it. Covert processes powerfully resist change actions and therefore require identification at the earliest possible moment. Failure to do so will render attempts at adaptive work impotent.

Adaptive capacities

Taking a systems view facilitates understanding the adaptive capacities of systems. Uncovering meaning-making and value systems helps one see how and why new realities provide adaptive challenges to the organization.

One organization that seems to have an enormous stumbling block in this regard is Apple Computers. Despite several years of very obvious new realities, they have refused to adapt. The Apple story provides another example of the power of relationships based on values. The founding inspiration of Apple lay in it assuming the role of 'friend'. To thousands of computer-shy administrative staff, academics, and hobbyists, the Apple and then the Mac became their 'desktop friend'. In the early seventies, when computers were perceived by most as intimidating black boxes a friendly computer was a great bonus. The Macintosh Apple 'friend' addressed the needs of the fearful. This 'friend' was as familiar as an apple, never caused humiliation by expecting the user to participate in complex routines and instructions, was fun to use, speeded up processes, was reliable, and empowered its users. Due to this highly valued friendship role, many users are committed to an Apple computer as a friend for life.

This 'best friend' devotion between the Apple organization and its users has culminated in a myopic resistance to the new realities. An advanced, more complex relationship is the more adult requirement. The new reality is that powerful networks, linked through open systems, with capacities for huge storage and speeds, is needed. The Apple 'friend' has failed to mature with the industry. Simple friendship is no longer sufficient. Apple's founding value of being a provider of a 'desktop friend' does not necessarily need to change, but what a desktop friend *means* has now changed. By comparison we seek different things in a friend when we are aged 11 or 12 than when we are 30. At 11 or 12 we seek simple and empowering relationships. At 30 we thrive on something more complex and challenging; we are better able to empower ourselves; we are prepared to take a few risks; and the rules of give and take are more subtle.

Apple management's refusal to adapt provides an example of the power of resistance to meeting adaptive challenges. Apple remains deeply vested in its founding values but has not seen a way of adapting those values to the new realities. The various attempts at bringing in new executives, dropping prices, providing new technical features, and participating in the laptop war were all technical fixes to an adaptive problem that would not go away. The resistance became so entrenched that management even resorted to bringing back Steve Jobs, one of the founding partners, in an attempt to bring back the good old days.

Apple is an example of an organization that has lacked true leadership for many years. Over the past decade the leadership has not challenged the company to face the changing realities in the world of information technology. It has shied away from dealing with the tensions between organizational values and the changed values of its customers. The adaptive work that it should have undertaken was not given over to the people of the organization as their work to do. Instead, management floundered in all directions in an attempt to find easy answers, technical fixes, and leaders who would shoulder all the responsibility. Apple clearly lacks the adaptive capacity required of an organization to survive in the future. Even their current 'Think Different' campaign reflects their resistance to change. It will be interesting to observe how Apple deals with the Microsoft liaison and whether it will now be mobilized to do its adaptive work.

Making the organization attentive and adaptive

Systems thinking encourages one to downplay the reliance on linear cause-and-effect explanations. Systems thinking encourages one to see the multiple activities that are occurring at any one point in time. In a living system the activity of each party in a network affects the activities of the other parties at the same time. As all activity is occurring simultaneously, it is exceedingly difficult to isolate not only the timing, but the sequence of events. This focus places emphasis on being in a state of preparedness to respond, rather than being dependent on devising specific responses.

Most organizational strategies begin with analysing the environment and the current competitor behaviour, followed by predictions of the likely future environmental and competitive panorama. Strategies are usually formulated based on sequential cause-and-effect diagnosis and prognosis. Environmental changes and competitor actions are analysed and assessed on an 'if this happens, then that is likely to happen' basis. The problem for organizations arises when the 'likely to happen' scenario, does not happen. It is even more confusing and disorienting when a multiplicity of scenarios occurs at once. Management is often dumb-struck at how to formulate a rapid and potent strategy to deal with unexpected events or system tensions.

While it may be necessary to use the analytical 'what-if-then' approach in order to get a handle on key performance drivers, relying on this approach is not only simplistic, but denies the realities of a dynamic world where all of life is in simultaneous motion. Systems thinking advocates being attuned to the many motions that are occurring simultaneously. It prompts one to pose questions concerning the value tensions that the entire system might be facing. The emphasis is not on what might happen next, but rather on being in tune with all the many things that are happening now, and being sensitive to the uncertainties of tomorrow. Preparedness is not strategizing about a sequence of events.

Preparedness is about being ready to adapt to events whichever way that they might unfold. It means being mentally agile and strategically nimble-footed. It requires flexibility, rapid learning, responsiveness, and customer focus. These are correctives that should be part of the self-organizing behaviour of all learning organizations.

The greatest learning comes from finding new questions, not new answers. Systems thinking causes one to delve into ever more subtle questions instead of generating hosts of potential answers.

Identification of patterns

Systems thinking encourages one to identify patterns. Identifying patterns of relationships and establishing patterns of behaviour facilitates seeing how a system is configured. Knowing its configuration, i.e. understanding how a system is constructed, can provide great insights into the system's ability to be adaptable and flexible.

Systems thinking is the ideal mindset for scenario planning. The strength of scenario planning lies in seeing the pattern of relationships within a narrative. Living systems live, and move, and have their being, in narrative. Relationships exist within a narrative. Conventional linear cause-and-effect analysis dilutes the integrity of the narrative within which living organisms dwell. Systems thinking reasserts this reality and assists in being sensitive to the multiplicity of narratives that are in continual co-existence.

The Systems Thinking Mindset

From a leadership point of view a systems thinking mindset that continuously seeks out systemic issues is critical. It is also a vital disposition for those engaged in the strategic planning process. Understanding underlying values is a requirement for Adaptive Age thinking, as meaning-making is a priority for all stakeholders in human living systems. People want to be in meaningful relationships and want to engage in activities that are meaningful. They will no longer tolerate temporary superficial relations or participate in technical solutions that are not consonant with who they are and what enhances their identity. As discussed in Chapter 3, self-identity, i.e. what makes us who we are and how we are different from others, is a powerful globalizing theme.

THE ADVANTAGES OF SYSTEMS THINKING

1   Enables the organization to perform better macro analyses.

2   Improves the ability to understand stakeholder relationships.

3   Informs the organization as to how it meets the meaning-making needs of its stakeholders.

4   Assists in the understanding of covert processes.

5   Facilitates understanding the adaptive capacities of the greater system as well as the organization's own stakeholders.

6   Makes the organization attentive to the here and now while also being intentional and adaptive to future events.

7   Helps with the identification of key behaviour patterns.

Performing a Systemic Analysis

Systems thinking is about looking at the larger picture and getting a feel for its pattern of colours, shapes, and contours. It is about understanding the dynamics of relationships, especially covert processes, understanding adaptive capacities, and identifying patterns.

What we now need to consider is how to use systems thinking to organizational strategic advantage. We need to delve into the specifics of systems thinking so that it reveals the implicit relationship arrangements that give organizations their dynamic and synergistic properties.

Systems thinking is manifested by carrying out systemic analyses. This is a rigorous activity. It is the type of work that a research biologist might do when studying nature in the wilds. From a tent in the environment which embraces an object of study, the biologist will continuously observe, take-in, or screen out, both the macro and micro phenomena that pertain to the enquiry. The biologist will move backwards and forwards between macro and micro issues as he or she starts to see relationships, define patterns, and identify key influences. These are the activities that comprise a systemic analysis.

The prime purpose of carrying out a systemic analysis is to distinguish and understand the network of relationships that make up a system and its environment. In order to identify the organization's adaptive challenges, an organizational systemic analysis is conducted to uncover any incongruencies and inconsistencies between the values held by the organization and the changing values of its environment, notably, the country, community, ethnic group, or local society in which it is embedded.

While we refer to systemic analyses as a way to explicate systems thinking, it is important to note that part of the analyses is syntheses. This means that one is not only engaged in breaking systems down into comprehensible parts, but, by taking different perspectives, one is also trying to see how different parts fit together and give a system its uniqueness and vitality. Just like the biologist, sometimes one will consider the whole or a part of the whole and sometimes one is only concerned with a tiny segment of the whole. As for the biologist, for the organizational systems thinker, the more attuned one is to the terrain or the subject matter, the more adept one becomes at moving between macro and micro issues and between analysis and synthesis.

Who should Perform the Systemic Analysis?

Formal responsibility for carrying out systemic analyses should be given to those responsible for strategic planning. The systemic analyses, while being an ongoing activity, should be explicitly discussed with the organization's management at least twice a year. Informal discussions should be ongoing. During the formal discussions there should be an interchange of ideas between those responsible for operations and the strategic planners. This should focus on observations about what is going on within the systems that interface with the organization, e.g. government, the community, customers, and competitors, and how the dynamics in these systems affect the organization. The organization should be viewed both as an entire system and as a system comprising multiple sub-systems.

The systemic analyses is intended to uncover, amongst other things, the value tensions that are occurring between and within systems. It should also reveal early warning or change signals to which the organization needs to pay attention.

Members of the organization who are not engaged in the strategic planning function and who are not responsible for operations should also be encouraged to do their own systemic analyses within their sub-system. Achieving this could be of great advantage to the organization as a whole as they get an opportunity to see the interactions between macro and microcosms, i.e. between the larger and the smaller systems. This will assist in assessing the congruence between the organization's mission, values, and goals, amongst some of its most important stakeholders, notably its employees. Testing this congruence with external stakeholders, e.g. customers, is a far more complex, time consuming, and expensive exercise. Teaching and encouraging employees systems thinking and the steps in carrying out a systemic analysis also fortifies the foundations of a learning organization, something to which all organizations currently aspire.

Steps in Performing the Systemic Analysis

Establish the Boundaries of the System

In our highly interconnected world, a world comprised of living, vibrant, networks nested within networks, which adapt and self-organize at a multiplicity of levels, grasping the dynamics of the whole is difficult. The questions that are always posed are: 'Which whole?' and 'At what level of aggregation should one carry out one's analysis?'

Performing a systemic analysis means setting the boundaries for the system that one is about to study and then identifying the meaning-making and value systems at stake for the system as a whole. The boundaries selected are perforce arbitary, as systems have an infinite number of links. From a practical point of view it is not possible to include all of these in the analyses.

Taking the organization as a system, the boundaries will most likely be dictated by the size of organization, e.g. multinational or local, and the number and influence of stakeholders. For example Coca-Cola as a system is enormous. It is also made up of many, many sub-systems. One key strategic decision is to decide on the level of analysis of each of these systems. If the analysis becomes too large and complicated, no one will be able to grasp the larger picture. If the level of analysis is too small or too limited, important information about other influences will be omitted. Just as the naturalist has to decide the extent of the terrain which needs to be studied in order to understand the specific object of study, so does the organization. There will always be compromises and trade-offs. What is important is knowing which compromises and trade-offs one is making and understanding their implications.

Once one has selected the level of analysis, the principal guide to deciding which systems to evaluate lies in performing two initial exercises. The first step includes reviewing *all* those systems with which the organization has boundaries or interfaces. This may include systems within systems and sub-systems that cut across other systems. The main focus is on identifying their value systems and the nature of their relationships along the lines outlined above. Special attention should be given to those systems that are directly affected by, or affect the organization's own meaning-making and value systems. These may be complementary (competitor) systems, or the systems of partners, e.g. suppliers, distributors, investors, and employees.

For example, a key system that affects many organizations is the government. Within the government system, however, the organization may deal with the regulatory system and the grant or subsidy providing system. Even though each sub-system may still retain the right to make its own financial decisions, there may also be the government's central payments system that serves both of these sub-systems. The organization will, therefore, be dealing with four interconnected systems that are also systems in their own right. Each sub-system will have certain properties and ways of being that reflect the government system and the values that it holds, yet they will also have their own distinctive properties and ways of being which reflect their own values. If a new government comes into office, for example, and the organization is very dependent on its links with government, it is not only expedient but a critical necessity that the organization continuously monitor the values and relational aspects amongst these systems. For instance the new government may no longer place much importance on investing in industry through grants and subsidies. This could prove to be an enormous adaptive challenge to organizations who depend on a government that embraces that particular value.

The second step is to try to define the systems of *all the stakeholders* in the organization. While in principle all stakeholder systems will have boundaries with the organization and therefore should have been included in the initial analysis, sometimes there are more subtle or less obvious stakeholders than an initial review based on boundaries might identify. An example might be the spouses of senior management whose individual or combined actions might have a significant explicit or implicit affect on the values of the organization. Another might be a family trust on which the organization's founding entrepreneur is dependent for credibility and capital. These organizational interfaces and pressure points need to be understood as systems. In my experience, often the subtle, covert, or opaque stakeholder systems that exist have a disproportionate amount of influence over the organization's value systems and capacity to adapt.

Identifying systems that are relevant to the organization from these two angles, is always helpful. Not only does it provide a check and balance, but often it reveals a variety of implicit or covert systems and relationships that are pertinent to the organization's own values, relationships, and behaviours. It usually results in insightful and creative discussions regarding the attributes of different systems which lead to a deeper understanding of why the organization is the way it is. It also facilitates identifying who, within the system or organization, needs to learn about the new realities and adapt in order to change things.

Establish Links and Relationships

The systemic analysis helps to establish the nature of the systemic properties that belong to the whole system as distinct from those properties that belong to the parts. Systemic analysis includes clarifying the key links within each system or network (establishing all is rarely possible), mapping the relationships within the system, and defining the nature of the relationships themselves.

Defining the nature of the relationships entails:

- Eliciting the meaning-making and value systems at stake for each system stakeholder and specifying how the different system participants meet one another's needs.

- Understanding the various roles played by each participant/ stakeholder in the system and recognizing the tensions that participants/stakeholders experience as a consequence of having more than one role.

- Identifying the extent of dependency between the various system relationships.

- Recognizing the value tensions that might exist between the parts of the system, the whole system and its environment.

- Seeing both the formal, and especially the informal, partnerships that might exist between system participants and organization stakeholders (see also Figure 5.2).

The box below sets out the main steps to be taken for each system's analysis. If the organization is performing several analyses the results need to be viewed in conjunction with one another. This combined analysis and synthesis is further explained in the next chapter, 'Leadership and Strategic Planning'. It may also help to re-read Chapter 2, 'Adaptive versus Technical Work'.

FIGURE 5.2   Mapping the relationships within the system

THE SYSTEMIC ANALYSIS PROCEDURE

1   Identify key trends and new realities being made manifest in the macro environment. Remember to have broad horizons.

2   Select a level of analysis e.g. the country or community as a system.

3   Identify boundaries to the system of analysis.

4   Identify the key systems and sub-systems that make up the larger system, e.g., the government, the communities in a country.

5   Establish the systemic properties of the larger system (e.g. the country or community) with emphasis on its manner of meaning-making and values.

6   Establish similar properties of the sub-systems within the larger system selected.

7   Define the organization as a system. Clarify its values and the way that it makes meaning. Define the role that it plays in the larger system. Determine its sub-systems.

8   Identify the key stakeholders within the organization and within each sub-system.

9   Identify stakeholder values.

10   Clarify the nature of relationships between all stakeholders identified.

11   Establish any value tensions that exist between the system and its environment.

12   Establish any value tensions that exist within the sub-systems, and between their stakeholders.

As described above, the systemic analysis process is an ongoing one. It is not something that should be carried out behind the proverbial closed doors. It should be part of the dialogue and interchanges going on both within the organization and by the organization with its external stakeholders. This continuous dialogue and interaction provides a certain amount of reality testing. It is also serves to ensure that attention is being paid to the present, ongoing, perpetual change and motion that occurs within living systems. The organization is stimulated to be intensely alive and attentive to the here and now as its source of key change signals of the future.

While the organization, led by its executive management and the strategic planners, is paying attention to the multiple system dynamics, there is a call to exercise leadership. Exercising leadership denotes making constructive and creative interventions in the daily life of the system.

Leadership Intervention

In the context of systems thinking and systemic analyses, exercising leadership means:

- being in tune with new realities

- understanding systemic relationships;

- recognizing value-tensions within those relationships;

- and intervening with a creative response.

Recognizing new realities for what they are and the value-tensions that they represent is not easy. Either the new realities are not seen at all (Apple

Computers), they are misinterpreted (Hunt and Blake, McDonald's), or they are denied (IBM).

Exercising leadership means recognizing the existence of these problems and working with them. Making a constructive *intervention* means holding up a reality which needs to be acknowledged and understood for the value-tension that it creates. The goal of the intervention is to prevent work avoidance and to curtail repetitive ways of seeing and doing things. The intervention serves as a direct challenge to entrenched values and attitudes. By holding up new realities, leadership intervention enables people to make progress on the value conflicts that they experience. A successful intervention will stimulate, inspire, and encourage new perspectives and new behaviours. An effective intervention will lead to organizational (system) development, inspire the co-creation of ideas and solutions, and stimulate co-evolution with other organizations. Good and appropriate interventions stimulate the systemic analysis process, both at formal and informal levels.

'On target' interventions act as a stimulus to the growth and developmental phase of the organization. They stretch its adaptive capacity and alter the organization's pattern and structure so that it can move to a new phase or stage in its path of development. Poor or inappropriate interventions encourage work avoidance, stimulate technical rather than adaptive solutions, and alienate people.

EXAMPLES OF POOR INTERVENTIONS

- Devising ways of tinkering with the system rather than proposing ways of changing the system.

- Suggesting old strategies that have been successful in the past.

- Re-assuring people that things are 'not that bad'.

- Interpreting new realities only from the perspective of one stakeholder group.

- Telling people to shape-up or ship-out.

- Discussing profitability or the share price.

- Avoiding the issue of values and emotions by focusing on technical problems.

- Blaming people or things for the feeling of disequilibrium.

Identifying the Adaptive Challenge

If an organization is faced with a challenge to its meaning-making and value systems, it is facing an adaptive challenge. Identifying the adaptive challenge and explicitly articulating its nature and the consequent implications, are significant parts of exercising leadership. The identification of adaptive challenges is one of the prime goals of performing the system's analysis. Identifying adaptive challenges and performing a systemic analysis, therefore, go hand in hand.

The focal point of the systemic analysis is to identify the adaptive challenge.

Hunt and Blake's adaptive challenge was to adapt and reshape its traditional values of attention to personal relationships and loyalty to the modern values of time efficiency and price. They upheld the value of traditionalism and tried to introduce modernity through the route of the technical fix. They did not orient the values of the organization's stakeholders to the new values. Lack of congruence led to their demise.

Apple's adaptive challenge is to orient the organization to the way that PCs now provide meaning to their users. PCs can no longer just be friends. They need to be powerful partners, capable of providing power, speed and communication links. Being a specialized computer provider is only valuable if one can do all the other things considered to be industry standards. Word processing, making presentations, and desktop publishing is no longer in the hands of the trusted secretary. Everyone wants to be able to do these things, and to interlink their programs with myriad other programs. Apple needs to grasp how PCs now make meaning for their users. They need to understand that the value of partnership and competency has now changed. Idolatry from old customers will not save them from this new reality.

Identifying the organization's adaptive challenge is strategic work. It is prior to any strategic analysis. It precedes all other analysis. It is the heart of exercising leadership and is the most critical activity of the strategic planning function.

Self-Organization and Adaptive Capacity

As we discussed under the findings of the new sciences, one of the greatest attributes of living systems is their ability to self-organize. Self-organization occurs in response to information flows from the environment and as a result of self-generated changes that are an inherent feature of all living systems. This ability to self-organize is an organism's capacity to adapt. It would seem that all living organism's have this capacity. We know from Darwin, however, that this adaptive capacity differs from organism to organism.

The responsibility of executive and strategic management teams is to enhance this capacity. Darwin and the new sciences tell us that the fittest survive. Survival and fitness are about adaptive capacities.

From an organizational perspective, strategic fitness means being able to identify new realities and to respond appropriately to them. New realities invariably require a change in values, followed by a change in behaviour. The most well-known example of those who couldn't make this shift are the dinosaurs. Hence our referral to intractable, unresponsive organizations as dinosaurs. Similarly, the ostrich is now a protected species. These animals have been unable to adapt to the reality that sticking their heads in the sand no longer confuses their predators. Their inability to unlearn old behaviours and to learn new responses has made them easy prey to agile prowlers. Apple, the premier example of an ostrich organization, now has the protection of Microsoft. Not all ostrich organizations will have the benefit of this reprieve!

Strategic management is responsible for assessing the adaptive capacity of the organization. The measure of adaptiveness is the ability of the organization to orient its values to those presented by the new realities. This is reflected by the organization's ability to change existing values, systems, and behaviours rather than just tinkering with old ones. It requires making shifts in thinking. It calls for organizational transformation. It implies new patterns and new ways of doing things. It calls for new forms of analysis and a focus on synthesis, i.e. attention to new shapes and forms as a result of creative combinations. It demands letting processes drive relationships, and letting the organization's structure form as a result. It means being attentive and mindful to the present and not being overly preoccupied with the future. Above all, it requires giving creativity free reign to create both chaos and new directions, as we have now learned that even chaos has order (Wheatley 1992).

An adaptive organization is a learning organization. In order to foster a learning organization, all the members of the organization should be encouraged to bring their individual adaptive capacities to bear. Harnessing this adaptive energy in an inclusive and meaningful way calls for sensitivity and an attentive ear from those exercising leadership. The processes prompted by the strategic planning function should inspire people to augment the creativity that is part of their ability to adapt rather than curbing it through planning limitations and constraints. This will be addressed in greater detail in Chapter 6, 'Leadership and Strategic Planning'.

Dealing with Distress

Despite their outstanding leadership skills, Jesus, Gandhi, and Martin Luther King were not able to contain the distress of all the factions in their communities. The realities that they held up as leaders were too unpalatable for some people, and so they had to be removed by crucifixion and assassination.

Dealing with the distress experienced within an organization as people orient to the new reality and try to realign their values is an important part of exercising leadership. Dealing with distress requires being attentive to the discomfort that many people will feel. It means identifying the level of distress experienced by the various stakeholders and being attentive to the pain that they are feeling.

Part of dealing with the distress is to moderate the heat. This means that holding up new realities requires both firmness and sensitivity. Forcing people to change at a pace faster than they are capable of will engender resistance rather than co-operation.

Exercising leadership requires providing a holding environment where people can feel relatively safe while being somewhat challenged. A holding environment allows people to feel that the ground has not been totally swept from underneath them. They can still revert to some safe ground or hold on to some old behaviours while going through the change process. Being attentive to subconscious process, covert behaviour, and the existence of multiple realities is part of a leader's behaviour skills. Authoritarian commands to change or to adjust will not help here, nor will the implementation of more exacting or scientific methods of planning or market, competitor, or customer analysis. Value changes have to be dealt with first. Not even great attention to people's distress, especially in the fundamentalist faction, will guarantee that everyone will be on board. Some will continue to avoid, misinterpret, or deny the new realities. We have lost many great leaders due to resistance by a fundamentalist few.

Mobilizing Resources

Leaders help us to see that we live in a world of possibilities. They change our level of consciousness, enabling us to move with the rhythm and flow of life rather than attempting to control it. By deepening our understanding of reality, leaders help people to participate in shaping the future. These are some of the reasons why we empower people to exercise leadership.

Exercising leadership entails mobilizing people to do something. As Peter Drucker says, everything must devolve into work, otherwise it has no substance. This means that dreams, ideas, hopes, visions, and new understandings should mobilize people to do something.

The measure of whether leadership has truly been exercised is whether as a consequence, some kind of work is going on. This work can be internal as much as external work. Dealing with adaptive challenges requires first and foremost internal work. Exercising leadership mobilizes people to do this internal work so that the external work may follow.

The organization, as a living system, has to do its internal work, too. In order to be strategically effective the internal work is prior to any external work. Mobilizing people to do this work is difficult, partly because it is difficult work and partly because its progress is not easily apparent. It is difficult to measure internal work. Exercising leadership within the organization requires being in tune with the extent to which the internal work is going on and knowing when or how to turn up the heat should this be required.

Cosmetics Inc. – A Case Study

Cosmetics Inc., a nationwide cosmetics manufacture and retail organization, has been losing market share for the past 18 months. A variety of customer and competitor analyses reveal that customers are switching to less expensive products being sold by an array of new cosmetic chains. The new competitors are positioning their products at the lower end of the market. Their primary target market is teenagers, followed by those in their twenties and thirties.

Cosmetics Inc. has tried everything in the book. They have lowered prices. They have changed their packaging. They have added new products to their product lists. They now advertise their abstention from animal testing and they use reusable containers. Still they continue to lose market share. What they have not grasped is that there are new realities in the market for cosmetics.

The New Realities

Cosmetic Inc. has not come to grips with the changing realities of the cosmetic industry. The old industry metaphor, attributed to the marketing skills of Revlon, was 'hope'. Revlon identified that the business of selling cosmetics meant selling 'hope'. Cosmetically enhanced beauty held the promise of fulfilled dreams, hopes, and aspirations. If the right cosmetics were applied, loneliness, rejection and dejection would supposedly disappear.

Now we have a new metaphor in the cosmetics industry. This one is 'creatureliness'. Hope is no longer the prevailing value. Enhancing one's creatureliness is what matters. Cosmetics are now bought and used so as to enhance the creatureliness of the earth's most beautiful, intelligent, and exotic creatures – humans. Especially for the younger market, in the case of both men and women, cosmetics are used to accentuate the person as a beautiful creature. This creature is invested in its self-identity, its unique physique and its looks. This creature is one of earth's greatest creations and it wants to reflect that in its looks and smell. Being earthlike is being authentic and true. It is about being real, who you are, being incarnate, being individual, being embodied, being connected, being relational, and being bonded to Mother Earth. These are the new values.

Beautiful creatures enhance their features by exposing them rather than disguising and concealing them. Rouges and powder packs are gone. The earth's beautiful creatures want to use earth colours, radiate earthly smells, and want creams, potions, balms, and salves from sources close to the earth. The earth's beautiful creatures want to feel part of universal earth so they desire products from all its corners. They want the products to come from native lands bearing native colours and native smells. Beautiful creatures want cosmetics that have not been concocted in artificial laboratories but are the real thing. Wearing 'earth' cosmetics is what beautiful earth creatures do.

While a market for the more expensive perfumes and colognes exist, this is not the new, growing market. Even the older crowd are following the lead of the sons and daughters and younger siblings in trying out new 'earth' cosmetics.

New earth products that enhance creatureliness are called 'Earth', 'Forest', 'Everglade', and 'Harmony'. They are packaged in recycled earth coloured materials bearing earthlike insignias. Earth colours are sky or sea blue, forest green, and earth red. Advertising and promotion focuses on the congruence of the entire product with authentic earthly creatureliness.

Cosmetics Inc. has not come to grips with this new reality. They have not grasped that there has been a radical shift in values. They are rooted in trying to address their adaptive challenge with technical fixes.

Systems Thinking and a Systemic Analysis

Cosmetics Inc. would benefit from adopting a systems approach and performing a system's analysis.

Step 1

Key Trends and New Realities

Cosmetics Inc. has recognized that there are new trends in the environment. They should create a list of the new realities affecting the cosmetics industry as they see it. Enquiry into the nature of these changes should bring out the new value placed on being more authentic and creature-like. An investigation into the nature, ingredients, smells, and colours of the new products should provide key indicators as to the new values that they represent.

The new emphasis on care for the environment, making young people conscious of their reliance on and duty toward the environment should provide Cosmetic Inc. with signals that natural substances are to be bonded with and appreciated.

In-depth enquiry will reveal that cosmetics are now being worn to expose one's real features rather than trying to conceal them. The value related to cosmetics is that they uncover who one is rather than conceal parts of oneself. Transparency rather than opaqueness is the new goal. An investigation into trends and new realities will reflect this radical shift in values and meaning-making associated with cosmetics.

Step 2

Select the Level of Analysis

Cosmetics Inc. must define the level at which it wishes to perform its systemic analysis. In this case it would seem appropriate to take the nation as the first cut. Cosmetics Inc. also has to decide to what extent the even larger system, for example the continent, or all English speaking western countries also seem to be experiencing changing realities, i.e. they need to enquire as to whether this changing trend in cosmetics is a world-wide, geographical, or country phenomenon. If new realities are evident at a wider macro level, they need to consider its extent and specifically how it is affecting changes in their nationwide scene.

Step 3

Identify Boundaries to the System of Analysis

Cosmetics Inc. must decide where to set the limits of their analysis. Are they going to investigate the changing trends and values of their direct stakeholders or are they going to include an investigation of the changing values and trends of indirect stakeholders. For example, do they need to investigate trends in surgical cosmetics, or cosmetics for the elderly? Do they need to investigate changing values and trends in the chemical industry, or the retail industry? They also need to consider the definition of nationwide. Will they review all potential cosmetics buyers throughout the nation or will they only consider the markets that they want to be in? Cosmetics Inc. may need to redefine its target markets in light of the new realities that it uncovers.

FIGURE 5.3A Setting the boundaries

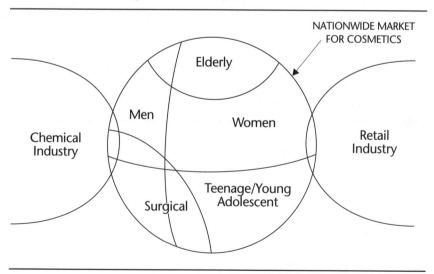

Step 4

Identify Key Systems and Sub-systems
Cosmetics Inc. should define the key systems and sub-systems that make up the larger system that they intend to analyse. This might look like this:

FIGURE 5.3B   Cosmetics Inc's key system and sub-systems

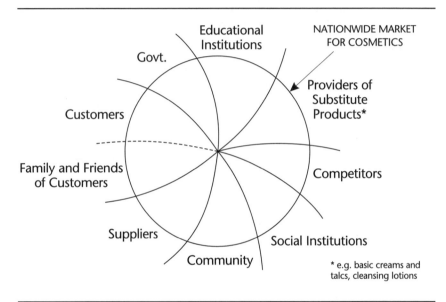

Step 5

Establish the Systemic Properties of the Larger System
Cosmetics Inc. should establish the values and relationships within the larger system.

Step 6

Establish Systemic Properties of the Sub-Systems

FIGURE 5.3C Systemic properties of cosmetics market

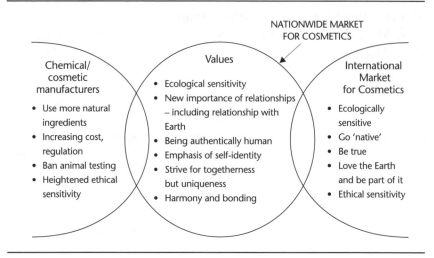

FIGURE 5.3D Systemic properties of sub-systems

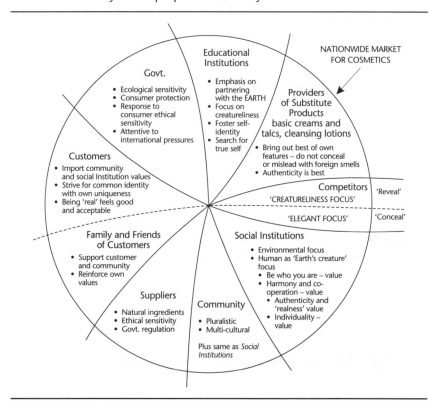

Step 7

Clarify the Organization's own Values and Ways of Meaning-Making. Define its role and determine its sub-systems
Cosmetics Inc.'s values are to promote upmarket cosmetics. In the past their prime focus has been on enhancing the beauty of women by providing elegant cosmetics with classic odours packaged in elegant wrapping. The value that they have emphasized has been 'simply elegant' and they have followed this theme through their entire product offering.

FIGURE 5.3E   Cosmetic Inc. as a system

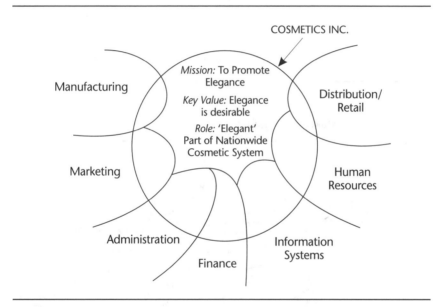

Step 8

Identify the Organization's Key Stakeholders
Cosmetics Inc.'s key stakeholders are mapped below.

Step 9

Identify Stakeholder Values
Cosmetic Inc's stakeholder values have been identified as follows:

FIGURE 5.3F Cosmetics Inc's key stakeholders

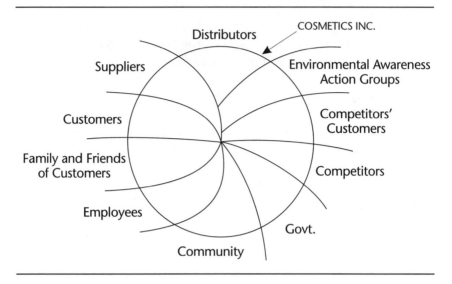

FIGURE 5.3G Stakeholder values

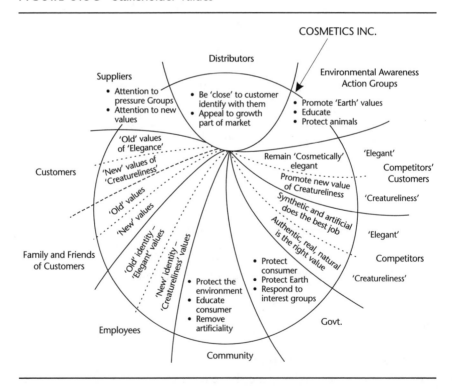

Step 10

Clarify the Nature of Relationships between Stakeholders

Cosmetic Inc' stakeholder relationships have been determined as follows:

FIGURE 5.3H Cosmetics Inc's stakeholder relationships

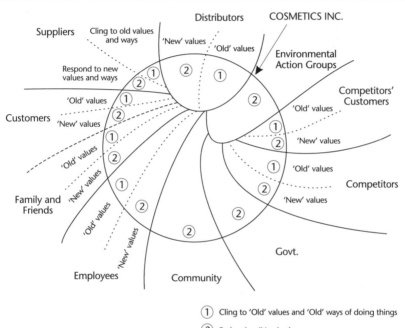

① Cling to 'Old' values and 'Old' ways of doing things

② Embracing 'New' values

Once these have been determined, Cosmetics Inc. needs to assess which groups represent the growth and profitability portion of the market they want to be in.

Step 11

Establish Value-Tensions

The value tensions between the new environment for cosmetics and that of Cosmetics Inc. can be summarised as:

Cosmetics Inc. faces the value tension between 'simply elegant' and 'creatureliness'. This is a big shift. People who want to look simply elegant do not want to smell of earth smells. The value of 'simple elegance' conveys looking flawless in an unostentatious way. Flawed features are elegantly concealed and strong features are elegantly accentuated. With 'creatureliness' all features are presented equally, there is nothing to hide or conceal. The concept of a 'flawed' feature is no longer relevant. Flaws apply to inauthenticity of a person rather than an irregularity of their features. This is a radical shift in the values associated with cosmetics and how they provide meaning. The 'old' value of elegance rejects the idea of artificiality or syntheticness in the interests of looking elegant. The 'new' value of creatureliness outrightly rejects artificiality, imitation, or syntheticness in order to look more appealing. What is appealing is real. Being real is the new 'hope'. It is what is valued and hence desirable. Respect, romance, fun, companionship, and love will be the reward for being true to oneself, being real, and being a beautiful creature. Simple elegance now appears fake, untouchable, unromantic, ornate and artificial.

Value-Tensions

New Values	Old Values
'Modern Countries'	Conservative Countries
Government	
Community	Elderly
Environmental Action Groups	
Younger Customers	Older Customers
Younger Employees	Older Employees
In tune Family and Friends	Outdated Family & Friends
Ethically Sensitive Suppliers	Old Fashioned Suppliers
Market Driven Distributors	Dated Distributors
Market Driven Competitors	Dated Competitors

Step 12

The value-tensions that exist between Cosmetics Inc.'s sub-systems are as follows:

Cosmetics Inc.'s entire operation is geared to simple elegance. Marketing invests in 'simply elegant' advertisements, sales staff are dressed in 'simply elegant' clothes, offices have 'simply elegant' decor, and the warehouse is modern and efficient. The R&D laboratory has scientific equipment and instruments and exudes a variety of simply elegant smells.

People who work for Cosmetics Inc. see themselves as being simply elegant. This makes them feel good. It defines who they are. They buy 'simply elegant' cars and live in 'simply elegant' homes in 'simply elegant' neighbourhoods. They buy 'simply elegant' clothes and enjoy 'simply elegant' cuisine. The idea of creatureliness is a very different value system.

Cosmetics Inc. is facing value-tensions with a significant part of its environment as well as within its own sub-systems. The rift is growing between those who identify with simple elegance and those who want to be up to date with the 'creatureliness' image. Amongst its own employees there is a tension between their own values and the organization's values. At work they are supposed to exude simple elegance. At home within their social and communal groups, they relate to 'new' values. They buy earth cosmetics rather than simply elegant cosmetics. They wear jeans and cords rather than stockings and skirts. They visit ethnic restaurants, cycle, camp, and watch birds and whales.

Cosmetics Inc. needs to understand that simple elegance now means something else. Elegance means being real and who you are, rather than being a well made-up, gracefully arranged clothes horse. Cosmetics Inc's management now needs to evaluate which stakeholder group has what to learn and how this should be communicated.

Identifying the Adaptive Challenge

Cosmetics Inc's adaptive challenge is to change its values to that of creatureliness. This is the new reality. Creatureliness is what is beautiful and authentic. Being 'simply elegant' is outdated and unauthentic.

Cosmetic Inc's adaptive challenge is to inculcate these new values into their organization. They need to ensure that stakeholders can embrace these new values and identify with them. This means more than just changing the packaging and refraining from animal testing. It means altering values and injecting a new mindset.

New employees have already been importing this new value. They do not see themselves as 'simply elegant' and represent the dissenting voices with Cosmetic Inc.'s mission. They insist that Cosmetics Inc. needs to change. Until now they have been ignored or discredited, yet they represent the new reality. Young people identify with their creatureliness. It makes them unique yet the same, and it makes them feel real. Cosmetics Inc. needs to begin the adaptive work. This means altering stakeholder values to embrace the new reality.

Distress

All changes spark resistance, especially new values. For Cosmetics Inc. there has to be a radical shift in values if they are to survive in the growing cosmetics market. They could, of course, decide to pick their niche in the smaller, traditional market with which they are familiar. Whether they can hold out forever by always selecting the traditional corner of the market is hard to say. If they have a classic name and a strong share in that market, they may pull it off – for some time at least. But even the nature of that market is sure to change with time, so all they will have bought is limited time before they will have to bite the bullet and change.

Cosmetics Inc. is going to experience substantial distress. The shift in values is a large one and many will resist. Some customers will switch, employees will complain and leave, and investors may pull out. Cosmetics Inc. needs to hold steady and to give the adaptive work to its stakeholders. This is a significant part of its adaptive challenge.

Barriers to Exercising Leadership

There are many personal and institutional barriers to exercising leadership. At a personal level, most often people do not know how to use their informal authority to best strategic effect. At the institutional level, many organizations inhibit people's leadership potential either through overt oppression and authoritarianism, or through covert processes that instil angst and lack of confidence. People become afraid to present a new perspective or to be a dissenting voice.

There is also a great deal of risk to being a leader. Leaders attract the distress and anger of the community and are inclined to experience very lonely times. Standing apart from the group is not easy. Those with entrenched values that are under threat will distance themselves from leaders who hold up unpleasant realities. Old friendships and allegiances can turn to enmity and irretrievable conflict when those who exercise leadership challenge people to change.

Exercising leadership is hard work.

Barriers to exercising leadership are as follows:

- cannot shift mindset to embrace the new realities;
- cannot identify the adaptive challenges;
- own cherished values too tightly held;
- lack will to change;

- just do not want to deal with the challenges;

- cannot unlearn old behaviours;

- bruised too often from previous leadership experiences;

- assassinated once too often;

- lack confidence and courage;

- lack motivation – cannot be bothered.

Summary

In summary, exercising leadership is about recognizing new realities, taking a systems view, performing a systemic analysis, making constructive and creative interventions, and formulating the organization's adaptive challenge.

Exercising leadership is about understanding the dynamics of the system both internally and externally. This requires identifying the system's dynamics, recognizing authority and cultural issues, and identifying the value systems on which the organizational system is based. It means grasping the main relationships and key drivers that give the system its dynamism.

Exercising leadership necessitates judicious use of one's formal or informal authority. It means understanding the roles of all the players within the system. It requires knowing when to get onto the balcony and watch others on the dance floor.[2] It requires recognition of work avoidance techniques and the ability to provide a holding environment while moderating the heat. Exercising leadership entails realizing the value conflicts between stakeholders and grasping the gap between new realities and old, cherished views, paradigms, assumptions, and mental models about the world.

Exercising leadership is about persistently holding up new realities and giving work back to the people. It means meeting people where they are and being in touch with both your own and others' emotions and baggage that is brought to the issue. Constructive and creative leadership interventions manage to alter dynamics and usher in new perspectives and behaviours.

Exercising leadership means realizing that the leader will become the target for the distress of the organization and knowing, as a leader, how to distinguish oneself from the issue.

Exercising leadership means staying alive!

Key Points Raised in this Chapter

▶ Foundational principles for the exercise of leadership exist.

▶ The focus of leadership is on the activity of leadership rather than on the person.

▶ Leadership begins by being in tune with new realities.

▶ Systems thinking has many advantages.

▶ There are distinct steps in carrying out a systemic analysis.

▶ Guidelines are given for identifying the adaptive challenge.

▶ Organizations depend on their abilities to self-organize and their adaptive capacities.

▶ There are many difficulties and barriers to exercising leadership.

SUGGESTIONS

■ Identify the new realities facing the organization.

■ Compare the values inherent in new realities with the values of the organization.

■ Evaluate the value challenges that these might represent to the organization and its stakeholders.

■ Identify the adaptive challenges that the organization is facing or could face in the future.

■ Consider whether there is any evidence of organizational distress or an over dependence on technical solutions.

■ Take time to consider (or reconsider) the themes of those in the organization who have represented dissenting voices.

■ Evaluate the extent to which the strategic planning function has assisted in the identification of new realities and their appropriate interpretation. Take action if this activity has been neglected.

Further Reading

Capra, F. (1996) *The Web of Life*, Doubleday, New York.

Heifetz, R.A. (1994) *Leadership Without Easy Answers*, Harvard University Press, Cambridge, MA.

Senge, P.M. (1990) *The Fifth Discipline*, Century Business, London.

Notes

1 Peter Senge in *The Fifth Discipline*, says that systems thinking is the discipline for seeing wholes (page 68).
2 The idea of getting onto the balcony and off the dance floor is discussed in *Leadership Without Easy Answers*, by Ronald Heifetz.

CHAPTER SIX

Leadership and Strategic Planning

Strategic Planning Defined

For many people, the words or the phrase 'strategic planning' conjures up various notions, concepts, memories and frustrations. Strategic planning is frequently viewed as that arduous, painful, and drawn out activity, which every organization is obliged to undertake (usually under duress) and which seems to take place too frequently. Many consider the strategic planning exercise to be a burden rather than an aid to strategic decision making.

To some, strategic planners are the people who crack the corporate whip and drive the planning process through most ordinary humans' limits of endurance. Planners ostensibly generate myriad piles of paper, pose thousands of difficult and perplexing questions, and surreptitiously influence the powers that allocate and re-allocate resources. The use of complex mathematical formulae and arcane algorithms, beyond the comprehension of most, are seen as providing justification for many decisions that ostensibly uphold the ultimate goal of increasing the value of the firm.

Henry Mintzberg, in his book, *The Rise and Fall of Strategic Planning*, goes to some lengths to arrive at what he considers to be an acceptable definition of planning. According to him, planning and strategy-making should be linked, and planning's systematic formalization of strategy over time, should be emphasized. His definition of strategic planning is as follows:

> Planning is a formalized procedure to produce an articulated result, in the form of an integrated system of decisions. (Mintzberg 1994:12)

This definition implies that the formalization process of strategic planning serves to decompose, articulate, and rationalize the processes by which decisions are made and integrated in organizations (ibid.:13). A prime purpose of planning thus lies in the process of rendering things explicit in terms of processes and their consequences (ibid.:14).

Despite the in-depth discussion, he adopts a somewhat reductionist approach. Possibly he strives for a simplistic tack in an attempt not to assign strategic planning a grandeur or a notion of eruditeness that it does not or should not possess. I would argue that, as with all reductionism, there is the risk of eliminating some of the richness of the essence of that which is being reduced. In this case, Mintzberg tends to dilute the richness of the potential power of a well-executed and integrated strategic planning process.

Strategic planning is much more than planning. While its importance lies undoubtedly in its process, I would insist that this process is far more than just analysis, articulation, and synthesis. The process for which strategic planning is responsible is the enhancement of the adaptive capacities of the organization. This process is aimed at galvanizing the organization into action to do its adaptive work. This is then followed by the technical work which will serve as the execution of the organization's devised strategies. The work of strategic planning is to encourage, motivate, and hone the organization's ability to self-organize. This work is fundamental to the organization's ability to survive and thrive. Being reductionistic about strategic planning's role ill serves both the organization and the planning function.

Strategic Planning as the New Business Leadership

Contrary to many books and courses on strategic planning, I am proposing a redefined and refined approach to the strategic planning function. The role of strategic planning has changed quite significantly from the past. Now the planning function is expected to play a leadership role within the organization in line with the new definition of leadership. The activity of strategic planning is the activity of exercising organizational leadership.

Based on the new leadership definition, strategic planning is responsible for formally and explicitly identifying new realities and identifying the adaptive challenges that these present. The strategic planning function is engaged in envisioning the future and co-creating a vision for the organization that resonates with organization stakeholders. As part of business leadership, the strategic planning function focuses on the organization's ability to self-organize by helping it to reframe its assumptions and renegotiate its relationship links.

The new approach to strategic planning requires a new lens and a new focus in seeing and interpreting the world. Planners have to read the times in a new way. They need to adopt systems thinking and they need to invoke the macrocosm-microcosm principle. They need to be able to distinguish adaptive from technical work, and they need to place their primary focus on the adaptive work. The technical work, i.e. the analytical assessment of markets and products, should be left to the operating divisions. Once the adaptive work has been done, they can focus on product/market analysis and work the numbers. Strategic planners should know when the technical work should begin and they should be in tune with the organization's tendency to go into technical mode before the adaptive work has really been done. The strategic planning function needs to know how to turn up the heat without disillusioning or alienating stakeholder factions to the extent that they subvert the planning process.

The strategic planning function should also hold up the organization's ethical principles. While business goals require constant change, ethical principles should not be sacrificed along the way. The strategic planning function sets the moral tone of the organization. If strategic planners act as ivory tower sycophants to powerful senior executives, the moral slippery slope will be well set in place. If, on the other hand, those responsible for strategic planning demonstrate commitment and integrity to the greater good of organizational sustainable growth and profitability, this will inculcate an atmosphere conducive to moral relationships and interactions. This sort of atmosphere is a basic requirement for a healthy learning organization. New realities identified by the strategic planners should also include awareness and attention to the increasing demands of environmentalism and corporate social responsibility.

As the Shell Group's executive management has so clearly and persistently publicized through its various books and courses on the topic of strategic scenario planning, an insightful strategic planning function, comprising well-informed and sensitive members, is critical to organizational life and to its adaptation to new realities.

The strategic planning function within the living organizational network is the key node that drives organizational self-organization. As such, the strategic planning process is the organization's claim not only to what it is, but what it would like to become. Strategic planning is far more than an articulation and systematization process.

Strategic Planning – An Alternative Definition

My definition for strategic planning that both distinguishes the new approach to planning from the old and highlights its leadership role is as follows:

> **Strategic planning is a formal process designed to interpret the organization's environment for the purpose of identifying its adaptive challenges and guiding its responses so as to optimize longer term competitive advantage.**

Although planning undoubtedly produces a series of integrated decisions, this serves a secondary purpose. The very process of monitoring and evaluating the environment is the sharp end of the strategic planning process. It is the critical link between the organization as a living network and the infinite number of networks that defines its environment.

Many different interpretations and results may follow from this process and certain important decisions will necessarily flow as a result of this activity, but this is not what distinguishes strategic planning from other decision-making processes. Many important decisions flow from non-planning activities as well.

This new approach to strategic planning requires a new mindset and new methods. First we shall turn to the new mindset.

Who are the Strategic Planners?

The strategic planners addressed in this book are those members of the organization deemed responsible for mobilizing the organization's resources in a direction that is consonant with its mission and the realities of the environment. This group includes those executives who are responsible for creating a vision that responds to the new realities and to which the rest of the organization can relate.

From a broader perspective, strategic planning is not the preserve of only a few privileged and chosen people who have the skills necessary for interpreting crystal balls. In a truly learning organization, all participants are engaged in continuous adaptation and self-organization, which is what learning is about. The process of learning is part and parcel of the strategic planning process; therefore, the ideas put forward here have relevance for those who do not have strategy or planning as part of their official titles.

The Strategic Planner as Prophet and Leader

In the past, the role of the strategic planner has been somewhat multivaried and contentious. He or she was supposed to guide, advise, facilitate, question or educate those who are actually responsible for achieving the plans that they have been charged with preparing. He or she has been considered excessively analytical, unempathic, and other-worldly. In more friendly environments, the strategic planner is viewed as the financial whiz, the computer buff or the insightful forecaster. In conflictual circumstances or difficult times, he or she is viewed as the politician, the number cruncher or the academician who has no real understanding of actually being in the world.

In the face of the new millennium, the strategic planner will play a far more proactive and pervasive role. The planner is no longer the objective outsider, burdened with presenting bad news or devising organizational constraints that impede the profit opportunism of divisional management. Nor can the planner remain a removed individual of the organizational elite who guides and educates. No, the planner now has a hands on, responsible and responsive role to play.

An effective strategic planner, who can help organizations read the times and who can provide a suitable holding environment for those who have to take difficult steps to deal with those times, is what is now called for. The skills and competences required for effective strategic planning into the next millennium exceed those of numeric analysis, market and product evaluation, and creative strategies for growth. The strategic planner, previously notoriously poor in people skills, now has to excel in dealing with people; energizing them, mobilizing them, holding them, stretching them, and providing the tensions and slack needed to get the difficult job done of making and owning those plans. This strategic planner is a new breed.

The Strategic Planner as Prophet

Contrary to popular belief, prophets are not just divinely inspired forecasters. Rather, they exhort others to fully see and face present day realities in order to avert future harmful consequences. Prophets are concerned with the needs of their immediate contemporaries and with the near, rather than the distant future. Prophets are not just proclaimers or pronouncers regarding the next eschaton; their moral political analysis is directed at contemporary society as they attempt to keep the nation or group on course here and now. While biblical prophets were supposedly gifted with profound moral insights and exceptional powers of expression, chosen by God to ascertain and communicate His will; nowadays authentic prophets have a no less important role. Their work is to hold up the difficulties that the changing world inevitably presents. They encourage dealing with worldly vicissitudes in a manner considered congruent to the values and beliefs of society and its traditions. Prophets are primarily concerned with core human values, morality, and choosing the road less travelled. Prophets raise awareness, inform, admonish and call to account. The prophets and sages of the past have typically called for a 'change of heart', a return to a conscious sense and commitment of what it means to live the good life. Translated in business terms, this means a reawakening of or revisiting the commitment to integrity, honesty and service to customers, staff, shareholders, the community and the environment.

The role of the strategic planner is to be the modern day prophet. He or she is charged with holding the complexity of tensions in balance, of understanding the important and relevant questions, and revealing trade-offs associated with pursuing various courses of action. The modern day prophet, as in the past, is concerned with actions and consequences, proactive to their occurrence. This does not mean that the strategic planner takes on the role of organizational moral arbiter. On the contrary, the strategic planner plays the role of questioner, prober and reflector of both the company and the individual to themselves. The aim is to enhance self-understanding at both corporate and individual level. Particularly in turbulent, uncertain times, profound self-understanding gives identity, authenticity and groundedness. The strategic planner plays an influential role. Authorities and leaders have been known to ignore prophets at their peril. A good strategic planner needs to be able to instil a similar level of confidence.

In summary, the strategic planner as prophet is responsible for monitoring the changing environment and identifying new realities. The strategic planner holds up these new realities to the organizations and both persists and insists on their appropriate interpretation. In the face of resistance, the strategic planner needs to hold steady by not altering course. Instead he or she needs to moderate the intensity with which the new realities are presented, so that people can integrate changes at a rate they can tolerate. The strategic planner helps the organization to articulate what the changes mean and how it is likely to affect future performance.

The strategic planner helps the organization to identify the gap between its current values and attitudes and those presented by new realities.

The Strategic Planner as Leader

The strategic planner has another key role – leader. He or she needs to exercise leadership by mobilizing the resources of the organization to effectively honour their values and commitments. Mobilizing resources is not limited to resource allocation based on strategic cost-benefit analysis. Mobilizing is energizing and bringing forth the emotional and creative spirit that exists within the people of the organization. It means providing space while inspiring and activating energy. These leadership responsibilities of the strategic planner are often substantially under-estimated if not overlooked.

The functions of a leader are to help unveil a vision for the future that reflects a balanced and comprehensive view of reality. The leader sees what others cannot and/or choose not to see. The leader coaxes out a vision that has appeal and that can be embraced and owned by others. The vision is a common one for the benefit of the group, and not for the self-aggrandizement of the leader. The leader helps set others free to maximize their potential and to achieve their visions. The leader does not impose, coerce or manipulate, but rather gives space, provides direction, holds and stretches.

A primary role of the leader is to assist his or her followers to embrace change and to deal with the value conflicts that these might entail. The leader holds steady when others do not want to face their adaptive challenges. The leader gives the work of adaptation back to the people, so that it is their work and their change process. He or she does not provide easy answers nor does he or she propose technical solutions. These come later, after the adaptive work has been done.

The leader makes constructive and creative interventions so that the organization does not lapse into the old ways of doing and seeing things. The leader understands the implications of multi-pluralism and multi-culturalism by being sensitive to the multiple realities existent amongst the organization's stakeholders.

The leader helps stakeholders find common viewing points and assists in shaping a sense of a common and valuable destiny.

This then is the role of the strategic planner within the framework of the planning exercise. He or she is prophet and leader focusing on the new realities and the identification of adaptive work. This fundamental role is foundational to the creation of a learning organization.

Insight, foresight, and sensitivity are critical requirements for the strategic planning task. Strategic planners need to understand the heart (what it is that stakeholders value and desire) and the mind (what it is that they think, rationalize, understand, acknowledge, and appreciate). Without these skills, the planner will not be able to get others to do the work that they need to do and the strategic planning exercise will not have the potency that unleashed creative energy and commitment generates. Survival in the twenty-first century calls for maximum heart and mind potency. The strategic planner needs to assist in optimizing the mind-heart balance as the organization adapts to new realities and responds to key change signals.

The Objectives of Strategic Planning

As we have discussed, strategic planning is about exercising organizational leadership in a new way. Under this rubric there are several objectives that the planning function should meet. The prime objective is to *identify key change signals*. In identifying change signals, the focus should be primarily on the external environment. Bearing in mind the macrocosm-microcosm principle, internal change signals are also important as they reflect changes in the outside world.

Identifying key change signals is what enables the organization to anticipate and respond appropriately to the future. It enables the organization to be proactive in a thoughtful, rather than hurried manner. It alerts the organization to new values, behaviours, and actions, and empowers the organization to participate in creating its own future.

Identifying key change signals serves as the guiding light to envisioning the new world and to the co-creation of a refined and retuned organizational vision. The envisioning and revisioning process seeks to take advantage of structural changes that the key change signals foreshadow. This process is at the root of organizational learning and adaptation, and serves as an integral part of the feedback loop that takes the organization forward to higher ground.

Identifying key change signals ahead of the competition enables the organization to recognize and take advantage of strategic growth opportunities and threats. Once everyone recognizes the same change signals, the future has already arrived and there is little opportunity for strategic leverage. The ability to identify and interpret change signals ahead of the pack provides the organization with its greatest, longer term strategic advantage.

The New Versus Old Strategic Planning

At this point it may be beneficial to spell out some of the key differences between the old and new approaches to strategic planning. As we discussed in Chapter 3, new business metaphors have arisen. New metaphors always imply new images, new mental models, new paradigms, and different jargon. Coming to grips with these changed images of the world and learning the new jargon is not easy, especially since the old images have become so well entrenched.

Table 6.1 (see p. 172) sets out the different concepts, principles, and language that can be associated with the old and new strategic planning approaches. The new concepts, principles, and language adhere to the principles of living systems, as revealed by the new sciences, and accord with the notion of exercising leadership.

New Planning Methods

Since the emphasis of strategic planning has now changed from technical to adaptive work, and there is a call for planners with a new mindset, actual strategic planning methods have also changed. First the evaluation and assessment of stakeholder values and relationships now takes precedence over the previous focus on product/market analysis. This is not to say that the detailed evaluation of products and markets is no longer an important exercise. Understanding stakeholder values, allegiances and factions is a prior activity, and is one that is performed by the strategic planners. The technical analysis of products and markets has now devolved to divisions, departments, strategic business units (SBUs), and strategic networks.

Second, scenario planning as a planning method is gaining favour as organizations realize the benefits of this technique as a method for dealing with uncertainty, complexity, and a great deal of interrelatedness. The technique and benefits of scenario planning are discussed in greater detail later in this chapter.

Capabilities versus Capacities

Strategic planning no longer places its greatest emphasis on the organization's capabilities but rather on its capacities, i.e. its capacity to adapt, its capacity to learn, its capacity to cope with uncertainty, its capacity to grow, its capacity to serve, and its capacity to be flexible without abandoning its mission or principles.

The difference between capability and capacity is that the emphasis of the former is on technical ability, usually in relation to a specific task or accomplishment. Capability relates to a talent or skill, which can be learned or enhanced. Capacity, on the other hand, relates to a power to experience, learn, produce, or retain something. Capacity is the innate potential for development or accomplishment which defines the extent to which people can be capable. The greater the capacity, the greater the potential to learn, grow, and understand. People with great capacities can be taught to be very capable. People who have limited capacities will soon reach the limits of their capability. Capacity is therefore the power that defines capability. Capacities grow and recede. Capabilities change or stagnate.

The purpose of the strategic planning function is to grow the organizations' capacities. Skilled operational management will channel this into the appropriate capabilities. Their responsibility is to ensure that people's capabilities do not stagnate but are aligned to changing organizational needs.

Forecasting versus Imagining

The new approach to strategic planning places less dependence on forecasting or the extrapolation of past results than previously. While the strategic plan does eventually result in a financial planning framework with a range of numbers with which to work, the new focus is on a range rather than a deliberate set of forecast results. Instead, the new planning effort tries to encourage the organization to imagine its future. This is where scenario planning comes into play. Various scenarios are developed and explored as to their impact on the organization. Chosen scenarios serve as the strategic plan rather than a definitive projection of target results.

By imagining the future, the organization starts with where it is now. It takes the present narrative of the organization as its starting point and weaves a story about what the future might be, given the present environment and the key change signals. The process of imagining encourages engaging all the creative responses that the organization can envision. It focuses on 'what if' questions, and prompts the organization to consider the style and pace of its steps in anticipation of the impending dance. It makes the organization attentive to the present while being intentional about the future. It queries the organization's adaptive capacities and its ability to turn this into strategic capabilities. The focus of imagining is far more holistic and creative than the closed box approach of forecasting. It requires both emotional and cognitive engagement and situates the organization squarely within the dynamic realm of a living organism. To imagine is to be alive, creative, and free-flowing. To forecast is to be excessively rational, constrained, and boring.

Certainty versus Uncertainty

We plan because we try to mitigate uncertainty. If there was no uncertainty we would not need to plan. Part of our planning psychosis is an endeavour to measure and thereby control risk. Risk is uncertainty that matters, i.e. its effects have a negative impact on the organization. Strategic planning is supposed to find ways to generate sustainable returns while understanding the risks.

Risk includes the upside as well as the downside. This means that the risk of missing or squandering opportunities is as important as recognizing and protecting the downside. In the past, planning has been inclined to focus on protecting against downside risk at the expense of protecting the organization against the possibility of lost opportunities. Risk management tactics have been aimed at eliminating uncertainty and thereby giving organizational management a sense of being in control and command. Regrettably this is false comfort. And, even if it works, it is likely to be a short-lived success.

The new approach to planning makes far less attempt at eliminating uncertainty. On the contrary, it seeks to prepare the organization to deal with uncertainty by holding this up as a very poignant reality that should not be denied. Developing the organization's adaptive capacity is strongly correlated with its ability to deal with uncertainty in a positive and constructive manner.

Cause-and-Effect versus Real Time Response

Most strategic planning efforts place a great deal of emphasis on cause-and-effect analysis. We are learning from the new sciences that this can be a deceptive way of analysing the world. The reason for this is that it is impossible to isolate the behaviour and impact of certain variables when all the parts of all living systems are in perpetual motion, the path of which is determined by possibilities rather than deterministic probabilities.

The new approach to strategic planning does not eliminate attempts at trying to come to grips with causality; however, it is far more realistic and modest about the ability to determine causal principles from a series of events. Rather than depend on isolating causes and effects, the new approach to planning looks at a number of simultaneous events and focuses on the organization's ability to respond in real time. Developing the organization's adaptive capacity focuses on the multiplicity of events that the organization can assimilate and respond to rapidly and effectively. It makes the organization attentive and mindful of 'here and now' as the starting point for the future. Many organizations are so busy planning for the future that they neglect the present thereby vitiating the foundations on which their future is to be based.

Expansion versus Sustainable Growth

The pressure on organizations to grow mounts almost exponentially as globalization and international competition increases. Many organizations are realizing that sustainable growth is a more important goal than year-on-year growth. Sustainable growth implies finding a formula that will ensure growth long term but may mean less glamorous growth figures. This eliminates some of the inordinate pressures that the short-term pursuit of growth usually entails. Sustainability denotes the ability to sustain something based on its inherent foundations and fundamentals rather than as a result of chance, the quick fix, or windfall gains. Earnings sustainability is now gaining credibility and confidence over the promises of inconsistent and indiscriminate growth.

Strategic Planning and the Strategic Agenda

In Chapter 3, we discussed the need for the organization to develop a strategic agenda with the specific intent of doing new things in new ways in the coming millennium. While organizations usually have a rolling agenda which sets the objectives and goals for future strategies, the new strategic agenda should set a new tone. It should be illustrative of the organization's understanding of new realities and the ushering in of the Adaptive Age. This strategic agenda should herald the beginning of new approaches to strategic planning, creating a learning organization, and structuring of the organization.

TABLE 6.1 Strategic Planning Concepts, Principles and Jargon

Old	New
Technical work	Adaptive work
Environmental view	Systemic view
Analysis	Synthesis
Product/market focus	Stakeholder/relationship focus
Hierarchy	Network
Allocate resources	Mobilize resources
Reductionistic	Holistic/expansive
Focus on capabilities	Focus on capacities
Directing	Influencing
Forecasting	Imagining
Controlling	Self-Organizing
Do the work	Give the work back
Search for Certainty	Focus on Uncertainty
Cause-and-Effect	Virtual/realtime response
Expansion	Sustainable growth

Those involved in strategic planning, both formally and informally, should be directly involved in shaping the new agenda. Continuous attention to key change signals will form the more detailed rolling agenda and will inform the organization of new realities regarding the other living networks with which it is linked. The starting point for a strategic agenda as proposed in Chapter 3, is repeated below.

The Strategic Agenda:

1　Decide on the nature and form of the strategic planning activity. The nature will set the objectives and the form will set out how and by whom these will be achieved.

2　Consider the macro-environment, the specific implications of globalization, and the impact of a multicultural world.

3　Prepare for the new face of capitalism.

4   Evaluate the implications of new 'life' and 'business' root metaphors.

5   Identify all significant stakeholders and determine their values. These values need to be continuously monitored and revisited in depth over time. Consider any current and future value-tensions that exist or that may develop.

6   Evaluate present alliances and consider the need and potential benefits of new ones.

7   Establish or refine the process for seeking out strategic growth opportunities and identifying strategic growth threats. The sub-agendas that describe in detail how each major agenda item will be achieved will naturally depend on the type and size of the organization.

In Chapter 3, I also made some proposals regarding the nature of the strategic planning activity itself. This included:

■   deciding who should do the firm's strategic planning;

■   deciding on how the activity itself is to be performed;

■   developing a version of systemic analysis that is most suitable to the nature and purpose of the organization;

■   selecting the planning methods to be used e.g. a combination of forecasting and scenario planning;

■   setting up feedback loops from the strategic planning function to the rest of the organization and vice versa.

In light of both proposals it seems timely to discuss the strategic planning process itself. This will assist the organization in both fine-tuning its strategic agenda and defining or refining its strategic planning function.

The Strategic Planning Process

The strategic planning process comprises the following main activities:

1   Monitoring the external and internal environment.

2   Recognizing new realities.

3   Identifying key change signals.

4   Interpreting change signals – systemic analysis.

5   Identifying and formulating the adaptive challenge.

6   Mobilizing resources for adaptive work.

7   Identifying strategic growth opportunities and threats.

While it is the explicit remit of those engaged in strategic planning at both formal and informal levels to engage in these processes, it is vital that the rest of the organization be involved.

As a living system, the organization is an open system, open to environmental influences. Any and every part of the organization is exposed to changes in the environment. Part of enhancing the adaptive capacity of the organization (see below) is to encourage all the functions, divisions, and departments of the organization to be open and attentive to key change signals in the environment to which they are exposed.

A healthy living system also undergoes spontaneous internal changes that affect its development and growth. In an organization these changes are stimulated by the internal dynamics of its stakeholders. As organizational learning takes place management and employees are prompted to experiment with new relationships and new processes. New employees bring fresh ideas and suggest new processes. All this realtime activity is part of the organization's being as a living system. The strategic planning activity needs to hold a fine ear to the internal pulse of the organization as it responds to its external environment.

We will now discuss the strategic planning process in detail.

Monitor the External and the Internal Environment

Understanding how an organization makes meaning and the values associated with that meaning requires beginning one's enquiry with a very macro analysis. As mentioned earlier, it befits organizations aspiring to compete in a rapidly globalizing world to carry out an ever more macro analysis, i.e. the horizons of enquiry need to be continuously extended. This implies that planners should consider extending the boundaries of analyses to the point to which the analysis is still possible and meaningful. If Coca-Cola is thinking about the weightlessness of Coke and its suitability as a beverage on the moon, this provides some clue of how macro one might get!

To understand how the organization operates within the larger networks of the community, the nation, the continent, or the white Anglo-Saxon Protestant or the Italian diasporean network (and so on), means carrying out several analyses. Just looking at one system is insufficient. Strategic planners need to consider the manner in which systems overlay systems. They need to comprehend the way in which systems form part of other systems, and they need to understand the criteria which define these systems. Strategic planners are advised to adopt systems thinking throughout their processes.

The External Environment

Strategic planning's principal focus is on the external environment. Using systems thinking the planning process begins by identifying the major external systems that interface and/or affect the organization. These systems can be defined geographically, by country or nation; according to culture or race; or according to religion, language, or value systems. Any classification that meaningfully defines the organization's external systems is appropriate. It is important to consider value systems when deciding on the criteria for defining external systems, i.e. common values are a strong thread within a system.

Having defined the relevant systems, the planning process evaluates the principal political, social, economic, environmental, technological and demographic issues that affect these systems. This requires a great deal of work and should be an ongoing planning activity.

The goal of this exercise is to understand the key political, social, economic, environmental, technological and demographical issues that persist within the systems identified, and to identify key change signals in these areas. An example might be a country's change of government from a social democratic to a conservative one. It may be the forecast of a drought, the rise of a new political leader, the collapse of a major financial institution, the formation of new alliances (e.g. Israel and Turkey), a political scandal, the death of a well-known figure, or the ruling of new legislation. A change signal might be the introduction of a new official language, the sale of arms to new states, a rise in single-mother households, or the public announcement of a decrease in inflation.

Given a particular system and its context, each one of these examples may signal future changes. After recognizing a change, interpreting its implications is by far the more difficult activity. The systemic analysis process should assist the interpretive phase.

The Internal Environment

There will also be change signals that are internal to the organization. Change signals could include the redundancy of existing processes, changes in employee attitudes, acrimony between management and investors, and new relationships with customers and suppliers.

Rarely are internal signals isolated. Most often evidence of internal change signals is evidence that something is happening in the external environment. This should be checked out. If a match between the internal and the external holds up, this should be explored in detail as evidence of changing realities is becoming pervasive.

The Eagle and the Ant

The strategic planning function fulfils the role of both the eagle and the ant. The eagle rises higher and higher above the ground so as to gain an ever wider vista of its terrain. It soars, eagle-eyed across a growing expanse of ever wider horizons paying attention to the distinguishing nature and contours of the terrain. Simultaneously it eyes the earth below for the slightest sight or movement that signals danger, companionship, or food. From a position of great heights it can see the big picture and the detail. It also knows exactly when to swoop down in order to deal with the detail. These are the required attributes of the strategic planning function.

On the other hand the ant is very much earthbound. It dwells deeply attached to its immediate terrain. It knows every leaf and every blade of grass that it traverses. It patiently covers the ground in the purposeful pursuit of life. What it lacks in vision it makes up in groundedness, patience, persistent attention to detail, and purposefulness. Although, mightily different, these are also the attributes of the strategic planning function.

The competent strategic planner should be both like the eagle and the ant. He or she needs to be able to soar and to swoop, to see the big picture and assess its layout from great heights, to know when to swoop down to the detail, and to be able to pay attention to that detail tenaciously and patiently.

The strategic planning function needs to implement processes that can perform the functions of both the eagle and the ant. The ability to move back and forth between the large and small picture is critical to the identification of key change signals. Planners need to have a good eye and sensitive antenna. While this skill may not vest in one individual, it is important that the complement of skills within the strategic planning function provide these competencies.

Recognize New Realities

Part of monitoring the external and internal environment is the recognition of new realities. New realities by definition signal change. What the strategic planning function needs to be attentive to is not only new realities themselves, but what they signify. They need to consider the effect that new realities have on the values and meaning making activities of the system.

The discussion of leadership and strategic planning takes place in a highly interconnected world. Our increasing awareness of our inter-connectedness is in itself a new reality which radically influences the way that we observe, view, and respond to our environment. This new reality needs to be captured in the strategic planning process.

For example, if the South African Government were to legislate that Xhosa or Zulu become the second official national language in place of Afrikaans (English being the first) what will this signify to both black and white South Africans. How will it affect their sense of self-identity, their value systems, and their behaviour? Consider the enormous ramifications that this would have on the South African way of understanding him or herself. Consider how the Zulu or Xhosa person will feel about being South African. What about the Afrikaner?

How would South Africa as a system affect the rest of Africa as a system? How would it change South Africa as a trading partner, as a place of investment, as a major exporter of gold? How would it affect foreign businesses? What about the ethnicity of products and services. What about marketing, packaging, legislation?

What would it mean to the United Kingdom if they pulled out of Northern Ireland? What would it do to the identity of the Northern Irish? Who would absorb their anger if the Catholics and the Protestants did not have one another to hate? What would it do to the identity of the Southern Irish? How would it affect the European Community? What about trade? How might it affect the Irish in America? Where will they redirect their sentiment? And their money? What would happen to the Irish punt? What about sterling? Would Aer Lingus benefit? What about the UK banks in Ulster?

These are difficult, explosive, and tantalizing questions. They are intended to provide an example of the world's intricate network of systems whose activities are all highly interrelated. One new reality, e.g. a new Prime Minister in Downing Street with a different view of Northern Ireland to that of his predecessors, could be the precursor to enormous changes in not one, but many systems. His different values serve as a key change signal to the rest of the systems with which he interrelates.

New realities thus serve as both change signals and indicators of future key change signals. This is critical information for the organization's intelligence network. Being in touch with new realities is the strategic planning function's most foundational work.

Identify Key Change Signals

The strategic planning function is charged with combing the external and internal environments with the intention of recognizing new realities and identifying key change signals.

A key change signal is one that foreshadows a major shift in values, the way that people or groups make meaning, and new behaviours. Sticking with the example of Northern Ireland, a key change signal was the successful integration of AIB Bank, a Catholic Bank, headquartered in Dublin, with the Protestant Ulster Bank, headquartered in Belfast. This signalled the fact that peace and harmony is possible and economically expedient. AIB Bank read the new realities correctly. They identified change signals at the micro level, e.g. some of their Northern Irish customers were Protestant. When it came to banking, service and competitive offering is considered by a growing number to take priority over national and religious differences. AIB Bank's internal environment told them something about the external environment. They checked out this emerging reality, recognized a strategic growth opportunity and acted.

If peace and economic partnership can occur at the micro level why not at the macro level? Who are the stakeholders and what are the barriers? Which stakeholders have what to learn? From a business perspective, the example of this key change signal adumbrates future liaisons and future partnership potential. How might other organizations avail of similar strategic growth opportunities?

Interpreting Change Signals

Once new realities have been recognized and change signals identified, the really important part begins. How should these change signals be interpreted? How does one recognize a key change signal? How does one interpret the future ramifications of the change process that appears to be beginning?

Here are some suggestions:

1 *Review the change signals for the underlying value changes that they may signify.* For example, if Israel is cosying up to Turkey, what does this say about the values between Islamic Turks and Jewish Israelis? Consider whether the signal seems to infer a shift in values.

   If Eastern Railways is now using daily train commuters to fulfil the role of train guard in exchange for free train fares what does it say about Eastern Railways' values regarding their own safety procedures. What does it say about how they view their customers? What does it say about the service that they provide? What if the train guard/ commuter misses the train, does that mean that other commuters are no longer on a safe and protected suburban train? Any change that signals a change in values is a key change signal. *Key Change Signals signify a change in values which create new or different stakeholder tensions.*

2 *Consider the stakeholders in the system in which the change signal is taking place.* If a new or different conflict of interest is apparent, important value shifts are at stake, and a key change signal has been identified.

3 *A key barometer for identifying a change in values and hence recognition of a change signal is by monitoring one's own responses.* If you observe, hear, or read about something that seems different, is counter to your expectation, or unnerves you, take note – something is going on.

4 *To get a real handle on the ramifications of new realities and change signals, perform a systemic analysis.*
   (In the box below are the steps to be taken in order to perform a systemic analysis as discussed in detail in Chapter 5.)

5 *Check out the interpretation of the systemic analysis by discussion with members of the organization and with partners and other allies.* Spend time and pay attention to accurately articulating the implications of key change signals. This is one of those instances where semantics matter.

   Strategic planners and executive management could do well to use creative imagery and emotional language at this point so as to get a feel for the real value tensions and the repositioning that is at stake.

THE SYSTEMIC ANALYSIS PROCEDURE

- Identify key trends and new realities being made manifest in the macro environment. Remember to have broad horizons.

- Select a level of analysis, e.g. the country or community as a system.

- Identify boundaries to the system of analysis.

- Identify the key systems and sub-systems that make up the larger system. e.g. the government, the communities in a country.

- Establish the systemic properties of the larger system (e.g. the country or community) with emphasis on its manner of meaning-making and values.

- Establish similar properties of the sub-systems within the larger system selected.

- Define the organization as a system. Clarify its values and the way that it makes meaning. Define the role that it plays in the larger system. Determine its sub-systems.

- Identify the key stakeholders within the organization and within each sub-system.

- Identify stakeholder values.

- Clarify the nature of relationships between all stakeholders identified.

- Establish any value-tensions that exist between the system and its environment.

- Establish any value-tensions that exist within the sub-systems, and between their stakeholders.

Evidence versus what is Evident

The systemic analysis process needs to distinguish what is evident as distinct from what is evidence. There are many times in our lives or careers where we sense, observe, or integrate things that are evident. Often our intuition or knowing is brushed aside because we cannot provide rational, logical, or empirical evidence. We just know something is so, and we usually respond with a 'You will see, time will tell'.

Sometimes it is not just that we do not have the evidence, we may not be able to organize it in a manner so that it will stand up to rational scrutiny. Lawyers and courtrooms are the classical examples of the evidence versus evident game. Lawyers argue about the evidence and set aside what is evident. The OJ Simpson case should serve to illustrate this point.

Unfortunately organizations are inclined to do the same thing. Management wants evidence prior to decision making. This evidence needs to be collected and presented in an acceptable format before it will even be considered. While this process has some merit, often the evidence is unavailable, or it is manipulated to justify a decision, or it does not do justice to what is really evident.

Engaging members of the organization in understanding systems thinking and how to perform systemic analyses should eliminate some of this preoccupation with finding blatant evidence. Being engaged in systemic analyses people will gain greater perspicacity and greater confidence in their abilities to identify what is evident. This will enable the organization to move faster on decisions and will improve its general intuitive ability in reading the times as it becomes less dependent on the old ways of presenting evidence.

Identify and Formulate the Adaptive Challenge

The strategic planning process is not a linear sequence of events. The process is iterative, circular, and all parts of the process are mutually interrelated. The need and ability to move backwards and forwards between the large and the small picture; between stakeholder issues and competing value tensions; between observation and interpretation is a necessary capability and a process in itself.

The prime purpose for identifying key change signals is to identify the organization's adaptive challenge. The sooner and the more effectively that the organization can identify its adaptive challenge, the greater the opportunity for strategic leverage, the greater the possibility of identifying and exploring strategic growth opportunities ahead of the competition, and the better the chance of thriving and not just surviving.

From a strategic planning viewpoint, identifying the adaptive challenge is prior to defining strategy. There can be no appropriate strategy if the adaptive challenge has not been identified and carefully articulated. Developing a strategy for the organization always follows the identification of the adaptive challenge. It is important to bear in mind that both processes are ongoing. New realities are always presenting themselves. This requires an ongoing identification of adaptive challenges and hence a continuous reformulation of strategy.

A serious pitfall is to recognize change signals and to rush into the development of new strategies. This approach is hazardous. More often than not inappropriate strategies are developed that do not really address the value tensions and the adaptive issues. This is not to say that given strategies are not also being continuously reformulated and fine-tuned. This is a necessary strategic process. Devising strategies in response to key change signals is another matter. Developing strategies in response to key change signals without understanding the nature of adaptive challenges will simply serve as a technical fix. Technical fixes are not strategic solutions in themselves. Good technical solutions are the response and execution of a defined strategy. As we have discussed at length in the opening chapters, technical fixes cannot solve adaptive challenges.

Organizations are advised to take the time to identify and articulate their adaptive challenges. This is where the strategic planning function can play a key leadership role by holding steady and ensuring that the adaptive work gets done.

Once the organization has performed the systemic analysis and identified its adaptive challenge/s it will use its chosen planning methods so that it may formulate a suitable strategic response.

Mobilize Resources for Adaptive Work

The result of the iterative strategic planning process should be the mobilization of organizational resources for adaptive work. This means that as a consequence of the ongoing dialogue between the strategic planning function and the rest of the organization (see below), members of the organization are sensitized to the adaptive challenges that they need to face and the adaptive work that is required of them. The sensitization process occurs as a result of explicit formulation of the changing nature of the environment and what it means to the organization. Sensitivities should also be heightened as members of the organization become increasingly attentive to what is evident in the world around them. They should be aware of what they sense and what their intuition tells them. They should be encouraged to discuss and to act upon this information.

The role of the strategic planning function is to mobilize – not to allocate. Its leadership role is to prompt, motivate, encourage, and challenge the organization to respond to both adaptive opportunities and threats. The planning function, in conjunction with senior management, provides the rationale, the motivation, the insights, the foresight, the courage and the holding environment for the organization to make important changes. The better the interaction between the planning function and the rest of the organization, the faster and less fearful will be the shifts.

Mobilization needs to be a self-motivated and self-directed process. Here operational management can also play an important role. Once they are on board with what needs to be done, mobilizing their people is their leadership task. Allocating resources is an outdated method of re-aligning businesses. If people do not see for themselves why changes are needed, they will never buy into the process. Getting them to buy into the process is part of their learning experience and is part of what moves the organization to higher ground.

The systemic approach that has been advocated here lends itself to the use of scenario planning. Once several scenarios have been selected as being probable pictures of the future, operational management can focus on mobilizing the organization for its strategic and operational work.

Identify Strategic Growth Opportunities and Threats

Strategy Making

Organizations are continuously trying to remake and renew themselves through the development of new and innovative strategies. The purpose of strategizing is to respond to the evolving and changing needs of their customers and to reposition themselves *vis à vis* the competition. Unfortunately many organizations who are still in 'war' or 'game' mode are so busy beating the competitors that they forget about their real goal which is to serve their customers. They are like runners in a race who are so intent on watching the people next to or behind them that they omit focusing on the finishing line. Satisfying customers well is what it means to win the race.

Devising strategies occurs at all organizational levels. Strategies for the operating divisions usually occurs at divisional level. Strategies for the entire organization usually occurs at senior management level. The strategic planning function has a role to play in both endeavours.

At the overall organizational level, it is particularly concerned with the synergy of the entire group and developing the systemic properties that belong to the whole. At the divisional level the strategic planning function wants to promote systems thinking and guide operating divisions in understanding their roles in the various systems of which they are part.

Organizational strategies (at all levels) need to be in sync with changing realities and need to be well grounded in the changing values, ways in which people make meanings, behaviours, and actions.

Strategies need to take cognizance of the political, social (which includes cultural), economic, environmental technological and demographic trends, and needs to build on these where possible. Information and research on these critical aspects of the planning backdrop are often formally carried out by the strategic planning function. People in the operating divisions should be encouraged to be attentive to and aware of issues in their environment. Strategic planning, besides informing, also plays a role educating the operating divisions on how to monitor and interpret the environment.

A significant part of strategy making is identifying strategic growth opportunities and threats. Reality testing takes place against the organization's external and internal systemic analyses as well as by reference to the mission statement.

Strategic Growth Opportunities and Threats

The identification of strategic growth opportunities and threats is a critical outcome of the entire strategic planning process. To say that strategic planning is only geared to this end would be reductionistic. Its purposes are far greater than that. Yet, the strategic planning process needs to have as one of its important aims the identification of strategic growth opportunities and threats. This major objective and goalpost needs to be fulfilled in a variety of ways on a continuous basis. The identification of new opportunities and threats is not only an ongoing process but a critical deliverable of the strategic planning function. Without the identification of strategic growth opportunities and threats, the firm can neither grow nor survive in the longer term.

A strategic growth opportunity can be defined as a window of opportunity that will exist in the future, given that certain things will occur. The opportunity lies in the promise of a potential growth market into which the organization can sell its products or services. The opportunity will occur in the future based on today's emerging realities.

An example is Vietnam. German and Japanese businesses recognized several years ago that Vietnam had strategic market potential. They realized that a country strategically positioned in the middle of South-East Asia, with a large and growing population, would soon aspire to the economic benefits enjoyed by its neighbours. They predicted that despite internal strife and the officially unresolved animosity with the US, economic realities would prevail. They read the realities right and are now reaping the benefits of having identified a strategic growth opportunity ahead of many other international business organizations. Based on the political, social, economic, environmental, technological and demographic fundamentals at the time, German and Japanese businesses in particular, foresaw that the climate was right to invest. They invested in the future and are now reaping the benefits.

A strategic growth threat is the anticipation or expectation of a declining or negative market opportunity. The threat signals the need to exit the market. The exact timing of the exit is of course key to the disinvestment decision. If the organization leaves the market too early it may lose more revenues than it needs to. If it exits too late, the exit costs may be extremely high. The timing of a market exit is almost as critical as the timing of entry.

Strategic growth threats can also provide short period strategic growth opportunities. For example, if many banks are anxious to leave the Indonesian market, a good understanding of the market and the nature of its inherent risks may indicate that a short-term opportunity exists in taking on the business of the early exiters. Knowing when to quit oneself and how to off-load one's own loan portfolio is critical to the economic equation.

Identifying strategic growth opportunities and threats ahead of the competition, but not too far ahead, is not easy. Those that try to exploit market opportunities ahead of the pack also incur the cost of developing the market for the benefit of the late arrivers. Understanding the nature of markets, how they evolve and decline, and where they are in their life-cycle requires strong economic and market research support. Market and economic research teams should work hand in glove with the strategic planning department. This combination of skills and insights will have added potency if it is performed in the spirit of systems thinking.

Generating piles of statistical graphs and data as justification for the market research effort may provide market evidence, but may not reveal what is truly evident. The combined knowledge of economics, marketing, risk management, product development, and systems thinking should together generate a series of heuristics that guide the quest for strategic growth opportunities and threats (see Chapter 7 for ideas).

In sum, the strategic planning process is the internal motion created by the communication of the living network with its internal and external stakeholders, along a multiplicity of strands, moving in all directions, with many movements occurring simultaneously. The objective of this perpetual motion and movement is to survive and thrive by seeking out strategic opportunities that help the organization to develop, expand and grow.

The Future of Planning

Strategic planning will no longer be geared toward the detailed decision-making process. There will be a shift. The planning activity will be responsible for widening the organization's aperture to the outside world. It will seek to increase the information flow between the external and internal networks, and it will facilitate the organization's capacity to adapt and respond by holding up new realities and facilitating the systemic analysis process.

The strategic planning function will be geared to prompt and provoke questions, allowing detailed decisions to be made within divisions and departments that are responsible for business operations. Instead of being responsible for devising plans or formalizing processes, strategic planning will now facilitate the decision-making processes of others.

One of the prime purposes of the strategic planning function will be the synthesis of the ideas, learning, and experiences, along with the identification of strategic growth opportunities of the operating divisions. They will be responsible for guarding and enhancing the systemic properties of the organization that distinguish the organization as a living system, from any other. This is an exciting, creative, and responsible role. It requires a planning methodology that reflects the richness, complexity and diversity of information that is filtered in the process of giving the organization solid strategic advice and sound and prudent guidance about the risks inherent in future strategies. The planning methodology that fits this criteria is that of scenario planning.

Scenario Planning

Scenario planning has received a great deal of exposure of late. Many books and articles have acclaimed scenario planning as the tool to overcome the many weaknesses of conventional planning methods. My own experience in the field of strategic planning strongly supports this view. Scenario planning is consonant with our new understanding of living systems and overcomes the lack-lustre approaches of conventional planning methods. By looking at the future through the lens of various stories or scenarios we are encouraged to take a far more holistic view than that demanded by forecasting, budgeting, market/product analysis, or contingency planning. Scenario planning taps into the way that people in the world see and experience their lives; people relate best to the narrative.

Scenario Planning – What it is

Scenarios are stories about the way the world might be tomorrow. The purpose of the stories is to help us recognize the changing environment to which we need to adapt. Scenarios can help us order our perceptions about alternative future environments and allow us to play out various decisions that we would make under different circumstances.

Scenarios are written like a script for a film or a play. They have themes and plots that have been carefully selected to highlight significant elements of the world environment which challenge the future of the organization. By considering a number of different scenarios the organization can think through the consequences of a range of decisions. It can see how and what might change those decisions when the scenario theme or plot is changed. Working with and through scenarios is like rehearsing the future, where like an actor on the stage, different lines can be used depending on which play is being run.

The reader of the scenario has the benefit of observing all the events and players at a distance, and can explore the issues, options, and challenges from a vantage point which the actors in the story do not have.

The Benefits of Scenario Planning

The virtues of scenario planning are extolled in ever new revelations about the Shell Group and other organizations which have seriously adopted the scenario planning approach. A synopsis of some of the main benefits of scenario planning is as follows:

- It builds on the power of story telling.

- It is performed in the narrative – something to which most people can easily relate.

- It is useful when the future environment is difficult to predict and there are many variables.

- It is less intimidating and offensive than more quantitative and rigorous planning approaches.

- It provides the opportunity of looking at multiple perspectives which can be held in tension without forcing a decision on only one. This frees up the psyche to see creative and constructive alternatives.

- It can highlight the nuances of an environment by making things evident without reducing the many facets to just data or evidence.

- It provides the opportunity of combining both analysis and synthesis.

- It is suitable if one takes the systems thinking approach.

- Through the use of analogies, scenario planning provides a vehicle for turning up the heat on new realities without being overly confrontational.

- It enables one to move backwards and forwards between tomorrow's possibilities and today's potential and constraints.

- It enables one to move from the present into the future without the usual discontinuous leaps that are intrinsic in other planning methods.

In this age and in this precarious uncertain environment, scenario planning has many positive aspects which explains its use as a core strategic planning technique.

Developing Scenarios

Developing scenarios that interweave the realities of the external and internal organizational systems while also addressing its opportunities, limitations, and constraints, is both an art and a science. Scenarios are stories that describe a possible future with the organization as protagonist. Scenarios need to be crafted so as to address the issues that organization is, could, or should be facing. A key theme within a scenario should be the organization's adaptive challenges. New realities should be reflected within the scenario in a manner that reflects the real world. Key driving forces, for example political or demographic issues, should stand out so that scenario readers, later to become users, can identify causal issues to changes in the future environment.

Scenario stories are written in the narrative, describing issues, events, and players from various perspectives. Just as in any good story, the plot unfolds based on past events and on predetermined and unexpected things that occur in the future. A concatenation of events can present an opportunity or a threat to which the players or actors may or may not be able to respond. A key feature incorporated in a well-written scenario, just as in a good book, is a number of things happening at once. The story of the possible future should include a reasonable number of events that occur either in combination or in disordered sequence.

A well-written scenario incorporates the systemic issues of all the interlinking systems and pays attention to the explicit and implicit relationships that network the systems together. The scenario should inject novelty and creativity. The scenario should exude energy and motion, should have interesting real life plots filled with real people and events, and should be plausible yet stretch the boundaries of people's imaginations. I am not proposing sombre, tragic themes, but who could have imagined the death of Princess Diana? Consider the systemic repercussions of this tragic event. Consider how it has affected so many industries: fashion, the media, travel and entertainment. Scenarios need to be grounded in the world reflecting real-life possibilities.

The scenario writing itself should be well composed in good literary style. It should be easy and interesting to read. The scenario writer(s) should use imagery, prose, mythology, and poetry if that seems appropriate. The scenario should alert more than just the cognitive senses. It should prompt and provoke as many of the senses as possible. It should also leave sufficient unsaid that people are required to use their intuition in uncovering all that there is to uncover.

The scenario itself needs to be developed in conjunction with other members of the organization. This should ensure that the scenario incorporates the internal constraints and tensions of the company in a realistic and well-balanced manner. It also ensures that future users of the scenarios have bought into the process and feel that the scenarios developed are credible pictures of the future.

Turning Scenarios into Plans

In my experience turning scenarios into formal plans depends entirely on the organization. In some companies, the selected scenarios are confined to the thoughts and concerns of senior management who use the scenarios purely as a backdrop to the more conventional planning process. In this case, scenarios are used to provoke thoughts and ideas that might influence and help shape forecasts and future plans. Attention to alternative scenarios facilitates flexible thinking if plans need later alteration.

In other organizations, the market and product implications of chosen scenarios are rigorously converted into numbers, and the 'most likely' scenario is used as the basis for the numerical plan. In this case, ongoing discussions and attention to alternative scenarios provide input to addendums to the formal plan thereby facilitating later adjustments.

In a less frequent number of instances, the organization relies on the chosen scenarios as the basis of the planning effort. The previous targets are extrapolated forward on the basis of growth forecasts and strategic goals are set based on the occurrence of different scenarios. This results in a different plan for each scenario. This is sometimes referred to as contingency planning. The problem with this approach is that management is not quite sure which plan to adhere to. In this case they might either keep switching plans as events unfold, or they may delay decision making to see which plan seems most appropriate.

In my experience, this latter approach is the least successful. Using scenario planning as a backdrop that drives the assumptions of the formal plan and/or selecting a main scenario and planning around that one, appears to work best.

The Limitations of Scenario Planning

As I have alluded, integrating scenario planning into the organization's normal processes is not easy. Here are some of the difficulties and limitations:

- Getting an organization accustomed to being driven by numbers, deviations from plan, and hard data may present difficulties when buying into the scenario approach. Holding the tension between certainty and uncertainty, hard and soft data, tight and loose control, is difficult and requires leadership and management skills. While this is not really a limitation of the process, poor execution results in limiting scenario planning's effectiveness.

- Arriving at a suitable number of scenarios that provide appropriate alternatives while not trying to address every possible alternative.

- Integrating scenario planning into the rest of the planning activity.

- Devising some numerical basis on which to measure plans.

- Including the flexible thinking engendered by the scenario planning process into the achievement of formal plans.

- Developing and evolving scenarios over time as the environment changes.

- Knowing when and how to prompt the development of new scenarios.

- Educating and engaging the organization in scenario planning is time consuming. Getting senior management to devote quality time to this exercise is always difficult.

Despite these difficulties and limitations, the scenario planning process is consonant with the new world in which we find ourselves and is highly beneficial to fostering the learning organization.

The SWOT (Strength, Weakness, Opportunity, Threat Analysis)

The SWOT remains a popular method of looking at the organization's current strengths and weaknesses and its potential opportunities and threats. Strengths and weaknesses refer to factors that are internal to the organization, while opportunities and threats are factors that are external to the organization.

The purpose of the SWOT is to make the organization look at its present situation and to juxtapose the external environment against the internal one. One of the principal ideas of the SWOT analysis is to provide a focused picture of internal and external issues and to motivate the organization to deploy its strengths so as to maximize its perceived opportunities. Similarly the SWOT should highlight the organization's key weaknesses especially in light of environmental and competitive threats.

The SWOT analysis is a good method for providing a snapshot of the organization's current position plus generating some indicators about the future. The limitations of the SWOT lie in its tendency to become an unfiltered laundry list of the good, the bad and the ugly. While this has some value, it is important and necessary that the list generated is refined so that it can communicate important messages rather than adding to the noise and clutter of the organization's general information stream. Often the SWOT includes a list of all the frustrations experienced by members of the organization disguised in the form of technical problems, e.g. the telephones don't work, the security guard is never there, the parking lot is too small, marketing brochures are the wrong colour, delivery vehicles block customer collection points, and so on. While this is all important information, sorting the wheat from the chaff requires the eye of both the eagle and the ant. Many of these technical problems are the symptoms of larger adaptive problems. Exercising leadership in this case will be the art of sorting out the adaptive from the technical issues.

Carrying out a SWOT analysis either simultaneous or subsequent to the development of scenarios is, recognizing its limitations, undoubtedly a valuable exercise. Issues that are raised during the SWOT analysis exercise can provide direction to the development of scenarios. This would support the view that SWOTs should be done before or during the scenario development activity. Especially if a number of SWOT analyses are prepared by several different departments, groups and networks, their combined view of the organization's current position can provide a suitable reality test to the way the organization might respond to particular scenarios.

If the organization has been monitoring its environment by using SWOTs, putting these aside and developing scenarios that are more externally driven may free the organization from its entrenched mindset.

This reminds me of the story about the illiterate Jewish *shammes* (sexton in a synagogue), Polotski, in Wroclaw. On finding out that the *shammes* was illiterate, the Rabbi called him in for a chat. Explaining that the synagogue was a centre of great learning, the Rabbi explained that it would be inappropriate for someone illiterate to hold the exalted position of *shammes* and that regrettably he would have to let the *shammes* go. Sadly Polotski left his beloved city and went to work for his cousin in Warsaw. After a number of years of diligent work in his cousin's garment factory, Polotski started his own fabric business. With his usual attention to detail and diligence, over time his business blossomed and by the time he was 50 he was a millionaire. A local TV station hearing of his success invited him for an interview. The TV broadcaster amazed to hear that he was illiterate asked him how he had managed to come so far. At one point she said, 'Imagine what you would have been able to do if you could read or write!' To which Polostski replied, 'I have. I would have still been the *shammes* in Wroclaw!' I rest my case.

FIGURE 6.1 Diagram of a SWOT analysis

Internal Factors	External Factors
Strengths	Opportunities
Weaknesses	Threats

The Core Competence Concept

The idea of an organization's core competence has evolved over several decades of organizational studies. It reached its crowning point of clarification and definition under the phrase 'core competence' as a consequence of the work done by CK Prahalad and Gary Hamel. Prior to that it was referred to, amongst other things, as distinctive strengths, skills, competencies and capabilities.

Prahalad and Hamel define core competence as an integrated bundle of skills and technologies; 'a messy accumulation of learning' which contributes to a business's competitive success (Prahalad and Hamel 1990). This concept promotes the idea that a combination of complex capabilities are critical to a firm's success. Some refer to this character of an organization as its 'distinctive competence.' The existence of this distinctive competence is supposedly the source of the organization's competitive advantage.

The core competency concept promotes focus on the essence of the bundle of skills and technologies on which the organization continues to build and adapt. To use an analogy, the core competence of an organization is akin to the roots of a tree. The roots of the tree will dictate the tree's capacity and its capabilities. Capacity relates to its power to grow, change, and adapt. Its capabilities relate to its height, colour, shape and growth potential.

The core competence motif is intended to encourage organizations to nourish the roots rather than to be preoccupied with painting the leaves. It also champions the idea of sticking to one's knitting and building on one's capacity from which the appropriate capabilities will follow. This orientation, many argue, is the only way that true long term, competitive advantage can be developed and sustained. In this instance organizational effort is centred on developing, fine-tuning, honing and researching inherent competencies, building and developing them so that they provide a long-term source of competitive advantage.

Usually a core competency is an innate strength or ability that an organization has developed over time. In other words it does not develop quickly. A foundational element of this competency is that it typically stems from the founding formula of the organization and has a highly developed, implicit learning element factored into its explicit manifestation. A core competency is what gives the organization its greatest strengths and momentum provided it is suitably nourished and fostered. This implies attention, investment, and nurturing to ensure that the competency remains practical and appropriate to a changing world.

The systemic analysis performed on the organization's internal environment should pay attention to the organization's core competence and should identify the relationships and capacities that give it its uniqueness. The identification of strategic growth opportunities and threats should also take cognizance of further building on this competency or protecting it from threats. The SWOT analysis and the development of scenarios should be sensitive to the organization's distinctive competencies and should ensure that these are suitably addressed in the analysis of the present situation and the trends of the future. Testing future strategies and plans against the organization's competencies in order to measure the explicit and implicit business impact is an important part of reality testing the strategic plan.

The Benefits of Keeping the Organization's Core Competence in Central Focus

By keeping the organization's core competence in central focus it:

- brings together a focus on the collective learning of the organization;

- encourages a trend towards harmonizing key activities e.g. information technology;

- facilitates the idea of thinking in terms of networks and is part of the process of eliminating organizational boundaries;

- facilitates acceptance of the sharing of competencies across functions;

- views strategy as a more unified activity rather than just a functional, divisional, or departmental endeavour;

- enables the organization to understand the benefits of forgoing short-term opportunities in order to invest in longer term competencies;

- encourages sticking to the knitting in new and radical ways;

- assists the organization in understanding that the enhancement of the organization's adaptive capacity is directly related to building on its core competences;

- provides insights into the possible development of new strategic alliances.

In summary, the core competence focus can enhance self-understanding and organizational groundedness; it can provoke innovative strategic alternatives; it can provide a united focus for the future, and it can set the basis for the negotiable and non-negotiable terms for future alliances.

Strategic Planning Fallacies

The function of strategic planning has been radically misunderstood by many in the past. This is not a department of Shamans and Soothsayers who can use magic to alleviate or dispose of uncertainty, discomfort, and ills. It is also not a cadre of ivory tower specialists or staff officers who manage the organization from the drawing board. The strategic planning function is within the web of organizational life and should not have any hierarchical position. Planners need to dwell in the world and within organizational life. They should be part and parcel of both the formal and the informal communication network. They should spend time with people involved in operations. They should experience the tensions of daily decision making and they should be expected to spend regular periods working within divisions performing divisional tasks. Contrary to most sabbaticals where people get away from it all, strategic planners should have periodic sabbaticals where they have to partake in actual daily decision making.

The strategic planning function is well known for some cliché phrases which regrettably often have a negative impact on some of the positive strategic work that is being done.

These include injunctions like:

- We need to respond as quickly as possible.

- If we don't do it our competitors will.

- Trying to put a number on anything and everything. (The fallacy of misplaced concreteness.)

- Deviations from plan are signs of failure.

- Analysis is solely a rational activity.

- Everything has a price.

- Good service means efficient use of assets.

- The stock market knows best.

- If we create value for shareholders everything else is acceptable, i.e. the end justifies the means.

- The strategic plan is the overlay on top of everything else that the organization does.

- Reward systems should be directly linked to the achievement of plans.

Senior management should endeavour to prevent putting these sayings into practice. They belong to the old order and are not suitable for exercising leadership, systems thinking, and responding to the challenges of the Adaptive Age.

Summary

The strategic planning exercise is amongst other things a learning exercise. Strategic planning is about learning about the environment and the adaptive challenges that it poses. This is a continuous learning process in that reality is continually changing and new value conflicts are continuously surfacing. New strategic planning skills lie in actively encouraging transformative learning. This type of learning changes the things that the organization does and the way that it does them. This is only possible if the members of the organization can respond to adaptive challenges by working on the challenges that these represent.

Leadership through strategic planning should align the organization to the challenges of the future. It should stimulate the organization to be vibrant and alive to the changing world. It should encourage members of the organization to value relationships. And, it should be attentive to key change signals that foreshadow new futures and new challenges.

Key Points Raised in this Chapter

- Organizational leadership is exercised by the strategic planning function.

- Strategic planners need to be a different breed to those in the past.

- A major objective of the strategic planning function is to identify key change signals.

▸ The strategic planning function is responsible for adaptive work. The operating divisions should be responsible for the technical work.

▸ Scenario planning is a suitable strategic planning tool in present times.

SUGGESTIONS

■ Review the objectives of the strategic planning function. Do these include the identification of adaptive challenges and the identification of key change signals?

■ Consider the role of the strategic planning function. List their activities. Do these include a great deal of analysis and technical work? Can these activities be passed onto the operating divisions?

■ Is the strategic planning function responsible for the identification of strategic growth opportunities and threats? Do they do this in conjunction with divisional management? Review the formal or *ad hoc* method by which this handled.

■ If the organization has not tried scenario planning, maybe it could experiment with a scenario that relates to a part of the organization's activities. This may prove to be a great learning exercise.

■ Consider placing members of the strategic planning function into line positions on some rotation basis. This need not be a high profile position with a great deal of responsibility, however the position needs to be an important one to the organization.

Further Reading

Mintzberg, H. (1994) *The Rise and Fall of Strategic Planning*, The Free Press, New York.

Van Der Heijden, K. *Scenarios: The Art of Strategic Conversation*, John Wiley & Sons, Chichester.

CHAPTER SEVEN

The Evidence – Strategic Planning in Action

The Nature of Strategic Planning

So far we have discussed the leadership role of strategic planning. I have emphasized that strategic planning is a humanistic task that requires extensive engagement with people and their issues. It requires understanding the world as a conglomeration of an infinite number of systems that have both common and unique aspects.

The strategic planning function provides input and guides the strategy process. Strategies are devised by grounding the organization's mission in new realities, exploiting strategic growth opportunities, and preparing against strategic growth threats. New or renewed visions are co-created by the members of the organization under the guiding hand of senior management and those engaged in strategic planning.

In order to engage in strategic planning in a manner that reflects the changing world I have suggested that we need to take a systems view and to become adept at carrying out systemic analyses. Rather than emphasizing analytical techniques and rational methods, I have proposed the use of scenario planning as being an approach for identifying the key drivers that will influence the actions of organizations in the future. I have also stated that the primary, but not single, objective of strategic planning is to identify key change signals, especially those that challenge the organization's adaptive capacity. One of the prime activities of the strategic planning function is to distinguish adaptive from technical work and to develop the adaptive capacity of the organization. Strategic planners should work on the adaptive challenges leaving the technical work to operational management. This does not mean that they should totally divorce themselves from the technical solutions that flow from the adaptive work. Through continuous dialogue and communication strategic planners and operational management need to move back and forth between what is considered to be adaptive and what is technical work. Planners are naturally interested in the efficacy of the technical solutions as they want to ensure that the adaptive work has been correctly translated to the operations.

In devising strategies for response to environmental changes I have proposed the use of well-crafted scenarios, the execution of a SWOT analysis, and the identification of organizational core competencies.

Using the dance metaphor, the aim of strategic planning is to assist the organization in understanding the size and shape of the dance floor and the nature of the dances that are being performed. This includes learning about the style, rhythm, and tempo of likely future dances. The planning function should help the organization see how well it dances, the typical steps that it prefers, its capacity for developing new dances, and its ability to dance new dances in the future. It should also help the organization recognize when to sit out a dance and when and how to find new partners. It should hone the organization's ability to recognize and understand the relationships between dancers and the end for which they have been formed. The nature of strategic planning can be summarized as follows:

- it is a humanistic task;

- guides the strategy process;

- recognizes new realities;

- facilitates co-creation of new visions;

- uses systems thinking;

- engages in systemic analysis;

- places emphasis on relationships;

- understands how values link the network;

- uses scenario planning;

- identifies key change signals;

- finds strategic growth opportunities and threats;

- pays attention to adaptive capacity;

- performs the SWOT analysis;

- focuses on core competencies;

- evaluates current dance steps;

- evaluates future possible dances;

- proposes and finds new partners.

Strategic Planning in Practice

The question may arise as to what extent the strategic planning approaches recommended here are actually used in practice. My response, based on my experience, is that some organizations engage in some of these methods some of the time. Some are more committed to systems thinking than others. And, more and more organizations are beginning to realize that social, cultural, and religious issues are important factors in devising plans. Regrettably a vast number of organizations are still fettered to the numbers game and tend to subdue creativity, novelty, and intuition in the interest of reaching targets. Numbers tend to remain 'Lord of their Dance'.

Many organizations are, however, starting to be more innovative and adventurous with regard to their strategic processes. Spurred on by rapidly changing markets and competitive pressure, the search for new ways of doing new things will doubtless accelerate in pace.

Over the past 20 years I have had experience with many strategic planning processes in a diverse number of organizations. These have included manufacturing, service, financial services, and a number of non-profit organizations. While all strategic planning processes have as their prime deliverable the production of a strategic plan, the way that this is achieved varies greatly. The output is usually in the form of an array of computer spreadsheets plus a bound hardcopy of text and spreadsheets. Once the planning process is complete, there is usually a sigh of general relief as many people feel that they can now get back to doing the real work. The weight of the tomes produced also varies from a few ounces to several kilos. (Their physical weight is often inversely related to their intellectual weight!)

The purpose of this chapter is to provide some evidence that the ideas championed in this book can, and are, being put into practice. For the purposes of further explanation and illustration I propose taking the reader through a detailed, real life, case study. This case study describes the development and process of a strategic planning function which incorporates a significant portion of the ideas that we have discussed. I will also draw on examples of other planning systems to further explicate points not addressed in the case study.

The Evidence – A Case Study

Background

A few years ago I was fortunate enough to be asked to assist one of the world's largest international banks ('the Bank') in the reconceptualization and reformulation of their strategic planning process. The project took place at the London Head Office which was responsible for all strategic planning activities, both local and international.

In the past the Bank had used conventional strategic planning approaches. This process included product/market analysis, evaluating input from their extensive economics department, synthesis of a range of market research efforts, and feedback from the operating divisions regarding their assumptions about the future. The Bank recognized that in the over-banked, highly competitive financial service market more creative and innovative planning was needed if they were to outperform their closest rivals. The board decided to appoint a new planning director. They encouraged him to be creative and challenging. He certainly took up the challenge.

This case study is a good example of an organization trying to do new things in new ways. The objective of my assignment was to assist the planning director in developing a new strategic planning process while simultaneously developing an advanced decision support system that would encapsulate this new process. At the time, I owned a consultancy organization that specialized in the development of strategic planning systems and processes and also designed and built expert systems (knowledge based systems). Most of our expert systems were specifically intended to aid planning processes. This project was not an untypical assignment. Besides participating in developing new planning processes, we were asked to program the knowledge inherent in the new process into a software construct known as an expert system shell. The expert system would serve, amongst other things, as a computerized expert planning consultant. In order to do this we needed to capture the relevant heuristics that related to the Bank's revitalized strategic planning process and encapsulate this within the expert system. For those readers who have been engaged in the development of expert systems and in the complexity of identifying and tracking expert heuristics, I am sure that you will recognize that this was no small task.

The champion behind the Bank's new way of thinking, and hence the driving force for the implementation of the new process was the Group's Planning Director, Peter Matus ('Matus') (a fictitious name).[1]

Peter is a man with remarkable skills. He is both highly numerate and he also understands the importance and complexities of the softer issues that cannot be described by or converted into numbers. He has a mindset that fits in with the notion of exercising leadership and he believes that the strategic planning function should play a leadership role. In 1992 Peter was ahead of his time.[2]

The project took place over a period of two and a half years. The initial, very broad brief that I was given was to develop a strategic planning process that incorporated systemic analysis interwoven with scenario planning. The brief evolved as the planning process itself evolved. Each new idea was developed, tested, developed further, and integrated with other ideas so as to create a coherent process. This naturally took time and required a great deal of internal selling. People resisted those parts of the process that demanded recognizing new realities and required new ways of doing things. Once people learn how to work the numbers, there is great escape in continuously manipulating spreadsheets or tweaking formulae. Dealing with the underlying assumptions is a far more challenging exercise.

The planning concepts which were foundational to the design of the new process included systems thinking, scenario planning, the SWOT analysis, evaluation of core competencies, identification of key change signals, identification of strategic growth opportunities and threats, and the assessment of the strategic planning gap. The planning process was driven and guided by a networked PC-based expert system. This computer system was designed to act as an in-house consultant to the strategic planning process and could also be used as a powerful decision support tool. This meant that the computer system not only included all the knowledge concerning the planning process itself but could act as a facilitator to the process. The system was designed to provide a dynamic framework of decision trees that could lead the user down the relevant path based on his or her inputs.

The system was named 'Aristotle'. Its principal purpose is to act as a consultant, intelligent assistant, or aide. Its motto was 'Planning the Future with Confidence'.

In order to describe the new strategic planning process I shall describe the design and content of the Aristotle system.

Strategic Planning Expertise

The strategic planning expertise which the bank drew on in order to revamp its planning process included both internal and external experts from a variety of multi-disciplinary fields. Workshops and focus groups were held with planning staff, people from staff functions, management from operating divisions, board members, major clients, and external experts. Part of my role was to screen and synthesize the concepts and ideas that these meetings generated, and to add some of my own.

Information

One thing that most organizations, least of all banks, do not lack, is data. The Bank, like many other organizations, suffered from an inundation of data as well as insufficient ideas and directives on how to filter the enormous amounts of data available. A critical process of the strategic planning activity is how to analyse data to maximum effect. This is where systems thinking and systemic analysis can have high payoffs.

At the commencement of the project, a great deal of attention was given to the available data and the method of data collection. Through workshops and discussion, systemic analyses were performed in order to fine-tune the Bank's data collection process. The aim was to make data collection more focused and purposeful so that it would assist in the identification of key change signals and the identification of strategic growth opportunities and threats.

Changing the data collection task was extremely difficult and met with a great deal of resistance. As we have discussed, systems thinking requires a different mindset and a quality rather than quantity mentality. The Bank had been generating the same economic research reports for decades. Obviously many could not understand why this should change. Inculcating a systems thinking mindset that can readily engage in systemic analyses requires a great deal of education and persuasion. Despite enormous efforts in this regard, obtaining relevant information in a manner that was meaningful to the new strategic planning emphasis, remained one of the biggest hurdles to the entire planning process.

Group Mission Statement

The Bank had recently revamped its mission statement. The new statement took cognizance of the changing realities in the world and in the international and domestic financial services industry. The new statement sought to present a vision that would appeal to both internal and external stakeholders.

Return to shareholders, globalization, customer focus, quality, social responsibility, and organizational integrity were some of the issues addressed. The mission statement also included some guiding principles that provided key benchmarks for the strategic planning process. These included expected returns and guidelines for investments in markets and products. Investment criteria and return benchmarks are updated from time to time.

The Aristotle expert system began every consultation by displaying to the user the mission statement and its guiding principles. At various points in the system users would be reminded of the Bank's mission so that they could factor this into their decision-making processes.

The Objectives of the Aristotle System

While it is recognized that the real world is exceedingly complex and that it is impossible to foresee the future, foresight and planning enhance the agility of people's mindsets and hence improve their ability to cope with predetermined and unforeseen events. The purpose of the Aristotle expert system is not only to assist in data gathering and assimilation, but also in the interpretation of the dynamic forces in the world that are continuously at play.

The underlying rationale for the Aristotle system is to assist the user in identifying key change signals and strategic growth opportunities and threats. The system enables the user to compare the strengths and weaknesses of the entire organization or any one of its operating divisions with industry opportunities and threats and/or country opportunities and threats.

The specific objectives of the system include:

- To provide a strategic planning framework that can be used as a guide to the strategic planning process.

- To act as a storehouse of the bank's culled knowledge of countries, industries, and organizations. This would include past issues and performance statistics, forecast issues and performance goals.

- To serve as a reservoir of strategic planning knowledge regarding specific issues that pertain to the Bank group and each of its major operating divisions.

- To act as a prompt and a devil's advocate when thinking through various strategic planning issues.

- To act as a dynamic aide-mémoire when performing certain processes.

- To encourage consistency in approach without eliminating creativity and innovative thinking.

- To encapsulate trends and changes in the macro environment and thereby assist in the identification of key change signals.

- To facilitate the capture and manipulation of information and data held on the world and on relevant industries.

- To act as a training tool for new members of the strategic planning function.

Overall Structure of the System

SYSTEM STRUCTURE

- Key Trends (database on world events and trends)

- Macro Module (systemic analysis and scenario planning section)

- Industry Module (financial and non-financial sector analysis)

- Groups and Operating Units (Divisional, department, business unit plans)

- Strategy Review Module (Review and SWOTs)

- Takeover and Valuation Module (Compare Bidder and target companies, perform valuations)

- Summaries Module (Access summaries of reviews)

- Reports Module (Generate reports of reviews)

The Function of the System Controller

Aristotle has been designed so that the main rules, heuristics, and performance benchmarks that are included in the system can be altered by a designated user. Accessing the rule base in this manner requires knowing a series of passwords.

This functionality enables the 'System Controller', i.e. the planning director in the case of the Bank, to alter either the path of analysis that a system user might follow, or the decisions that might be reached. For example if the System Controller alters the rules that affect the extrapolation of a business unit's current results, the strategic planning gap over the planning period could be larger or smaller. This would mean that the operating unit has more or less work to do in order to close the gap. Another example might be the SWOT analysis. Here too the System Controller can alter the weightings assigned to certain SWOTs, thereby affecting the performance assessment of the organization being reviewed.

The role of the System Controller, is to test and retest the ideas and procedures encapsulated in the planning process. He or she should also be responsible for the integrity and the appropriateness of the rules. In the case of the Bank, Matus was continuously rethinking the procedures and rules. He held many discussion groups and workshops in an attempt to make these reflect the changing world as much as possible. With or without a computer system, the exercise of rethinking the nature of the process and the underlying assumptions is fundamental to any strategic planning process.

Operating the System

The Aristotle system is entirely menu driven and requires no computer expertise to run. At various points the user can call in notepad facilities, databases, or spreadsheets that interface with the main system. All information that is entered, created by the system, or altered from a previous consultation can be saved under a unique filename that is accessible at a later date.

Only designated users may access the system via their unique password. All the information that they gather, generate, or create is saved under filenames that include their passwords. Dependent upon the name or position of a user, he or she may or may not access the files of other users. For example members of the planning department cannot access or review the files created by senior members of the board. Access of any file created by someone other than the user remains on a read-only basis so as to ensure that other people do not corrupt one's own files.

As the system is networked, a group of users can complete a planning review of an organization, (their own or a competitor organization), where each member of the group need only deal with an aspect of the process. For example one user may create the macro scenario, another the industry scenario, while another may perform the detailed SWOT analysis. Group members can save their results and their thought processes in designated files that only the group may access at a later date.

Key Trends

This section of the system provides access to a database of major world issues and events. Here the user can review data on different countries, world industries, world demographic and population trends, and a host of other issues.

The purpose of this section is to apprise users and planning departments of the major issues that are in the forefront of world news and on the top of the agenda of many of the world's leaders. The database is intended to show the user the interrelatedness of world issues and the significance of events at a number of levels. This section requires continuous review and updating.

Macro Module

MACRO MODULE STRUCTURE

- Strategic planning base scenarios

- User scenarios

- Projections and divergences

- Scenario comparisons

- Summaries and reports

The world macro module is a pivotal part of the Aristotle system. This module is specifically designed to promote systems thinking and to take a systemic view of the world. By holding up the world as the system in which the Bank exists and operates, it encourages those engaged in providing direction to the Bank to think about the world as one large integrated system rather than a group of isolated land masses defined by geographic and political contours. Despite the fact that the Bank has been operating on an international scale for decades, a separatist and fragmented view of the world prevailed. Groups called the South-East Asia Group and the North America Group existed. Seldom did these groups gets together to discuss their regions' commonalities or differences. One of the aims of the new processes developed for viewing the macro environment was to overcome this fragmented approach to planning.

The macro module included in the expert system enables the user to re-perceive the world. Through the use of scenarios the user can explore the world in a creative manner. He or she can evaluate the events, uncertainties, and the major issues by either looking at them in isolation, or considering them in combination.

The user can develop an infinite number of scenarios about the world. He or she can create the profile of possible future environments and can see the system generated consequences to the scenario as profiled. He or she can also see the impact of different decisions made and can consider the anticipated consequences.

In creating the world to be modelled the user can either look at the 'world' and treat it as if it is a country, or he or she can include up to 20 countries and so constitute the world.

The user can also invoke a number of world issues that overlay a combination of country issues thereby creating a world picture. This means that users can create an infinite number of systems or scenarios in order to make up a world system or scenario. The user can also just create a scenario of one country.

Base Scenarios

These are scenarios of the world and of certain countries created by the strategic planning team in conjunction with specific members of the organization. These scenarios are the main scenarios which form the backdrop to the strategic planning process. They include specific issues and events that members of the organization feel are pertinent to the current planning process. These scenarios have been modelled at both world and country level. This means that users can see how the world is perceived as an integrated system, as well as how countries are perceived that make up that world system.

Users reviewing these scenarios can see how they were compiled, can query the underlying assumptions, and can print out reports that describe the systemic analyses that resulted in the conclusions drawn. They may not, however, alter these assumptions. By selecting the 'compare scenarios' section, they can compare their own scenarios with the base scenarios. They can also query the differences between their assumptions and those of the base scenarios and they can see the implications.

User Scenarios

Here the user may create his or her own scenarios. As mentioned, users can create as many as they like, and they can create an infinite combination of countries while varying aspects within those countries. The Aristotle system has enormous amounts of information on 55 countries embedded within its knowledge base. There are also certain points within the system where the user may ask for more information and may then access other on-line databases that provide pertinent information to the creation of a particular scenario.

At any point users may access a notepad where they can record any key change signals of which they are aware or, they may review key change signals identified by other users of the system. System maintenance includes updating key change signals. All input of information is not only saved to a file but is recorded by user password and is date and time recorded. The scenarios themselves can relate to either one year or up to any 10 year period forward.

The user may also create five-year world or country scenarios and projections based on certain trigger events. The system itself includes several scenarios generated by the planning team and selected members of the organization based on their choice of trigger events.

Projections and Divergences

Based on chosen trigger events, here the user can compare his or her five-year projections against any number of other projections, including those created by the planning team.

Compare Existing Scenarios

Here the user can compare up to five different scenarios that have been generated. The system reminds the user of his or her inputs, shows the decision path that has been taken, and comments on similarities and differences between scenarios.

Summaries and Reports

Each completed scenario results in a number of summaries. A key summary is one that prompts potential strategic growth opportunities and threats. The system explains the rationale that underlies its results. If the users do not agree, they may record their comments on another notepad, which is automatically assigned for the System Controller's attention.

The implications for the organization in availing of the strategic growth opportunities and threats are also prompted by the system. For example, if the system suggests that the Vietnam market for Small Business Lending is very promising, it will also comment on what this means for the organization. These comments will be presented under at least the following headings:

- management competence;

- required staff skills mix;

- market/product opportunity and threats;

- customer influence;

- technology;

- innovation;

- operational factors;

- geographic location issues;

- financial issues;

- risk.

At another point in the process these implications can be compared against the SWOTs of the organization. The system will make the comparison, highlight the gap and make recommendations.

In this section the user can also compare the results of up to five different scenarios. Here the results, including the potential strategic growth opportunities and threats, can be reviewed.

Modelling the Scenarios

In modelling the scenarios the user is provided with a menu-driven framework that guides the creation of scenarios. Users can elect either to consider all aspects, or they have the freedom to bypass an issue when they deem it appropriate. The system will not only track their responses but will record those issues that they have been bypassed.

The system framework for the development of macro scenarios is built around the following:

1   *Force majeure issues can be included that might have positive as well as negative effects.* These include issues relating to the global effects such as:
    – nuclear explosion;
    – epidemic;
    – environmental catastrophe;
    – major disaster;
    – harmonization;
    – technology breakthrough;
    – oil price impact.

2   *Creating World or Country Scenarios.* In creating scenarios at the macro level, users are asked to input their views on the following:

    (a) Political factors (internal)
        – control over the economy;
        – distribution of wealth;
        – corruption;
        – strength of political institutions;
        – political tolerance;
        – quality and direction of leadership;
        – role of the military;
        – internal tensions.

    (b) Political factors (external)
        – stability of the area;
        – conflict with neighbours;
        – potential disputes (territories/resources);

- inward migration of workers;
- alliances;
- incidence of capital flight;

(c) Social and religious issues
- religious fanaticism;
- human rights issues;
- health;
- distribution of wealth;
- skills of labour force;
- infrastructure;
- willingness to change (psychological profile);
- mobility of labour force;
- level of literacy;
- population growth rate;
- racial tensions;
- new regulations;
- bill of rights (social charter).

(d) Economic issues
- employment;
- inflation;
- population;
- demographics;
- standard of living;
- GATT issues;
- EC Issues;
- availability of resources;
- capital flows (exchange controls);
- taxation;
- business confidence;
- technological advance;
- technological substitution.

(e) Environmental issues
- adverse weather;
- pollution;
- disaster;
- ozone layer impact;
- regulation;
- discovery of natural resources.

(f) Key change signals notepad facility
This facility enables users to refer to key change signals

identified by the strategic planning team and notes made by other users. They can also record their own notes. Key Change Signals are stored under the following headings:
- buyer power;
- supplier power;
- substitute products/services;
- new entrants;
- alliances/joint ventures;
- technology (distribution);
- human assets;
- consumer expectations;
- risk;
- other.

(g) The Trigger Events that can be used as key drivers for a five year projection include:
- substantial oil price hike;
- death of a key figure e.g. the Pope;
- change of government;
- the Euro put on hold;
- environmental disaster affects world agriculture;
- major war;
- rise of fundamentalism;
- civil wars in Eastern European countries;
- breakthrough in medical science.

Suggestions for trigger events form part of the ongoing discussions between the strategic planning team and operating management.

At any point during the consultation the user can ask for assistance. This is available in a number of ways. First they can query the system as to why a particular question has been asked. The system will respond by giving examples and explaining its relevance. Users can ask for help by way of input regarding for example, a political or economic issue about a country. They can request that certain statistical information be downloaded and they can call in economic research reports where relevant.

Industry Module

Aristotle's industry model allows the user access to a range of information with respect to industries both in the financial services sector, and in the non-financial services sector. This information is also available on a geographical basis.

Users can enter the system and gain information or add to the information that is stored there. They also have the facility to define and create a new industry which they can compare with other industries.

INDUSTRY MODULE STRUCTURE

- Key Strategic Changes

- Political Profile

- Industry/Size Positioning

- Profitability/Economics

- Merger and Acquisition Activity

- Operational Influences

- Forces of Competition

Key Strategic Changes

Here the user is encouraged to input key strategic changes that appear to be incurring in the industry sector which they are reviewing.

Political Profile

In this section the user is guided through a series of questions regarding the effect of the current and future political environment on a particular industry. This includes questions on for example legislation, regulation, political cronyism, corruption, and political support.

Industry Size/Positioning

The industry size and positioning module is the front end to a database on a host of industry statistics. This includes the number of players, the number of recent entrants, turnover, income, and profitability statistics. Certain users with designated passwords may alter and update these numbers.

Profitability Economics

In this section the user is asked a range of questions regarding the profitability and business economics of the sector being reviewed. It addresses revenues, costs, profitability, market share, break-even, taxation, the average capital base, and the state of the industry life cycle (emerging, maturity, or decline). Help in answering the questions is available to the user at all times.

Merger and Acquisition Activity

This section is the front end to a database on the merger and acquisition activity (M&A) that is occurring in the industry sector. Users can add to this information and they can download summaries and reports held in the M&A files.

Operational Influences

In this section the user is asked to respond to a number of questions regarding the major operational influences that exist within a particular sector. The emphasis is placed particularly on distribution systems, how these are responding to customer needs, and how these are altering the economics of the business.

Forces of Competition

This section guides the user through Michael Porter's model of the five forces that define an industry's intensity of competition (Porter 1985). The user can either do his or her own analysis or see the views of the strategic planning team with input from the operating divisions. Users can also compare different industries and are given ideas as to the implications of operating in high or low intensity industries. The system also addresses the industry's barriers to entry and how these might be overcome.

The purpose of the Porter model and its use is explained in detail and information that is relevant to assessing the power of players in an industry is readily available through the help facilities.

FIGURE 7.1   Forces of competition (adapted from Porter's model of five forces)

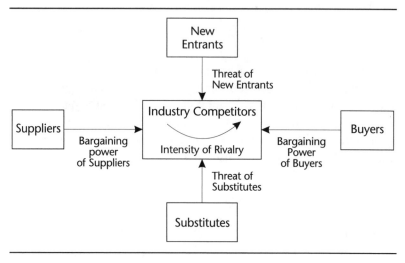

Key Change Signals

At any point the user can investigate the system identified key change signals or add his or her own key change signals. Key change signals are prompted or collected under the following headings:

- strategic changes;

- geographic/market diversification;

- customer values and needs;

- growth plans of key players;

- quality of service/product;

- technology;

- distribution;

- alliances/joint ventures;

- risk management;

- human resources;

- pricing/payment policies;

- management style/organization structure;

- equipment/processes.

Operating Division/Business Unit Module

The purpose of this part of the Aristotle system is to enable divisional and business unit operating managers to review the output of their own strategic plans in the light of a forecast macro scenario and the state of the industry. They are asked to input the name of a macro scenario which they wish to work with as well as selecting the relevant industry sector. For the formal plan they are obliged to view their plans against the backdrop of the base scenarios created by the strategic planning team and other senior executives.

They are then asked to input the following details regarding their strategic plans:

- the strategic mission;

- the strategic objectives and key milestones;

- their 'Balanced Scorecard' (Kaplan and Norton 1996);[3]

- business unit core competencies;

- financial numbers (these are directly accessed from spread-sheet files).

The system processes their input and provides feedback under the following headings:

- A review of strategic objectives.

- Comments on core competencies.

- Competitor positioning.

- Past performance assessment.

- Forecast Financial Analysis and Ratios.

- Shareholder value analysis.

- SWOTs.

- Overall feasibility of plan.

- Strategic planning gap.

Inferences for the SWOTs are derived both from information on the industry and from the strategy review section.

The strategic planning gap is system generated. It takes the organization's past performance, knowledge about the industry and projects these forward. This is compared with the organization's forecast plans adjusted by:

- the core competencies assessment;

- identification of strategic growth opportunities and threats;

- industry opportunities and threats;

- organization strengths and weaknesses;

- the success rate for achieving previous plans.

The system concludes this section with summaries, recommendations, and reports.

Strategy Review Module

The purpose of the strategy review module is to carry out a strategic audit of an organization. Its focus is on internal factors. It culminates in a detailed Strength and Weakness analysis and sets this against the respective industry Opportunities and Threats. The structure of the module provides some indication of the many aspects that management is invited to review.

STRATEGY REVIEW MODULE STRUCTURE

- Organization profile

- Review of the industry – access to industry module

- Competitor analysis – access to industry module

- Management evaluation

- MIS/Technology review

- Market attractiveness analysis

- Structure review

- Risk analysis

- Company performance – access to spreadsheets

- Resource review

- Organization evaluation – generation of SWOT.

Takeover and Valuation Module

In the takeover and valuation module the user can compare any two organizations on a variety of criteria. Any organization and any industry that has been reviewed with the guidance of the Aristotle system can be called into this module and evaluated as both a bidder or a target *vis à vis* another organization.

The user can input criteria for the merger or acquisition and can review how a variety of organizations stack up. The system will also carry out a company valuation and will comment on the synergies if the chosen entities are combined. It will also highlight the implementation difficulties and give an overall prompt as to whether it thinks that the merger or acquisition is a good idea.

Summaries Module

This section provides access to any and all of the summaries generated by the system.

Reports Module

The reports module allows the user to print out any of the system recommendations, comments, summaries or reports. This includes the identification of key change signals, the generation of strategic growth opportunities and threats, the strategic planning gap, detailed SWOT analyses and organizations' Balanced Score cards.

The System Audit Trail

Each computer consultation creates an audit trail. This means that every scenario developed, every SWOT analysis performed, every core competency assessment, and any assessment, summary, or report generated is automatically saved to disk. This means that the user can resume a consultation at a later date from the point at which they exited the system. It also means that as scenarios and organizations are evaluated using the system, a database of consultations is created. This provides users with the possibility of comparing the results of one scenario with any number of others. These comparisons are also saved, thereby enabling users to review the results of comparisons. They can then compare and evaluate the results of one comparison with another set of comparisons.

The audit trail and savings facility enables operating divisions to develop scenarios that can be played off against other scenarios at head office. It also enables the planning team to review the decision paths followed by users of the system at different operating levels and thereby gain an understanding of how other people perceive their world and how they assess the strengths and weaknesses of an organization or industry.

The New Strategic Planning Process

As I mentioned, the strategic planning process of the Bank had been rather conventional. It had been a mixture of budgeting, forecasting, and a range of product/market analyses. The Bank did not pay much attention to market life cycles, assumptions were largely based on economic factors, and they did not use scenario planning.

The economics department generated hosts of reports that focused on the economic issues of countries and market sectors. While these reports were full of information, for the layperson they were difficult to read and interpret. Many of them did not address key change signals. Instead they included screeds of quantitative data which supposedly conveyed important messages. A large majority of the reports were not used in any strategic or intentional way.

The strategic planning process itself was also previously carried out at senior management level. Plans were prepared and then foisted on the divisions with little bottom-up input. The record for achieving plans in the past was unsurprisingly poor. The Bank used to jokingly refer to this as the J-curve effect.

The purpose of the new planning process as envisioned by Matus, was to break the hierarchical approach to planning by putting the process back into the divisions where it belongs. He wanted everyone to have some input, or to have at least the capability of understanding other people's input. He believed in the top-down and bottom up approach, and in the necessity of dialogue and negotiation between head-office and the operating divisions. He assigned members of the planning team to certain divisions with the aim of getting them to work more closely together.

He also believed in the scenario approach and the richness of inductive reasoning that this could elicit. He believed that planning is an ongoing activity and not something that is done periodically just for the purpose of generating a plan. He advocated that the more we plan the better we get at it. The better we get at it the more we plan. Planning needs to be internalized if it is to be effective and evoke commitment. Matus hoped that by making planning part of every day's work and part of every activity, these benefits would follow.

Through the creation of a networked PC-based strategic planning system, the strategic planning process is now devolved downwards into the divisions. Divisional management can now participate in any or all aspects of strategic planning. They can allow their staff to have input into the system too, and/or at least create their own plan and see what it looks like.

Using an expert system, the planning process is now transparent to the user. He or she can see the links that are made, the nature of and importance of assumptions, and the implications of certain decisions. Using the system is intended to increase people's awareness of their environment, the effects of globalization and the world's interrelatedness, and the importance of being in tune with new realities. By being attentive to the world and its new realities, Matus hoped to make people attentive and proactive about envisioning their futures. He was always challenging people to see whether they could turn what seemed like adversity to their advantage. He wanted to foster an atmosphere of dynamic interchange where people would be encouraged to use lateral thinking and be creative. By having Aristotle as their aid, he hoped to eliminate many of the conventional barriers to a highly dynamic and interactive planning process.

Matus envisioned Aristotle as being the central hub of the strategic planning. It would not only act as a consultant throughout the planning process, but it would educate members of the organization in the process of planning itself, i.e. people can learn while they do. By focusing on how we make decisions, and which assumptions are explicit and implicit, his aim was to use Aristotle as part of the process of developing a learning organization. According to Matus, recognizing new realities, identifying key change signals, and facilitating adaptive work is the primary activity of the strategic planning function.

Introducing the New Planning Process

Introducing the new planning process and Aristotle was no easy task. The first challenge lay in getting the rest of the organization to buy into the new orientation. Many were quite resistant. They were content with the way things had been done for decades and they saw no need for new ways of doing things. For them new realities were confined to the use of more powerful computer technology that would essentially do the same thing, but do it more accurately and faster than before. They shunned the idea of holding multiple workshops and sparking more interdivisional and interdepartmental dialogue. They wanted to get on with their jobs, as they saw it.

As a large number of senior members of the organization had either mathematical, finance, or accounting backgrounds they preferred to remain in the realm of formulae and calculations. To them only numbers had meaning. The idea of developing scenarios or focusing on non-quantifiable issues was a waste of time and served little purpose. Many of them also said that they had no time for all this chat. They had deadlines to meet, and all this dialogue was certainly not helping them meet those deadlines. At the time, many of the Bank's senior members still did not use computers. Computers were for secretaries, administration, and junior employees. If they had to use technology, they preferred to stare at the numbers displayed on the Reuter screens relaying movements in bond or stock prices. Developing scenarios seemed to be a tedious exercise with little quick pay back.

At the lower levels of management, employees tried to break the system. They seemed more attracted to illustrating what the system could not do for them, rather than what it could. At every opportunity, they would try to enter in garbage, and then howl with indignation when they got garbage back. Every opportunity would be taken to discredit the system's process, its underlying assumptions, or its recommendations.

Those assigned to maintain the system and to communicate changes to users also balked at the task. They preferred the old way of doing things. I cite one example of the Bank's old way of tracking change signals in the banking industry.

Step 1. A person was assigned to read all the UK banking newspapers every morning. Over the previous three years this task had been assigned to the most junior member of the department. This was typically someone in the Bank's management development programme who had been assigned to spend one or two years in the Bank's strategic planning department.

This individual would read four or five of the main newspapers every morning. He or she would make a red mark next to what they considered to be an important article and indicate its file reference.

Step 2. At around noon, when the papers had been read from cover to cover, they would be handed to a secretary. She would cut out the articles and place them in the appropriate file. The files containing all this information were kept in a large filing cabinet within the main planning office. Over the years the filing section had grown to five enormous filing cabinets.

Step 3. At the end of each year the oldest files, i.e. those over five years old, would be transferred to storage in a warehouse 50 miles away.

In between these three steps nothing happened to this information! Seldom if ever were these files accessed. The newspaper reader became very knowledgeable of course, but never communicated his or her knowledge. From time to time, he or she would be asked to do some research for a management paper or in-house presentation. This individual might then refer back to these files. Whenever a new individual was assigned this position, they invariably changed the filing system.

This then was the heart of the strategic planning department's research efforts into industry and competitor knowledge. No accessible knowledge bank existed. Everything was held within different individual's heads and was intermittently communicated through formal presentations or papers. People in the Bank preferred this method. They felt that the new process and input into the Aristotle system was a needless use of time.

In sum their resistance was articulated as follows:

- they are comfortable with the old way;

- the new way is too much work;

- maintaining the system is too tedious;

- there are not enough opportunities to play with the numbers;

- they prefer quick-and dirty approaches as they do not have the time for such detailed thinking and planning;

- systems thinking is too complex and should only be performed by a few people who have the time;

- if we need extra help we can get a consultant to tell us what to do;

- the system is too complex, we cannot be expected to understand how it works;

- creating shareholder value is all that counts;

- we are happy with our newly revised spreadsheets, they provide us with what we need.

As you can see, the underlying philosophy of the new approach to planning had not been understood by a significant portion of the organization. Only a few pockets existed where the new approach was appreciated and has been adopted.

A key mistake on our part (Matus and mine), was to underestimate the nature of the change. We introduced a technical fix to what was essentially an adaptive problem. The Bank's values and thinking process needed to be addressed first. We should have worked on the Bank's adaptive challenges long before introducing a new process.

The adaptive challenge was that banking is no longer just a numbers game. Banks play a systemic role in every community. Banking deposits are only possible where there is trust by the community in the banking system. The extension of credit only occurs when there is trust by the banking system in the community. This value of trust has become increasingly complex as community relations and institutional development has become more complex. Communities are no longer local and neither are institutions. Good banking now means understanding the many webs that form the community. Being a global player requires understanding these webs at a global level.

Banks are no longer institutions that just perform transactions. They now hold the community together. Using a body analogy, banks have become the skeletal frame that enables the rest of the body to perform its normal functioning.

Consider Japan. If the Japanese goverment pulls the rug from under the Japanese Banks, what will happen to Japan Inc? What will happen to the US? What will happen to a myriad international industries without the systemic role of Japan in the equation?

Banking is no longer about tweaking spreadsheets. In the case of 'the Bank', our first task should have been to hold up the new realities in banking. We should have spent time getting management in the bank to realize that the role of banking as an institution has changed. Banking values have changed. The Bank has become a pivotal player in the community at not just the economic level, but at the political, social, religious, environmental, and demographic level too. Banking profitability is only important in so far as the banking system is healthy and stable. Prudential banking, where banks ensure that the community can trust them to understand the nature of the risks, has become a far more important value. Trust as a value has assumed priority over profitability. Trust can only be assured if one knows what's at stake. Prudential banking means understanding systemically what is at stake. No spreadsheet can tell you this. What prudential banking will ensure, however, is long-term survival, not only of the bank, but of the community on which it depends. All the profitability in the world will not help if the system crashes around you. Due to the role of the economy in our modern world, banks and their communities are in symbiotic relationship. They feed off one another and their fortunes are intricately interlinked. This demands new values where care of the other is as important as care for oneself.

Not grasping this reality means being radically out of tune with new realities. As to profitability, holding the communities trust in good and bad times, will ensure sufficient profitability in the longer term.

RECENT BANKING VALUES	NEW BANKING VALUES
■ local trustworthiness	■ systemic trustworthiness
■ profitability	■ prudential process
■ direct stakeholders	■ systemic stakeholders
■ quantitative risk management	■ qualitative risk management

Many bankers might proclaim that this is old hat. They know all about prudential banking, they have been practising this for years, and this has been the hallmark of their success. In response I would like to clarify that I am highlighting a new type of prudential banking. Here prudence is exercised in favour of a much wider community of stakeholders. I am also advocating a far more integrated and complex understanding of risks. The first step in understanding risks is understanding what is at stake. I am proposing far greater attention to understanding what is at stake, for whom, and how. I am also proposing that banking customers are not only the ones who make deposits and take out loans. The entire community is a customer in so far as it trusts the Bank to give the community the benefits of its risk management skills. Communities look to banks to keep the system working; and the value that underpins banking is trust. This trust has far greater implications than 'my word is my bond'. Banking trust now rests on care for the community as being the bond.

The main objective of Peter Matus' new strategic planning process was to introduce these new values into the Bank, and to provide its members a means of enacting those values. He did not, however, pay sufficient attention to the enormous implications of this shift in values. We were too intent on introducing a sophisticated technical tool without realizing that people resisted the value changes that it implied.

Fortunately, some people did get it, and this gave us some fertile ground on which we could build. Dealing with the adaptive work is still keeping Peter Matus a very busy man.

Preparing the Organization for Strategic Planning

Regardless of whether the organization has an existing strategic planning function, or whether it plans to implement a different or new one, I would recommend that senior management pay attention to how this function will be positioned within the organization.

As I have illustrated, changing the nature of the planning process is often an adaptive challenge demanding adaptive work in its self. Organizations need a formal process that holds up new realities on a continuous basis. This is one of the new realities. Many would find this a rather challenging and uncomfortable reality and hence the need for sensitivity and attention to resistance. If the resistance is not dealt with, as in the case of the Bank, the strategic planning process could be rendered impotent. Countering this with authoritarian measures is also not the answer. This is the age of joint envisioning, co-creation, co-evolution and co-operation. Forcing compliance or assent is counterproductive. People need to learn what is at stake if they do not use new age strategic planning. If they do not they need to learn that they will not understand the world in which they live nor the organizations and institutions with which and for whom they work. They will also become victims rather than agents of their own futures. This topic will be discussed further in Chapter 8, 'Developing the Learning Organization'.

In Chapter 3, we discussed the creation of an agenda for the new millennium and therein we included the need for attention to the strategic planning function. The steps for establishing and/or refining the strategic planning activity as part of establishing the strategic agenda were described as:

- *Step 1.* Decide on who is responsible for the strategic planning leadership of the organization. Consider the trade-offs between a dedicated person/team and part-time members.

- *Step 2.* Decide on the nature of the strategic function itself. What does the organization need it to do so that the organization can meet its adaptive challenges? How best might this be achieved?

- *Step 3.* Decide on the systemic approach required so that the organization can evaluate and understand the values of its stakeholders and identify stakeholder tensions that exist or may arise.

- *Step 4.* Evaluate the alternative strategic planning methods and approaches that might be adopted, (e.g. budgeting, forecasting, contingency or scenario planning methods). Formulate an approach that appears to meet the organization's short-to-medium term requirements.

- *Step 5.* Strategize on an appropriate reporting and feedback method between those engaged in strategic planning and other members of the organization. Be sensitive to the need for strategic planners, line management, and staff functions to work well together. Remember that in networks there are no hierarchies.

To this I now add:

- *Step 6.* In conjunction with the strategic planning team, identify the adaptive challenges facing the organization. Ensure that these have been identifed in conjunction with other key representatives of the organization. Test these by holding discussions with external stakeholders.

- *Step 7.* Refer to steps 2 and 3 above and clarify the approaches and methods to be used to address the immediate adaptive challenges.

- *Step 8.* Communicate the adaptive challenges throughout the organization using every communication method and delivery vehicle available.

- *Step 9.* Elicit and encourage people to articulate their resistance to the adaptive challenge itself and/or the value tensions that it is creating.

- *Step 10.* Invite dissenting voices to participate in leading the adaptive work.

- *Step 11.* Ensure that the strategic planning function always includes members from the operating divisions. This may be based on short- or medium-term assignments.

- *Step 12.* Ensure that those assigned to strategic planning on a formal and long term basis spend at least six months to a year out of every five years actually working in an operating division.

A key principle is to ensure that strategic planning is embedded within the operations of the organization, and never stands above or apart from it. This means being in touch with the constituencies and the constituents. It means meeting them where they are. Peter Matus and I learned this lesson the hard way.

Summary

Implementing new strategic planning processes is not an easy task. People become used to the old way and resist new ideas especially if they change the nature of work. Plans to introduce new planning systems should be sounded out with key members of the organization, and care should be taken not to railroad through changes. New strategic planning processes say something about changing values within the organization. This is cause for adaptive work and should be paid attention to as such.

Notes

1 While this is a true case study fictitious names have been used for the Bank and the Planning Director in the interests of protecting strategic information.
2 The project took place during the years 1992–1994.
3 This book provides a framework for setting goals for the organization. It includes both qualitative and quantitative measures.

CHAPTER EIGHT

Developing the Learning Organization

The Reflective Practitioner

During the early part of 1994, I was asked to facilitate the strategic planning process of a non-profit organization. Prior to our first planning weekend, during which we were going to focus on new realities and the changing environment, I invited members of the planning team to perform a few preparatory exercises. One of these was for each member of the planning team to write down what they perceived as the most unexpected recent event in the world and in the USA. The purpose of the exercise was to gain some insight as to what issues stood out for these people, and to see whether these issues converged on similar themes. Of the seven responses included below, three were from women. All respondents were American, one of whom defined himself as an Irish-American. The following is an excerpt of the results.

The most unexpected world event:

- Israeli-Palestinian rapprochement

- Scientific breakthroughs in genetic/DNA research

- Palestinian-Israeli peace accord

- Japanese recession

- Preparing for black and white elections in South Africa

- British and Irish government working together for peace

- Reconciliation between Israel and Palestine

The most unexpected event in the USA:

- Getting serious about the US health system

- Natural disasters of earthquakes and floods

- Turnaround of the Clinton Presidency

- Harding-Kerrigan ice-skating affair (the physical attack organized by Tonya Harding on Nancy Kerrigan in an attempt to get her out of the Olympics)

- Waco, Texas incident

- Retrial of Byron de la Beckwith in Alabama state

- Respect accorded to Hillary Clinton

Naturally I was interested in the range of responses. It reminded me that people's interests are diverse and that different issues engage people's attention differently. This exercise provided me with some very important information about the group. It also reminded me of the sensitivity required when performing the role of facilitator.

By reading these responses I realized that members of the group came from very different backgrounds, had very different interests, and had very different personal narratives. This was borne out during later discussions.

Over the weekend I gained some knowledge regarding the background of the various participants. Three of them had spent some time either working or vacationing, in the Middle East. All three claimed this to have been a fascinating experience. One of the participants had overcome several serious illnesses, including cancer and the removal of a kidney. Another member of the team had worked extensively in the healthcare system. One of the team had lived in Japan, another had a sister in Alabama, and another was actively involved in relief aid for the states besieged by terrible flooding occurring at the time.

Gaining these insights, confirmed yet again, that people see the world through lenses that have been adjusted to their world and their interests. From both a leadership and strategic planning point of view, being sensitive to people's backgrounds, and the main factors that give them self-identity, helps one understand how they construe the world and its realities.

Being a reflective leader or reflective strategic planner goes further than just being sensitive to where people come from. It is also advantageous if this person can reflect on situations while they are in the process of unfolding. This means observing the dynamics of a particular situation and seeing the roles that people assume in situations while the interaction is going on. Donald Schoen (1983) discusses the art of reflection-in-action in the *Reflective Practitioner*. This he explains to be 'on-the-spot surfacing, criticizing, restructuring, and testing of intuitive understandings of experienced phenomena'. (*ibid.*:241) By seeing patterns of behaviour, the reflective practitioner is able to move to a deeper level of awareness of systems and how they work. This awareness, Schoen claims, increases the practitioner's own learning, which in turn makes him or her more aware in future situations. According to Schoen, the hallmark of the professional practitioner is if the practitioner is able to reflect on his or her own responses simultaneous to reflecting on others' responses. This is reflection on reflection-in-action.

Effective leaders and strategic planners need to be reflective practitioners. They need to be aware of what it means to meet people where they are. They need to be able to be observers and participants, (sometimes referred to as observer–participants), where they are able to move back and forth, being part of and apart from the dynamics of a situation as they reflect in real time on the roles being played, including their own.

Self versus Role

Leaders and strategic planners need to be able to divorce themselves from their role. They need to realize that the anger and distress that is levied at them refers to their role in the system. They need to be aware that people are objecting to what they represent. Although it may often not seem like it, the affront from antagonistic factions is not intended personally. It is the role and what it represents that people object to and not the person as an individual. Unfortunately, most people are not able to make this distinction, hence the unbridled animosity that can emerge. It takes mettle and confidence to be on the receiving end and to hold steady in the face of a negative onslaught. Being reflective-in-action can help leaders see the dynamics of the situation and help them to see that their competence or worth as a person is not the issue. Avoiding retaliation is critical if the leader or strategic planner wishes to 'stay alive'.

Action Strategies

Here are some guidelines for the reflective professional engaged in guiding a change process:

- Know the people. Take time to know their backgrounds, their interests, their key experiences, their defining moments, their hopes and their fears.

- Remember that uniform information given to a group of people will be heard, read, understood and construed in many different ways. The way that information is perceived will be affected by the lens through which it is seen.

- Getting a general consensus of understanding, which harmonizes the differences in interpretation, takes time *and* patience. People will only see and understand what they are able to see and understand. Knowing what is at stake when stakeholders are asked to engage in a change process, is more important than forcing concensus on an issue. Seldom are all factions in a system in total agreement. Disagreement is not bad, it just needs to be managed – dissonance is a part of harmony.

- During the process of interacting with people, it is necessary to be reflective in action. This provides leaders and strategic planners with important information about the group and themselves.

- Systems thinking should be practised. The recognition and interpretation of roles within the system will help leaders and strategic planners focus the change process appropriately.

- Leaders and strategic planners need to be able to divorce themselves from their role, especially when factions within the system are antagonistic, angry, or demonstrate passive-aggressive tendencies.

- Wherever there is conflict this should be depersonalized by distinguishing the issues from the people representing those issues.

Learning to ask Questions

One of the great contributions that organizational leaders and strategic planners can make is to teach members of the organization some of their own skills. In fact, as MIT's Emeritus Professor of Management, Edgar Schein points out, in *Organizational Culture and Leadership*, an effective teaching method is to focus on the questions. In his books on *process consultation*, he describes how he teaches organizations to solve their own problems by first simply posing critical questions. He does not provide answers. He leaves his clients to co-create their own solutions under the guidance of his ever-more penetrating questions. Over time, his clients are not only more masterful in devising solutions, but they start learning to ask the right questions. As time passes their proficiency increases here too. Self-sufficiency is attained once people can guide their own change processes by knowing which questions to ask when.

Strategic planners are in effect the internal consultants to the organization. As such, their role as teacher is pervasive. They too spend a great deal of time learning which questions to ask and pose to members of the organization. Over time they should stimulate a corporate culture that is continually engaged in asking ever more creative and innovative questions. This is an empowering process for the members of the organization as they become more and more engaged in understanding the questions that drive the change process. Teaching members of the organization to ask the right questions as well as find the appropriate solutions is when 'giving the work' back has reached maturity. Achieving this stage of engagement in the change process is the goal of the learning organization.

The Learning Organization

A great deal has been written about organizational learning and the learning process. Every organization would like to say that it has the characteristics of a learning organization. Many claim that management is trained to be attentive to the softer issues, that staff go on a variety of skills-training seminars, and that the corporate environment is one that encourages creativity, innovation and healthy risk taking. But creating a learning organization takes far more than this. Learning is 'to know' differently. It is the process of exploring, enquiring, searching, reflecting, and in the end 'knowing the place for the first time' (T.S. Eliot, *Little Gidding* 1942). The learning process affects the way a person constructs or reconstructs meaning. It results in transformation. Learning is not the addition of information. It is not training in new skills. And it is not about devising new technical solutions. The learning we are focusing on is about one's adaptive capacity. It is not so much about enhancing one's capabilities, although that usually follows.

Building on the new sciences approach, the characteristics of a learning organization (organism) include:

- The organization is open to changes in the environment.

- It allows these changes to flow through the organization, unimpeded and unchecked, trusting in the organization's ability to find order, even when there seems to be chaos.

- The learning itself affects the way members of the organization construe reality.

- The learning is experiential, it is not just thinking and reflecting.

- The learning is affective, it changes how people are and how they feel, as much as how they think.

- The learning is of the type that it is perceived by all of the person. A fundamental change in 'body chemistry' occurs. The person feels and is different as a result. This is what makes true learning transformative.

- Organizational learning is created through dialogue. Here members co-create collective meaning and joint understanding of changing currents. Collective meaning helps individuals to internalize meaning giving them a sense of unity, ownership, and personal agency.

Learning is Subjective and Relative

In the learning organization it is readily acknowledged that there is no such thing as objective, value-free, uncensored, or unbiased viewpoints. These words are holdovers from an outdated scientific epistemology. It is not possible to be objective because our very observations affect what we see and hear. Our perceptual biases actually create the shape of our observations. We see things not as they are but as we are. Hence we do not believe what we see, rather we see what we already believe. This reality is critical to the development of a learning organization, the exercise of leadership, and the implementation of an effective strategic planning function. It underpins the saying, 'We must meet people where they are, not where we would like them to be'. This also explains why learning is such a personal endeavour.

Leadership through strategic planning promotes a people-centred and relationship-oriented way of learning. People learn best in relationship. They learn from people whom they love, respect and admire. They learn because they see in the other, images of themselves as they would like to be.

Creating a corporate culture that fosters a learning organization takes these factors into account. Organizational management need not pay excessive attention to innovation if a learning climate exists. 'Forcing' innovation is akin to growing artificial flowers – they never smell and bloom like the real thing. Innovation must come from the heart of the organization.

We know that given the appropriate holding environment, enough freedom and space, living organisms are naturally creative and innovative. It is part of who they are. Excessive attention to developing innovation is misdirected energy. Provide the right environment and innovation will follow. Nourish the organization's capacity to be innovative and people will develop the necessary capabilities.

A Key part of Learning is Unlearning

An important part of the learning process is unlearning old mental models and old ways and behaviours. Organizations, just like individuals, become accustomed to approaching familiar problems in familiar ways. Often the problems are not as familiar as they are construed to be; it is just convenient to categorize them in familiar ways. Differences are ignored and similarities are readily accentuated, so that the tendency becomes to treat an ever wider range of problems the same way. The successful outcome of problems also reinforces the fallacy that the same strategies can be used time and again. Discarding well ingrained, old behaviours becomes increasingly difficult over time. Unless organizational leadership keeps finding new ways to deal with both old and new challenges, past success can easily breed complacency and apathy. Getting the organization and its members to unlearn accustomed ways of interpreting the world and to relinquish old behaviours is often the greatest barrier to the next level of learning. Leadership through strategic planning must realize that this is one of the organization's greatest challenges. Like the ostrich mentioned in Chapter 5, reprieves for ostrich-like organizations never last long.

Organizational Structure in the Learning Organization

In our discussion on the findings of living organisms in Chapter 5, two important aspects were highlighted. The first is the self-organization characteristic of living organisms. This was described as the capacity of living organisms to continuously reorganize themselves in response to the changing environment. The other aspect was that the structure of the organization is what prescribes and describes its pattern of relationships. The self-organizing feature and the structure of the organism, therefore, go hand in hand. If the organism needs to reorganize, restructuring immediately follows.

In organizational strategy and design there has been a similar tendency, i.e. if the organization's strategy is altered the firm adapts its structure. The adage 'structure follows strategy' is usually quite diligently applied. Recently there appears to be a change. The spate of reorganizations and so called restructurings seem to place emphasis on the restructuring side somewhat independently of the strategy side. A question arises as to whether one can tinker and even radically alter the structure without working on the strategy.

Living systems raise a far more important question even than this. In living systems there is evidence that the structure and restructuring process is an extension of self-organization. This means that the living organism that is continually engaged in recreation and self-organization, lets the structuring occur as a direct output of these prior activities. No isolated attention is paid to the organization's structure. Once the organism knows how to self-organize so as to adapt to changing realities the restructuring is automatic. The system inherently knows the network and pattern of relationships that is required so that it can adapt to environmental realities.

Organizational structure and design theory should take their cue from living organisms. Less attention should be paid to structuring the organization. A learning organization, that is focused on self-organization should allow its structure to form for itself. Once people know what needs to be done, and they feel empowered to follow this through, they can organize themselves pretty efficiently. It is only when they are disempowered that they need to be allocated to boxes on organization charts or assigned to teams.

Learning organizations should pay less attention to the organization's structure and more attention to empowering members of the organization to participate in the adaptive and self-organizing process. Structure follows self-organization, which is after all the organization's strategy for adapting to the future. Structure does follow strategy but it should be allowed to form naturally for itself.

The Difference between Leaders and Managers

Just as confusion exists between authority and leadership, there is also some confusion between managers and leaders. Some people refer to these roles interchangeably, as if managers are or should be leaders and vice versa. This is an unfortunate mistake and leads to many unnecessary organizational tensions. For one, the emphasis should be on exercising leadership and not on leaders. Managers can of course exercise leadership.

Managers are, however, often those who have formal authority. As discussed in Chapter 4, 'Exercising Leadership', there are constraints to being in a position of authority and trying to exercise leadership. Further, the function of management is different to that of leader. Management is about allocation and control. Leadership is about mobilizing people to adapt to change.

Many claim that organizations are overmanaged and underled. Management typically pays excessive attention to short-term results. Leaders are more concerned with the longer term future. Managers seek order and consistency. They try to solve problems, especially technical problems. Leaders motivate change, establish new directions, and seek out new opportunities.

Exercising leadership, while focused on adapting for the future does not disregard the present. In fact it is by acute attention to the present that the future can be developed. Nevertheless, managers and leaders fulfil different functions. They need one another to effect a balance. Without order and controls, there can be no boundaries and no holding environment. Without change and discontinuities there can be no new opportunities.

Managers are inclined to be interested in facts and answers. Leaders are interested in values and questions. Managers try to preserve the status quo. Leaders try to inject change and transformation. Managers tend to be deductive, interested in results, and try to contain risks. Those who exercise leadership tend to synthesize, be inductive, be imaginative, and are prepared to take well intentioned risks.

The roles of manager and leaders are complementary. Both roles are necessary to the organization and should be understood as fulfiling important yet different functions. It is difficult, but not impossible for managers to exercise leadership. A powerful way in which they might achieve this is to partner across the authority boundary with someone who has informal, rather than formal authority and who is willing to exercise leadership. By lending support to those who can or want to exercise leadership a very powerful coalition between management and leaders can emerge. Many successful organizations do just this. The CEO and senior management encourage a cadre of potential leaders who have informal authority to create new visions and ideas. If they cannot find willing leaders within the organization, they often buy them from the outside. Managers need leaders and leaders need management. Strategic planners should encourage them to work together.

How Leadership through strategic planning enhances the adaptive capacity of the organization

Opening the organization to a continuous learning process is one of strategic planning's most vital roles. By exposing members of the organization to the perpetual winds of change the organization becomes more attuned to the nature and inevitability of change. Change is no longer seen as a disruptive process but is understood as being part of the organization's evolutionary and developmental process. Change programmes should no longer be dreaded *ad hoc* events that focus on the frightening future. Rather, dealing with change should be part and parcel of everyday corporate life and should inform decision making at all levels.

The ability to absorb and integrate change defines an organization's adaptive capacity. The adaptive capacity of the organization indicates its power to recognize, acknowledge, and appropriately respond to the demands implied by changes. The faster the organization is able to deal with value-tensions presented by the new environment, the greater its adaptive capacity. The less the organization resists change or pretends that simple technical solutions will drive the more difficult tasks away, the greater its adaptive capacity. Change has become a redundant word. Everything is in continual change and flux. Stable states no longer exist. A new definition of stability might be 'a process of change that is not too discontinuous or too volatile'. The mindset that the strategic planning function needs to inculcate is that perpetual change is the new reality. It is real, it should be acknowledged, and it should be worked with in a constructive manner. Above all, continuous change generates ever new opportunities. These opportunities are not a zero sum game, i.e. those that take advantage of the opportunities do not rob others from generating their own opportunities.

The new approach to strategic planning places emphasis on the following:

- The role of strategic planners is to identify new realities and key change signals, and to act as change agents.

- Their focus is on adaptive work and, in conjunction with other members of the organization, to interpret the adaptive work that flows from new realities.

- Strategic planners will take a systems approach to looking at both the environment and the organization. They need to be adept at systemic analysis and they need to understand the meanings that underpin relationships.

- Strategic planners need to have good people skills. They need to deter people from engaging in work avoidance and they need to hold steady in the face of organizational distress. They need to understand the emotive power of value-tensions. They need to be able to redirect that emotive energy into working with those value-tensions.

- Understanding the environment requires taking an ever more macro viewpoint. This means, compared with more traditional approaches, more perspectives and a wider range of issues will be included within the new strategic planning process.

- Strategic planning methods will include the use of scenarios and many forms of dialogue throughout the organization.

- Strategic planning will include a variety of models, both new and traditional, throughout the planning process.

The implications of this new approach include:

- new types of strategic planning skills are required;

- there will be greater inclusion of the whole organization in the strategic planning process;

- there will be more local strategic analysis at the operating level, especially of the more technical kind;

- the organization will place greater emphasis on the communication of the assumptions that underlie strategic plans;

- greater opportunities to work together between different operations within the organization will exist;

- the need for a networking structure will become paramount;

- real time thinking and responding will have as much importance and attention as planning for the future;

- the ability to improvise will provide indicators of the organization's adaptive capacity;

- mission oriented and core competence based opportunism will be practised;

- all members of the organization should sense greater empowerment in co-creating new visions and new strategies.

Summary

Developing a learning organization is a people-centred activity. The exercise of leadership by the strategic planning function should help create a corporate climate that is conducive to learning. The type of learning that occurs in a learning organization is more than conventional learning. This learning is transformative, it makes the individual 'know' differently. By challenging an individual's existing capacity to adapt, his or her capacity is further developed and strengthened in anticipation of future challenges. If individuals can adapt well the organization will be better able to adapt.

To facilitate the learning process organizations need both managers and leaders. These people have different yet complementary roles. Without management there will be no consistent holding environment and no measurement of the achievement of goals. Without leadership there will be insufficient impetus for change. Without change there can be no learning organization. Failing to embrace and drive through changes is maladaptive. The strategic planning function helps to drive through change and influences the shape and form of the learning organization. Continuous organizational renewal is a direct consequence of continual learning.

Key Points Made in this Chapter

▸ Leaders and strategic planners need to be reflective in action.

▸ Dealing with resistance, anger and distress during the change process requires being able to distinguish self from role.

▸ Learning is about asking questions.

▸ Learning is a personal process.

▸ Learning often begins with unlearning.

▸ The organization's structure should be allowed to form for itself.

▸ The roles of management and leadership are different and complementary.

▸ The strategic planning function should be actively engaged in fostering a learning organization.

SUGGESTIONS

- Evaluate whether senior managers and members of the strategic planning function are able to distinguish self from role. List the evidence that you have that does or does not support that view. If the answer is negative some remedial action should be taken.

- Ensure that senior members of the organization have some exposure to and competence in reflection in action processes.

- Encourage members of the organization at all levels to ask questions. Have a box or an office where people can leave their unanswered questions. Hold discussion groups or workshops aimed at both answering and posing new questions.

- List the strategies in place to create and foster a learning organization. List the evidence that you have to show that it is working. Carry out a survey within the organization to see whether people feel that they are experiencing transformative learning.

- Evaluate the extent to which the organization relies on previous successful behaviour in dealing with current challenges.

- List the number of restructurings that the organization has carried out over the past three years. Evaluate what the key driving forces were that stimulated the need for change. Consider whether management has ever left employees to structure the processes themselves. If this has been done consider how and why it was or was not successful. If this has never been done it may be worth a try.

Further Reading.

Haas, H.G. (1992) *The Leaders Within*, HarperCollins, New York.

Morgan, G. (1997) *Images of the Organization*, Sage Publications Ltd, London.

Schein, E.H. (1990) *Organisational Culture and Leadership*, second edition, Jossey-Bass Publishers, San Francisco.

■ CHAPTER NINE ■

Strategic Planning, Leadership and Ethics

The Hype surrounding Business Ethics

Business ethics, like leadership, is a hot topic. It has stolen the limelight from TQM and re-engineering. Business magazines, books and training programmes all pay increasing attention to the ethical issues facing businesses.

Modern philosophers have weighed in with renewed insights on the ethical writings of Plato, Aristotle and Immanuel Kant. Sociologists are researching the tensions of being a Christian in the workplace, bearing witness and coping with two masters, God and mammon. The demand for greater human rights (HR), individual freedom, and public morality is blending in with the cry for more socially responsible corporates.

In the United States a new business role has been established. This is the role of the 'ethics officer'. This person is someone elevated to the status of supreme moral arbiter and paragon of virtue in the corporation. He or she is above the tensions of the real world. He or she is responsible for devising eloquent codes of practice and rules of conduct that reflect the moral party line. He or she is supposed to ensure that members of the organization remain on the moral high road. There are courses, magazines, and institutes for these ethics officers.

As a business person who has over 25 years of business experience, and who is also a student in social and business ethics, I am rather perplexed and disappointed at the manner in which business ethics is being approached. I feel that, in many instances, business ethics is not understood, studied, or practised in a manner that addresses what it means to be in business. Rather, businesses are being treated as the object of ethical analysis in a rather generic way. By this I mean that the nature and context of business is not given sufficient attention. Further, adding another 'how to', and 'do and don't' manual to executives' and employees' collections simply amplifies the corporate watchdog mentality. Understanding why and how businesses find themselves in ethical dilemmas is surely more important than the actual dilemma itself. If businesses could understand when and how they are at 'ethical risk' they are more likely to be able to do something about it. It will also encourage greater proactive rather than reactive behaviour.

It is only by taking a systemic view that one can gain a comprehensive understanding of the nature of business and the inherent tensions and pressure points. Important questions include the purpose and role of business as a system operating within, and in relationship to, other systems. One must enquire into the nature of trade-offs when choosing between right and right. One should also evaluate the ethics of a business in the light of its stakeholders. Just as ethics itself is about human nature, so business ethics must be about the nature of business.

Why We Need Business Ethics?

What is it about business that seems to suspend personal morality? What tensions and complexities are inherent in the nature of business that stimulate, provoke, or facilitate moral misdemeanours and negligence. What is it that makes people check their ethical behaviour at the door of the corporation? Why do so many people feel that they have to suspend their capacities for care and concern, and compartmentalize their souls when they are at work? Why is there a 'company pays' mentality? Why do people at work do things that they would never do at home or with their friends? Why does being in business undermine the 'Golden Rule'?

Employees want to know why they do not get to see more of the profits. Owners want to generate more profits so that they can increase their wealth. Increased wealth, they say, makes for more jobs and bigger bonuses. The question is how much is enough profit? And, how much is enough bonus? Where does entitlement begin and where does it end? What role does justice, morality, and equity play in the system of business?

One of history's many lessons is that moral decay is usually evident during periods of either heightened, frenetic activity, or during times of communal complacency and apathy. The current period seems to be that of the former state, where our excessive drive for material satisfaction has eclipsed many of our other natural needs. Human nature, being what it is, we are seldom able to get enough of a good thing. Managing limits is one of our most significant ethical dilemmas. When is enough enough?

Business ethics is a far more integrated and complex subject than simply the analysis of business behaviour and actions. To do business ethics justice requires taking a business perspective. The starting point is to realize that all human activity poses ethical questions. The context of that activity determines the nature of the ethical problems that arise. Being in business provides a context of human activity. Different businesses, operating within different business contexts, pose different ethical challenges and dilemmas. Business ethics is about understanding why and how.

Since the economic marketplace and the activities of businesses dominate almost all aspects of modern life, the ethical issues that arise in this context are likely to have wide ramifications. We have plenty of examples of this as in the case of the Union Carbide gas leak in Bhopal, India; the rise and fall of Michael Milkin of Drexel, Burnham, Lambert; and the Exxon Valdez incident off the Alaskan coast.

The Nature of Business Ethics

Ethics is the critical analysis of morality (McCollough 1991). Its purpose is the analysis, criticism, interpretation, and justification of the rules, roles, and relations of a society. Ethics is concerned with the conditions in which moral decision making takes place, and the justification of the principles brought to bear in resolving conflicts of values and moral rules (ibid.:7). Business ethics means applying these principles to the business context.

Ethics is about critical awareness and reflection. It requires understanding what is at stake. It is about seeing relationships, asking questions, understanding how and why conflicts arise, and being able to make prudential decisions. Ethics is about more than behaviour. It is about the very nature of things. It is about being and making meaning. By reducing business ethics to the control rules on moral misbehaviour, we turn ethics into a policing activity, rather than an exercise in critical reflection. The former is a reductionist approach and does not foster moral creativity and maturity, far less an atmosphere of critical reflection. Our world already suffers from an impoverished moral imagination, let us not perpetuate this with a superficial approach to business ethics.

The Goal of Business Ethics

The goal of business ethics is to enhance ethical behaviour through upholding appropriate levels of trust and inspiring both corporate and personal moral agency in all of the organization's activities. In order to create an organizational atmosphere that is conducive to this spirit, it is necessary to grasp the organizational and personal tensions that the business context poses. Only by understanding both general and specific pressure points inherent in various business contexts, can one create an environment that stimulates mature ethical reflection at all levels.

The business ethics starting point has to be the subject, the business itself, and what gives it life and purpose. A business organization is no more than a group of individuals striving to attain united goals, often amidst a sea of troubles. Admittedly, groups prompt certain group role behaviour. This does not, and should not, allow the individual to disappear behind a corporate veil. While organizations espouse a communal value system and provide guidelines for identifying and dealing with an increasing array of conflicts of interest, individual accountability and responsibility must remain. The economic system hinges on a certain base level of trust. It is individuals, as moral agents for the institution or organization, who communicate and uphold that trust.

The key tension for organizations is the requirement to satisfy two ends, namely business sustained profitability concomitant with a focus on the sustained welfare of employees, customers and the larger community. How can one make this a win-win situation without compromising competitiveness or failing to meet the social obligations of human welfare? The goal of business ethics is to hold up these two juxtaposed ends and to avoid one advancing to the detriment of the other. Is this possible, or is this supposedly serving two masters? Which has priority, profit or human welfare? Can one have one without the other? If there is no profit, there is no organization, no new wealth, and no jobs. If there is poor attention to human welfare, in the long run there will be no profit. Therefore, this is not an 'either or' question. Being in business remains a continuous competitive and moral balancing act. This requires being able to analyse systemically what is at stake, knowing how to engage in prudential process, and being able to deal with value tensions both morally and pragmatically.

The Definition of Business

If one asked a hundred people for a definition of business one would probably get as many definitions. Many would say that business facilitates trade, brings buyers and sellers together, or creates jobs. The *Concise Oxford Dictionary* refers to business as a commercial house or firm, where a firm is described as a group of persons working together. This definition does not assist us in understanding what a business really *does*. It only tells us, in a very limited way, what it *is*. Many people, on the other hand, are not concerned with what business is, but rather what it does. One of the biggest problems about modern business is understanding what it does and coming to terms with the extent of its power and influence.

Without a sound grasp of the nature of business it is rather difficult to evaluate what it does, i.e. its performance. Before engaging in a discussion on how business ethics fits into the leadership and strategic planning aspects of a business, it is necessary to clarify the nature and function of business. The real nature and function of business has been lost and forgotten some time ago. Now we focus only on its ability to make profits.

First, I should like to begin by proposing a very simple definition of business:

A business is a group of people who work together on a regular basis in the interests of meeting a specific purpose or attaining a pre-determined goal. The purpose or goal may not necessarily be a commercial one, e.g., the goal may be to improve people's health or safety.

The prime purpose of business at the micro-level is to achieve its stated purpose or goal. Any profit or net benefit that it earns while pursuing this purpose or goal serves as a barometer of its performance. High profits or net gains signal superior performance, while low profits or no gains indicate that there is room for improvement. The prime business purpose is always centered on meeting the needs of a group or market. It is thus 'other-oriented'. This holds for both profit and non-profit oriented businesses. Profit or net gain is not the prime goal or purpose of a business. Not for the medium or longer term at any rate. To survive in the longer term, businesses need to pay attention to their real nature and function in the larger system. The prime systemic goal of business is to redistribute risk. Profit or gain is the payoff for businesses who do this well.

It is important to emphasize that making a profit is a necessary but not sufficient goal. Regrettably very many people have lost sight of the real purpose of businesses from a systemic perspective. Capitalism in particular, has lost touch with its grounding spirit which was to serve the community.

As we know businesses have a critical part to play in any society and, increasingly, across societies. Lack of attention to the systemic responsibilities of business has led them to be out of sync with their environment, thus attracting growing censure and criticism.

There are two major aspects to business ethics from which all other things flow. The first is understanding *what is at stake* and the second is *the concept of limits.* Before we can discuss these aspects it is necessary to consider the systemic function and role of business in some detail.

Business from a System's Perspective

In any system, every part has its function and role. So with business. Every business has an important and distinct function and role within the larger economic and societal system. Distracting it from this function and role harms the entire system.

In any system, it is important that participants have functions and roles. The interrelatedness, interdependence, boundaries, and limits of each participating part, is an intrinsic and necessary feature of the whole. These functions and roles may change given certain conditions or, with time.

In the western capitalist world, business is considered the prime creator, organizer and participator in the economic system. In fact the economic system is founded on and rests upon the activities of business. Business did not attain its pre-eminence and power by coincidence. Within the greater system it has a critical role to play. The power and breadth of business' influence has arisen for a purpose. That purpose is to serve the system. If business, as an economic entity, did not make a substantial contribution to the larger system, it would have been rendered redundant or non-functioning a long time ago.

So what is this critical role? From a systemic viewpoint, business is expected to redistribute the risks that buyers and sellers would face if they had to buy and sell without business as a vehicle. Consider the risks that a lone trader bears. His or her livelihood hangs on each purchase and sale. Without substantial personal resources, there is little opportunity to stockpile for holidays or rainy days. And then, what if the wrong stocks are piled, or if there is a fire in the store? As pre-Industrial Revolution history reminds us, before the advent of businesses, economic life was precarious. In a system where economic life is precarious, social life is precarious too.

As businesses have alleviated the risks of carrying the entire economic load on individual shoulders, social and cultural life has been freed of many burdens. Just consider how adversely social life is affected when businesses go out of business. People lose their jobs. Suppliers have to find new markets and buyers inevitably pay increased costs for their goods. The loss affects the whole system. When businesses are healthy the whole system is healthy. Business is the vehicle that keeps economic life in balance. Once it fails to do this, the entire system is corrupted. At the time of writing, the problems in Asia serve as a timely example. The Asian business system neglected their prime function of holding the economic system in healthy balance. They overlooked their systemic role of managing and redistributing risks in the interests of short-term gargantuan profits for a select few. They totally disregarded the concept of limits. They believed, along with many others, that there are no limits to growth, profitability, wealth, power. Every sage and wise person that has ever lived has repeatedly held up a reality that we dislike intensely. Starting with Adam, we refuse to acknowledge that there are limits – for others maybe, but not for us!

TWO MAJOR BUSINESS ETHIC ISSUES

- Knowing what is at stake

- Recognizing and respecting the concept of limits

The Principal Purpose of Business

The principal purpose of business is to redistribute risk. The payoff for doing this well is sustainable profits.

The principal purpose of business is to redistribute risk at a profit. Both parts of this definition are vital. One element does not make sense without the other. If a business does not redistribute risk, it does not perform its function in the larger system. The manner in which each business redistributes risk is specific and unique. It may choose to be a manufacturer, a retailer, a management consultancy, or an insurance broker. These are the strategies that organizations pursue so as to fulfil their risk redistribution function.

The other part of the equation is that organizations need to generate a profit. Without generating profits they will not be able to operate effectively or survive in the longer term. They will also not be able to attract further risk capital to assist them in performing their function in the future.

Many people insist that the prime function of a business is to maximize the value of the firm or the value of the shares for the shareholders. This places incorrect emphasis on the payoff that businesses receive for playing their part in the larger system. If they are effective, they will earn profits.

If one takes the human body as an analogy, where businesses fulfil the functions of the kidneys, we may be able to draw some parallels. The purpose of the kidney is to help clear the system, eliminate toxins, and decide what is waste. This is the body's risk reduction mechanism. That is the prime purpose of the kidney as an organ in the greater system of the human body. If the kidney is strong and healthy, it will perform its function well, and the entire body will benefit. If the kidneys for myriad reasons, do not perform their function well, deteriorate and become sick, then they will render the whole body system unwell. In fact, since the body is so dependent on the appropriate functioning of the kidneys, their malfunctioning may place the life of the entire body in jeopardy. Healthy functioning kidneys on the other hand, will grow, develop and support the body as it grows and develops. If the body and its kidneys work together in sync, the kidneys will hopefully stand the test of time until old age.

The payoff to the kidneys is the contribution to the whole which itself is totally interconnected with the kidneys' own healthy development and longevity. There is no cause and effect. The interconnectedness is an iterative loop that cannot be severed or disassembled into component parts. The prime purpose of the kidney is not growth or longevity (in business terms ever-growing profits), as these are useless goals without the interrelationship with the entire system. The purpose of the kidneys is to help keep the whole system healthy and to benefit along with the system.

In society the risk reduction activity has been made possible by the invention of the limited liability company. The vast majority of all businesses now operate under the protection of this vehicle as a limited liability against risk.

Limited Liability and Risk Reduction

The idea of the limited liability company is one of the greatest conceptual creations of humankind. This invention has altered every aspect of political, social and economic life. The foundational principle of the limited liability company is the limitation of personal liability. While this reduction of risk was originally intended mainly for the entrepreneurs of rapidly expanding businesses during the time of the Industrial Revolution, the proliferation and sophistication of business has now reached a stage where all of the stakeholders in business experience a reduction in individual risk.

The entrepreneur can raise money without carrying the entire financial risk alone. Management can remain in decision-making positions and exercise their expertise without being overly burdened with all the financial implications. People who do not wish to be entrepreneurs can obtain jobs where others carry the burden and responsibility of ensuring the survival of the business. Manufacturers and other suppliers can produce and sell in bulk and need find only a relatively few number of customers compared with selling on an individual basis. Buyers do not have to spend a great deal of time or resources, nor do they have to travel long distances to gain access to an array of goods and services. Competition between sellers ensures a reasonable market where opportunities exist to compare the quality and prices of goods and where, hopefully, not too many people are ripped off. Commodity markets are regulated to a certain degree and businesses are obliged to comply with certain health and safety standards. Imagine the cost, complexity and inefficiency of doing this, if millions of single traders were to exist.

From a societal viewpoint consider the benefits of the risk reducing function of businesses. People have more time. Psychologically they have greater financial peace of mind. The proportionate cost of most people's purchases is lower than in the pre-business days. This allows for greater disposable income thus providing opportunities for leisure and doing charitable works. Without business, we would be back to a few hours off on Sunday writing to friends and relatives who have left on long arduous journeys to secure needed supplies. While wealth might be more evenly distributed, nearly all of us would be extremely poor.

Risk-Return Strategies of Business

Taking a whole system's view, businesses exist to redistribute risk. This activity reduces the burden on the individual and reapportions it to a group of individuals who have expertise in managing risk. These people are known as managers. Their function is to manage the resources of the business so as to minimize the risks that the business undertakes in relation to the return that can be generated. This is what it means to maximize the value of the firm. The concept 'maximize' is a relative term. In relation to businesses, it means obtaining the highest possible amount in relation to the risks that the firm is prepared to undertake. The most junior student in finance knows 'no risk, no return'. Therefore returns are always considered in the light of the risks taken to earn those returns.

One of the main benefits of the redistribution of risk is that it fosters the creation of new wealth. It encourages entrepreneurship and serves as the breath of commercial life. Growing, successful businesses are continually taking on more risk through innovation and new product development. The pursuit of wealth occurs through new wealth creation and not continuous redistribution of old.

Innovation is akin to the creation of new cells within the body. New cells start a fresh life cycle that keeps the body alive and vigorous. Once businesses give up these risk redistribution activities, they become old, sluggish, malfunctioning, and eventually die. If, on the other hand, they become greedy and self-satisfied, preferring to pursue profits and serve their own self-interest, they will be like the overactive kidney that knows no limits, placing the whole system in jeopardy.

At the micro level then, businesses use their unique risk management skills so as to optimize the risk-return allocation. Some people manufacture garments, some sell property, some invest in small businesses, and some program computers. These strategies are used to satisfy the needs of a group or market in the most risk-effective, cost-efficient, and convenient way. Combined skills, economies of scale, and focused expertise, give the managers of a business far better opportunities for comfortable survival than any one individual.

The risk-return relationship is important. If returns do not reward the risks, then fewer and lesser risks will be taken in the future. This will inhibit future growth and wealth creation.

We know that living systems take risks in the form of development and self-initiated structural changes. Here too, they win some and they lose some. On balance it is important that they win more than they lose in order to ensure survival. Businesses too, need to be compensated for higher risks so that they can keep on engaging in the risk redistribution process.

Business Tensions and Trade-Offs

While performing their risk-redistribution functions businesses face many tensions and trade-offs. The most important tension is that their stakeholders have lost sight of their systemic function. Instead the entire system no longer realizes what is at stake, and no longer pays heed to the concept of limits. This results in excessive demand being placed on businesses to perform with only the profit goal in mind. The means has become an exalted end.

Far from being a free market system, no one is free, least of all businesses. The entire system and all its players are enmeshed in the web that they have spun for themselves. They cannot escape from the demand for more. More growth, more earnings, more dividends, more goods, more bonuses, more customers, more.... No one player dare refute the demands of the system. Those who have tried, continue to be half in and half out, and are going nowhere. Disentangling oneself from the economic web is close to impossible. Fortunately some enlightened organizations are prepared to keep trying.

As a consequence of the general tensions that businesses face, there are some specific tensions and trade-offs. These include:

- short-term high profitability versus longer term sustainable profitability;

- placing the organization first versus paying attention to individual needs;

- serving stakeholders with greater power and influence at the expense of those with less direct power and influence;

- allocating resources only to generate profits versus allocating resources to enhance the quality of life of their employees;

- putting profits ahead of corporate responsibility.

These tensions manifest themselves in a multitude of ways and are also the source of unethical behaviour. This context is relevant to the way in which we should approach business ethics. This does not mean that I am advocating a situationalist or relativist stance – it is rather to say that, by understanding the tensions, one has a better grasp of the ethical dilemmas and how they might be dealt with.

The Backdrop to Ethical Problems in Business

Before we consider the business tensions and pressure points that often cause ethical malpractice, I would like to discuss some foundational issues in businesses that create ethical vacuums or spark ethical conflicts. Many other issues or conflicts are usually subsumed by three main issues:

1   The problem of means and ends.

2   Depersonalization of institutions.

3   In over our heads.

The Problem of Means and Ends

Immanuel Kant's moral philosophy held that the dignity of human beings gave them a worth that was absolute and invaluable, not to be compared with economic or political values. Moral behaviour meant that humans were to be treated as ends and not as means to ends. The end to which all human action was to be directed, was to furthering the welfare of humans. These are the roots of rational behaviour.

Herein lies the primary tension of our economic system. Over and over again it is asserted, both directly and indirectly, that the goal of the organization is to make a profit (or maximize wealth) for shareholders, stakeholders, whatever. The end is 'profit' at all costs.

In particular in our 'downsizing climate', these words are anathema to thousands of employees. Many have lost their jobs, while others wait anxiously every day to see whether they might be next. Their perception is that business is greedy, that owners only care about lining their own pockets, and that employees are purely dispensable commodities. No matter how much interpersonal respect may be evident within the organization, few employees feel as if they are treated as ends or that the organization's profit is for their human welfare. This remains a real problem in most organizations. When times were tough, even the mighty, lifetime employing IBM shed staff by the thousands. Will organizations ever be forgiven for this era?

Prior to the introduction of any ethics programme, the first question that must be asked concerns the organization's corporate culture. Do people feel as if they are purely means to ends? If so, the atmosphere needed to uphold ethical behaviour and moral agency is missing. Any attempts at enforcing ethical codes are likely to be vitiated.

Depersonalization of Institutions

Institutions were originally created as means to ends. The idea of formally structuring the roles, responsibilities and activities of groups of people, began when people realized that their individual and combined interests could be better served through a group organization.

Nowadays, institutions seem to have taken on a life of their own. They have become ends in themselves and their original founding purpose or genesis has been lost. The institutionalization of our society has become a moral and motivational problem. An attitude of subservience to the institution has evolved where individuals feel robbed of personal agency, self-determination and true accountability. As institutions have grown, the distinction between owner-manager-worker has exacerbated the situation. Individuals feel depersonalized and unable to bring their full selves to work. Herein lies the first and greatest conflict of interest – 'I dislike work. I am only at work because I have to be'. Multiply this attitude by several hundred employees, and the scenario for moral bankruptcy has been written. It is difficult to be morally sensitive when one finds no meaning in what one does.

In many organizations, individuals feel a loss of control and self-determination. They need to work for psychological and economic reasons. Having work gives identity and dignity, and a place to go to. It is what society expects one to do, and it is what one's friends typically do. However, the individual could have this identity snatched away at any time. This sense of loss of control can result in a lack of taking responsibility for one's actions. Unless employees can see tangible results for their efforts, the incentive to sustain responsibility is diminished. Add this to the loss of a sense of self-determination, where the individual feels that the organization can arbitrarily determine the individual's dignity or sense of worth, and the organization becomes an adversary, rather than a benevolent friend.

In Over Our Heads

Robert Kegan's (1994) book, *In Over Our Heads*, points out that in general there is a lack of fit between what culture demands of our minds and our mental capacity to meet those demands. Building on his previous book, *The Evolving Self*, which explores the transformation of our consciousness through various stages of mental and interpersonal development, he asserts that contemporary culture is burdened with mental demands for which it is not yet consciously ready. He emphasizes that the information highway has geometrically increased the pressure on our mental capacity to receive and assimilate information. He also discusses at length the ever increasing claims that work makes on us and exhorts those who seek to teach, inspire or move others to action, to be more sensitive to these stresses.

Kegan's words resonate with my own experience. Many people are catapulted into performance frameworks for which they are not quite ready. Work is no longer a place where one is allocated a task and one's performance thereof measured from time to time. Often now, one has to invent one's own work. One has to be self-initiating, self-correcting and self-evaluating. One has to build one's own vision and see it through. The worker increasingly has to acknowledge his or her part in the whole system and not just in some well-defined and bounded task, in some bounded department. The borderless world is reflected in the borderless organization. The cross-cultural strains of global businesses are experienced in the cross-cultural strains of intertwined departments and disciplines. To deal with this increasing complexity, people require to be led, to be held and to be nurtured. Many cannot be expected to make the enormous leap in consciousness required of this new world. Fear, a sense of disorientation and disequilibrium results in erratic, and often unconsciously, unethical behaviour. Anything to restore equilibrium.

The informative book, *Can Ethics be Taught*, written by a group of researchers from the Harvard Business School (Piper *et al.* 1993), discusses the research findings regarding the ethical sensitivity and awareness of a selected number of talented and highly motivated students about to enter the Harvard Business School. It was found that despite their strong sense of interpersonal accountability, they had not had previous encouragement to critically reflect on moral issues, and they revealed only a limited consciousness of systemic harm and injustice. They were also limited in their understanding of what was at stake in any given situation. Their moral imagination was constrained by the limitations of the interpersonal model where complex relationships with competing claims could not be consciously construed. They were unable to make connections between different societal domains and were primarily interested in individualism, personal autonomy, achievement and personal empowerment. In sum, they were not aware of the bigger picture and the importance of asking the questions. The results of this research provided critical input into Harvard's ethics programme. Similarly, such an understanding of our corporate community should affect the organization's ethical programme. People should be taught a way of thinking, rather than how to read and apply the rules.

The insights from these two books point out two critical factors from an ethics point of view. First, where we are as people, in terms of our stage of consciousness and our mental capacity to deal with interdependent events, affects our ability to deal with the complexity of daily life. Foisting moral agency and accountability on people who are not ready for this is highly stressful for them and insensitive. The result can only be ethical confusion, especially between interpersonal demands and institutional claims. Second, ethics can be and should be taught. How this is done is critical to the moral maturity that will result. Mentoring is one very important approach. Different organizations will have people at different stages of consciousness and moral sensitivity. These factors are critical to the development of any business ethics sensitivity and should be thoroughly researched in advance.

Systemic Pressure Points

With these three factors as the backdrop to the business culture, I would like to discuss the external and internal systemic pressure points that influence a business's propensity for greater or lesser ethical risk. These systemic pressure points provide key indicators for the external pressures on the business and its own stage of moral development. A variety of pressure points exist in every business. What one needs to know is what they are and how they manifest themselves. It is by understanding these pressure points that an appropriate ethical climate and code of practice can be put in place.

External pressure points devolve from the larger system and are outside the organization's direct control. In this case, what matters is how leadership acknowledges these pressures and deals with them. Internal pressure points typically change over time, either organically, as the business develops and matures, or radically, as a result of external forces or events. A merger or takeover being an example of the latter.

The more complex the business the higher its propensity for ethical risk. Businesses in high ethical risk categories need mature moral leadership. They need a corporate culture that pays particular attention to moral issues and tensions. Senior management should ensure that some education in ethics is given to members of the organization at all levels. This does not mean that 'simple' businesses can remain morally inattentive or ignorant. All businesses need to pay attention to their ethics. However lawyers and bankers are probably exposed to far greater ethical tensions than bricklayers. The human activity provides the moral context and this should be considered when performing ethical reflection, evaluation, and assessment. The moral balancing act referred to earlier is only possible by being aware of the ethical pressure points that exist within the real world context of the business.

External Systemic Pressure Points

State of the economy

It is always easy to be gracious when one has a good bank balance, or so the saying goes. When the economy is booming, and profits are good, and motivation is high, people feel better about themselves and one another. During these times many ethical programmes are implemented and new ethical promises are made. When the economy is stagnant or in recession these promises are either not made or no longer kept.

Organizations that boast about their good ethical behaviour better have sufficient reserves to sustain their ethical standards during leaner times. Ethical behaviour includes paying attention to the reasons and the manner in which they lay off employees. After all, breaking promises is unethical, not to mention how adversely it affects organizational morale.

Country leadership

Organizations often implicitly take their cues from political leaders. If political leadership is strong and demonstrates consistent ethical behaviour then typically corporates, as country representatives, will emulate that behaviour. If ethical leadership is lacking, it is interesting to note the lack of ethical corporate behaviour. Bad ethical leadership is like an epidemic. It spreads rapidly and is pervasive. So when considering the leadership integrity of the organization, one should initially consider the strains that might be imported from the macro-environment.

Industry characteristics

Although some industries are more susceptible to ethical dilemmas than others, the general propensity for business ethical risk is increasing. Take the pharmaceutical or biotechnology industries. The ethical questions to which they are subject are ever on the increase. In fact, ethics is the most important feature of their industry. The approach to ethical questions in these industries requires a sophistication that exceeds that of the average person. Real experts in the field of ethics are essential to these businesses.

Number of competitors

The greater the number of competitors, the more likely that ethical issues are increasing as an inherent part of doing business. Where there are many competitors, consumer sophistication is high. As consumers, they have many suppliers from which to choose. The greater the choice, the more discriminating and the more ethically sensitive they become. Food and cosmetics are good examples. Ethics is starting to drive these businesses (animal testing, recycling, clarification of ingredients are some issues).

Nature of the competition

An industry characterized by intense competition is susceptible to greater ethical pressures than one less so. In intensively competitive industries, competitors sometimes take desperate measures to keep or gain market share. They may mislead customers or they may take quality and safety short-cuts.

If there are only a few mammoth players who dominate the industry, ethical responsibility has until recently been a low priority. Look at the ethics in the oil and pharmaceutical industries. In these cases, consumers have less power. It can take government intervention to make these organizations attentive to their ethical responsibilities.

International competition also creates many ethical dilemmas. Different standards may apply in different countries. This combined with different consumer expectations may result in a sloppy or relativistic approach to ethical standards. This means that the organization will try to get away with what it can in each country. Consider the nuclear industry and their differing standards across the world. Consider the garment manufacturing that takes place in the sweatshops around the world.

Internal Systemic Pressure Points

Leadership

The CEO is undoubtedly responsible for the ethical culture of the organization. He or she is charged with creating and sustaining a strong moral environment. This cannot be delegated to anyone else and particularly not to 'ethics officers'. Forget any ethics programme if the CEO is not heading the initiative. Assent won't do. Active participation is essential.

There should be evidence of proactive attention to future ethical issues. This ranges from employment procedures to the opening of new factories or outlets in foreign countries. Attention to moral issues should be a visible activity. It should not, however, result in righteous blowing of trumpets.

If a mentoring environment is not present this should be considered a negative factor. Mentoring is the most constructive and transformative way of teaching ethics. People learn ethics from those they admire, seldom from rule books.

Corporate culture

Inspiring people to be ethical requires transformation rather than information. While information is necessary in order to identify a potential area of ethical conflict, only those 'transformed' are morally sufficiently sensitive enough to be aware in the first place, and to know how to deal with the conflict in the second.

Shaped by the CEO, the corporate culture of the organization should be one of concern for relationships and for the exercise of justice. Consistent behaviour by senior staff that demonstrates concern for doing the right thing and not just things right, is critical for providing a supportive moral environment. No amount of rule books will replace the example set by senior management.

Stage in the Corporate Life-cycle

The organization's stage in the corporate life-cycle will also affect its moral sensitivity and propensity for ethical risk. The small, entrepreneurial business, where the founder adopts a hands on approach to most of the activities, is likely to be sensitive to relationship issues, however less sensitive to potential conflicts of interest which only become evident with the awareness of larger horizons. Struggling to stay alive and grow, may encourage maverick behaviour. Maverick behaviour is not necessarily unethical. The advantage of small businesses is that people usually retain a certain sense of personal agency. Added to this, market and employee feedback is often more effectively heard, and corrective action is more rapidly taken.

As the organization grows and matures, enter the owner-manager-worker triad. This dynamic immediately escalates the number of internal conflicts and lengthens the external feedback cycle. Organizations in the rapid growth phase, are likely to be in the high ethical risk bracket. They are typically preoccupied with growth, gaining market share, and implementing overdue management information systems. Many ethical conflicts are overlooked or will inadvertently slip through the over-stressed management control net. Successful, growing companies can often exhibit a certain bravado or high risk-taking attitude, usually a sign of cocky management. This can set the tone for future moral malpractice.

Large, mature businesses have the greatest personal agency problem amongst their staff. The organization, seen by employees as an impersonal monolith, finds it difficult to reignite the personal creativity and agency temperament evident in small entrepreneurial companies. They will typically develop large rule books, and in time have a cadre of ethics officers. While this may initially curb the more obvious misbehaviours, this approach is unlikely to foster ethical sensitivity or build corporate moral excellence. When people put their own moral agency on hold, ethical problems arise out of abuses of power and neglect.

Profitability

Organizations that are struggling for survival are more vulnerable to taking the moral low road. When survival is at stake, there is little time for ethical reflection and the testing out of moral behaviour in the face of value-tensions. These are times when it is most easy to rationalize an unethical course of action. Sometimes this is through active choice and other times through the unconscious screening out of potential ethical conflicts. Whatever the cause, organizations that are experiencing profitability or cash flow crises are often faced with very blunt ethical dilemmas, for example whether to take that contract with the enemy, to recall suspect products, or re-engineer the automobile that concertinas when rear-ended.

The CEO and senior management need to be on great alert to their own and their employees' moral decision-making sensitivity during these times. With no profit on the books or no cash in the bank there is sparse headroom for ethical decisions that might imply short-term sacrifice in the anticipation of longer term benefits. It is undoubtedly during this time that a large proportion of unethical activity takes place. Performance in the financial services and military manufacturing sectors bear ample testimony to this.

The consequence of unethical behaviour during the low profit-ability phase is typically twofold. If the organization gets away with it, the ground is fertile for further unethical behaviour. In some cases the organization struggles along from one marginally unethical deal to the next and ultimately collapses. The alternative is that the organization goes from strength to strength, where its dubious behaviour becomes an intrinsic part of its aggressive, competitive style. Where profits are excessively high (in relation to return on capital), beware, something is amiss. Our efficient capital market system does not allow this to persist for any length of time. Unethical behaviour is driving the organization and will be its downfall. Again I cite the financial service sector, not to mention Michael Milken *et al.*, as good examples.

Organizational size

Large organizations are forced to devolve into smaller, decentralized units in order to compete effectively. They are often under pressure from divisional management to support regional autonomy and may only manage these business units using very broad guidelines. Inevitably there are also feedback delays before the headoffice or holding company is apprised of any malpractice. By that time the ramifications could be astronomical. The larger the organization therefore, the more important the maturity and experience of local CEOs or directors. Performance and reward systems will also play a key factor in driving the ethical behaviour of decentralized units. While codes and rule books may play a guiding role, there can be nothing more important than the vigilant eye of the head CEO and carefully chosen co-directors. The non-executive board of directors should also play an active role in developing an intimate understanding of the culture and workings of the decentralized units.

With organizational size comes reporting structure complexity. Matrix management, usual in project type companies, is more vulnerable to ethical conflicts and risks than hierarchical reporting structures. Accountability and responsibility is inclined to greater dissipation in the former system. The more directly accountable people are, the better the chances that good business ethics is practised. The flatter the organization, i.e. the less hierarchical, the less opportunities there are for abuses of power.

Tangibility of the product or service

The less tangible the product, the easier it is to overlook moral laxity or less than honest behaviour. A product or service that can be visibly seen, touched or experienced, can be more readily evaluated and measured than a less tangible one. We all know when the new auto has been badly spraypainted, the airline departure time is delayed, or when the laundry returns soiled clothing. We can experience the pollution from automobiles, see the waste from paper products or the effluent from leather industries. It is less easy to see or fully understand the mortgage insurance calculation, the costs of the mutual fund management fees or the timing of the bank credit to our account. It is far more difficult for most of us to understand the implications of buying junkbonds than a microwave.

Understanding the nature of the product or service, what it purports to do, how it is made, constructed and delivered, gets more difficult the more intangible the product. The ramifications of what happens when things go wrong is also less well understood in advance. In this way service industries are more vulnerable to ethical risk than less complex manufacturing, distribution or retailing businesses.

Complexity of the product or service

The more complex the product or service the greater the propensity for ethical risk. By definition, complex products and services are not simply configured. They often require complex parts and processes. Obtaining these parts, or the processing skills can have many ramifications. The side effects in many cases are easy to overlook or not estimable in advance. Surgery, breast implants, complex software programs or advanced military espionage equipment are some examples.

With complex products and services, the ethical risk is heightened by the knowledge differential between the makers, suppliers or providers and most users or end consumers. Wherever large knowledge differential exists there is a power imbalance between suppliers and buyers. This makes for high ethical risks.

With complex products and services, it is often difficult to benchmark acceptable performance and the consumer can be bombarded with every form of obfuscation. Unethical behaviour is often concealed behind a barrage of technical minutiae. Environmental effects, if there are any, are usually dismissed as inconsequential in the face of meeting consumer needs.

The less tangible the product or service, usually the greater its complexity. Intangible, complex products and services are the highest ethical risk area. We have ample evidence of this in the markets for exotic financial instruments.

Customer base

The size and profile of the customer base has implicit and explicit ethical risks for the organization. A business that is highly dependent on a relatively small customer base will be torn between looking after the relationship and encouraging a high sales penetration policy. This means being concerned with the customers' welfare while at the same time maximizing sales. Losing just one customer could have a substantial affect on profitability.

On the other hand an organization that has many customers, who seem a faceless mass, may be tempted to treat them as such. They may be viewed as gullible objects who have only a desire to consume goods, and their welfare may never really be part of the organization's ethos.

Performance and reward system

The performance and reward system plays a highly influential role in setting the tone of the moral culture of the organization. Reward systems that focus on short-term results based on individual achievement encourage a climate where greed and self-interest prevails. Short-termism is detrimental to all stakeholders. Excluding the group from benefitting from the exemplary performance of its members denies the supportive role that they play. Failure to promote the concept of interdependence fosters a self-centered, immature morality where good performance is not considered valuable for any other reason than the immediate tangible pay-off. Multiply this temperament by several hundred staff and the organization and its associated communities are headed for moral shipwreck. Increasingly businesses are rewarding staff for group performance and for the quality of their commitment and participation rather than their quantitative input or output. The manner in which performance is valued says a great deal about organizational values.

Planning horizons

Planning time-horizons radically affect the organization's ethical risks. Industries where corporate performance is measured in short-term cycles encourages ethical malpractice. The insurance, mutual fund and investment management businesses are good examples. If the individual or the organization is considered only as effective as 'its' last quarterly report, moral behaviour goes out the window. These are high risk industries and ethically high-risk businesses.

A business' own internal planning time-frame also influences ethical behaviour. Medium- to long-term goalposts are invariably better than short time-frames.

Impact on the Environment

No organization is exempt from having some impact on the environment. As the environmental effects of production and distribution become better understood, it behoves businesses to take action proactively to mitigate the negative side effects.

Organizations whose products and services have a significant effect on any one of the earth's ecosystems are obviously expected to demonstrate ethical sensitivity and responsibility. These businesses are ethically high risk and require experts in their field to deal with these factors. Far more than just codes of practice and rule books are required.

While I have highlighted some of the systemic pressures (see Table 9.1 for a summary) that exist in businesses, this is neither a complete list, nor are these issues mutually exclusive. As we become more industrially sophisticated and more conscious of the interdependence of every sphere

TABLE 9.1 Systemic Pressures that affect Business Ethical Sensitivity and Moral Maturity

External	Internal
■ State of the economy	■ Profitability
■ Country leadership	■ Corporate leadership
	■ Corporate culture
■ Industry characteristics	■ Impact on the environment
	■ Organization size
■ Number of competitors	■ Stage in corporate life cycle
■ Nature of competition	■ Tangibility of product/service
	■ Complexity of product/service
	■ Customer base
	■ Planning horizon
	■ Performance and reward system

of life, our ethical awareness is continuously raised. With increased awareness comes increased ethical responsibility.

ANALYSIS OF DEGREE OF ETHICAL RISK INHERENT IN THE BUSINESS ENVIRONMENT IN SOUTH KOREA, MALAYSIA, AND INDONESIA

External factors

State of the economy	– frenetic activity, overheated
Country leadership	– weak, corrupt
Industry characteristics	– emphasis on manufacturing
	– dependent on volume
Number of competitors	– limited by protectionism and cronyism
Nature of competition	– limited by protectionism and cronyism

Internal Factors

Profitability	– erratic
Corporate leadership	– imported from country leadership – weak, corrupt
Impact on the environment	– high → pollution, energy needs, infrastructure effects, resource pressure
Organization size	– many large, many small
Stage in the corporate life cycle	– high growth, immature
Tangibility of product	– mostly intangible product services
	– industry undeveloped
Complexity of product	– typically uncomplex
Customer base	– wide, volume dependent
Planning horizon	– very short
Performance and reward systems	– limited, undemocratic

Evaluation: Ethical Risk – very high
Prospects: Violent Shakeout

Roles within the Organization

Just as one needs to understand the external and internal systemic pressure points that face the organization, one needs to consider the ethical dilemmas that are part and parcel of the roles of people within the organization.

For example, people in R&D are under pressure to remain within budget yet to devise suitably reliable and safe equipment or potions. Those in marketing are expected to generate customer prospects while also being truthful about the limitations of the product or service. Those in human resources are expected to oversee employment, promotions, and reward systems that satisfy the needs of the business and the aspirations of the employee. Those in finance are charged with advising on the most cost-beneficial allocation of resources. They are supposed to perform their analysis at arm's length and their advice should stand up to the scrutiny of the supposedly rational investor. So the list goes on.

When studying business ethics, these considerations need to be taken into account. The reason is not to provide moral excuses. On the contrary, it is to foster a climate that is alive to and conscious of the ethical dilemmas and risks that are inherent in the way of doing business. This attentiveness is the first stage in understanding what is at stake. Only once the collective organization has its finger on the ethical pulse can it promote an ethical climate.

The Problem with making Social Responsibility a Prime Goal

As I have pointed out, the prime purpose of business is to redistribute risk. The pay-off is profit. This is its purpose within the larger system of society. The purpose of business is not to 'do good', take care of others, or support the welfare system. Expecting this from business is not only inappropriate but unfair. That is not to say that business should not behave ethically or with attention to social concerns. It should not, however, define this as its primary goal. These benefits should flow if businesses are meeting their primary goal.

What business does need however is the imposition of limits. This should be exercised internally, as part of the self-regulating function of the system, and it should be imposed externally, by society as the larger whole.

In any healthy system the concept of limits is an inherent part of its nature. If we return to the analogy of the body, we know that the body has a limit-setting mechanism, the glandular function, and each organ has within its own intrinsic make-up, certain limit-setting characteristics. A kidney is not designed to grow to the size of the stomach. Both the kidney and the glandular system impose internal and external limits respectively, to keep the kidney to its appropriate size. In an unhealthy system, the kidney will grow too large or be too small. This will naturally affect its functioning and some form of remedial action will need to be taken. A malfunctioning kidney will not be able to exist for any length of time before the entire system becomes unhealthy too. An underperforming kidney that cannot be revitalized will need to 'die'. An over-performing kidney will need to be restrained. Interestingly, in general, the greater risk to the system is an over performing organ. This over-active sub-system threatens the life of other organs and is also difficult to contain. As we know, cancer is the over-production of the body's white blood corpuscles which causes further uncontainable growth. Excess growth rapidly becomes life threatening in any system. Regrettably, excessive capitalism evidences many of these features.

Leadership through the strategic planning function should address the two prime business ethical problems. The first is understanding the role of business and what is at stake, the second, is the concept of limits.

Ethical Leadership

There can be no discussion about leadership without talking about ethical leadership. Good leadership evidences ethical sensitivity and moral maturity. James MacGregor Burns' (1978) well-known book, *Leadership*, mentions his concern for moral leadership. He points out that 'leaders and the led have a relationship not only of power but of mutual needs, aspirations, and values' (MacGregor Burns 1978:4). Moral leadership should always be attentive to the fundamental wants, needs, values, and aspirations of the followers. Good leaders need to be able to orient to both general welfare issues and to a host of more individual values and responsibilities.

In our terms this means that those who exercise leadership understand the system and its ethical tensions and pressures. By taking a systemic perspective they understand who the stakeholders are, their interests, their power differentials, and their value-tensions. They know how to assess what is at stake. They understand the moral balancing act between rules, consequences, justice and fairness. They are able to see and soar like the eagle, and to dwell and abide in the messy particulars like the ant. Exercising moral leadership is done on the road. In other words, it is in the living of daily life, and being closely in touch with all that that means, that sensitive moral leadership is practised.

Exercising moral leadership is evidenced in the defining moments when ethical choices have to be made. These defining moments reveal priorities and set the ethical tone for the rest of the organization. Johnson

& Johnson, Union Carbide, and Microsoft, have all been faced with defining moments. They have had to make difficult ethical choices requiring understanding what is at stake, balancing moral alternatives, and making judicious decisions. These defining moments, described in Joseph Badaracco's (1997) book, *Defining Moments*, cast a shadow forward and shape the character of the person and the organization. Enhancing the organization's business ethics requires attention to these defining moments at all levels of the organization.

Exercising leadership implicitly implies moral leadership. Moral leadership means paying attention to values and relationships, and respecting the integrated networks that make up the living world, of which business organizations are a part.

Strategic Planning and Business Ethics

Leadership through strategic planning means that the strategic planning function has an explicit ethical role to play too. They are engaged in recognizing new realities, and this includes ethical realities. They perform systemic analysis and analyse relationships. The ethical dimension is an important part of this function. They should play a role in the setting of limits and in negotiating those limits with stakeholders. This refers to both external and internal limits. They should manage the boundaries of the organization in its relationship with other stakeholder networks. They should foresee ethical dilemmas that arise due to external systemic pressures and internal systemic pressures. They should initiate discussion on potential ethical issues in advance of these occurring. This might relate to new products, services, markets, or a potential takeover.

The ethical role of the strategic planning function is to make ethics part and parcel of all business decisions. Ethical discussions should be as readily heard in the corridors of the organization as discussions on sales targets, new employees, the need for a new telephone system, and the loss of a contract.

Business ethics has to be seen as a part of business decision making. It has to be attuned to the context of that decision making and it should be an explicit part of everyone's role, function, and vocabulary. Questions should be framed as to whether they are good ethical business decisions. If they are not, then open discussion should be held with all those involved as to why and how they raise ethical dilemmas.

In an environment such at this, there will be less need to focus on gender discrimination, sexual harassment and employee bribes. These activities are prevalent in an environment where ethics is not discussed, far less part of everyone's decision criteria, and vocabulary. Influencing the culture of the organization to be more ethically attuned is one of the most important roles of the strategic planning function. Effective business ethics is not a way of thinking, it is a way of being, organizational being.

ETHICS AND THE STRATEGIC PLANNING FUNCTION

Systems thinking
- understand the larger system
- recognize, interpret new realities
- co-create new ethically sensitive visions

Perform systemic analysis
- recognize systemic pressure points
- identify ethical risks
- help set external limits
- provide check and balance on internal limit setting
- combine limits in dynamic balance
- include ethics in all decision criteria

Summary

Business ethics is learning about the complex interdependence of the world and the ramifications of our actions in the name of doing business in their widest context. Business ethics is about more than just inappropriate behaviour. It is about the very nature of business itself. It should not be seen apart from the normal activities of the business, for business ethics is not *another* activity of the business, but is *part* of *every* activity.

Understanding the business as a system and identifying the ethical pressure points provides a better appreciation of how the business operates, and how the organization might develop increased moral sensitivity.

The starting point of ethics lies with the CEO and the corporate culture that prevails. Recognizing employee alienation, institutional depersonalization, and the moral maturity of members of the organization is critical to the form, content and style of any formal ethics programme. Simply developing codes of conduct to counter sexual harassment, discrimination and dishonesty, takes a reductionist view of business ethics.

In order to develop ethical sensitivity that is proactive as well as reactive, it is necessary to understand the business' systemic ethical pressure points. Knowing these and being attuned to the ethical dilemmas that are inherent in every role, is vital input to the development of a healthy ethical climate. A healthy ethical climate is where ethics is recognized as part of an activity and not as something apart from it. Just as individuals make ethical decisions within the context of their activities so must the organization. The criteria for doing business should include ethical criteria.

Exercising leadership implies exercising moral leadership. Unethical leadership is an oxymoron. It is no leadership at all. Ethical leadership can be exercised through the strategic planning function. Those engaged in strategic planning are well placed to influence the ethical corporate climate of the business. They should educate the organization to what is at stake and they should participate in setting and negotiating limits.

Finally, with respect to those ethical codes and rule books, let us take our lead from Moses, ten simple clear points will do!

Key Points made in this Chapter

▸ The key systemic role of business is to redistribute risk at a profit. It is not to be a 'do good' institution.

▸ Capitalism has influenced the nature of our institutions so that there are basic conflicts between the person and the business organization.

▸ Understanding business ethics means understanding the nature of business and the systemic pressure points that it faces.

▸ Key systemic pressure points can be identified.

▸ Roles and functions within the organization also experience ethical pressure points.

▸ Exercising leadership means being ethically sensitive.

▸ The strategic planning function has a role to play in forming the ethical environment of the organization.

SUGGESTIONS

- Analyse the organization's key ethical dilemmas over the past three years. Identify the systemic pressure points, both internal and external that came into play.

- Review the present situation of the organization, and see whether there might be any new systemic pressure points on the horizon. Reflect on any action that might be taken, e.g., if profitability is currently a problem, what actions are being taken to ensure that safety, reliability, and respect for employees is not being undermined.

- Review the organization's present method of identifying ethical dilemmas. Is this always after the fact? What proactive steps might be taken in the future?

- Draw up a list of the key functions and roles within the organization. What typical ethical dilemmas and value-tensions are these roles and functions faced with? Have the people concerned been involved in discussions relating to these dilemmas and value-tensions? Do they have an open, understanding forum in which they can discuss their personal feelings and any tensions that they might experience.

- Review to what extent the strategic planning activity pays attention to present or potential ethical issues. Could this procedure be enhanced?

Further Reading

Badaracco, J.L. (1997) *Defining Moments*, Harvard Business School Press, Boston, MA.

Chryssides, G.D. and Kaler, J.H. (1993) *An Introduction to Business Ethics*, International Thomson Business Press, London.

Piper, T.R. *et al.* (1993) *Can Ethics be Taught?* Harvard Business School, Boston MA.

Weiss, J.W. (1994) *Business Ethics: A Managerial, Stakeholder Approach*, Wadsworth Publishing Company, Belmont, CA.

CHAPTER TEN

Conclusion

An Invitation

This book is intended to be a dialogue and an invitation. It is a well-known saying that a book is completed by the readers. The completion is in the digestion, the ongoing questioning, and critique of the ideas presented. If the book comes to a halt on the last page it has failed to keep the dialogue ongoing. I hope that in this instance this will not be the case. Instead, I hope that the reader will take up my invitation by trying out some of the ideas presented and by developing them further.

This book is an invitation to businesses as institutions and to those people for whom being in business is part of daily life. It is also an invitation to the stakeholders in business. They are invited to understand the purpose of business and how and why it does what it does. Stakeholders can exercise leadership by recognizing their own realities and holding up changing realities to businesses.

As the reader will have inferred, this book is a synthesis of many ideas and disciplines. It provides an eclectic and syncretistic view of the concepts of leadership and strategic planning. It provides ideas about how organizational leadership might be achieved and enhanced. It distinguishes between the role of authority and leadership. It clarifies the differences between the role of leaders and managers. It discusses the organization and its need to enhance its adaptive capacities so that it will survive and thrive in the future. It presents a new approach to business ethics and it proposes that ethics, leadership, and strategic planning are all of a piece.

This book is also an invitation to alter our attitudes toward leadership. We can no longer rely on leaders that provide easy answers. We need to participate in creating those answers for ourselves. We need to take our own work back and do it. Doing our own work will enhance our adaptive capacities and make us more resilient for the future.

Business organizations, through the strategic planning function, have a key role to play. They need to respond to their adaptive challenges and do their work. Their first adaptive challenge is to recognize the fact that they have a systemic role to play. That role is not the anxious, greedy pursuit of profits. Their role is to sustain the health of the system by redistributing economic risks for appropriate profits. They need to adjust their mindsets and their value systems to the reality, which is not new, that everything has limits. Business organizations have a key role to play in setting and negotiating those limits. This should not be left to the policies and procedures of the IMF, the World Bank, or any other external policy driven institutions. This book is an invitation to businesses to take up the leadership challenge and to learn how to dance.

Where Have All the Leaders Gone?

As I write these concluding pages I am reminded of the question, 'Where have all the leaders gone?' The media is no longer preoccupied with 'Asia Rising',[1] but with Asia falling. The world economic system has been rocked by the Asian financial crisis which has probably affected every business in the world in some form or other. The United States is threatening to invade Iraq again, and its President is caught up in an embarrassing scandal that speaks of alleged infidelity to his family and the American people.

The mighty Microsoft Corporation is tied up in legal wrangling about whether or not it has a right to be mightier still. General Electric (GE), one of the world's largest companies with profitability that exceeds most rivals, wants to earn more profits. The present profit level is not enough, so retrenchment and restructuring has begun.

GE is not alone. It is part of the web of the so-called free-enterprise system that is in fact no longer free. Downsizing, retrenchment and corporate restructuring continue even though corporate profits on both sides of the Atlantic look good. Financial institutions are merging in an attempt to slim down overcapacity in the market. Cases of corrupt business ethical practices are on the rise. So where have all the leaders gone?

Business as a key player on the world stage needs to take up some of the leadership slack that exists in the political and social arenas. They need to acknowledge their systemic role and realize that roles have responsibilities. Business institutions need to reorganize themselves along the lines of the living organisms of which they are a premier example. Businesses are encouraged to alter their mindsets, to change their metaphors, and to lay down their weapons of war. Instead they are invited to participate in the cosmic dance of which they are part. They are invited to take a lead in this dance and in partnership, to co-create new steps. They are invited to exercise leadership and to encourage others to do so.

New Realities

In the early chapters I proposed that the world is moving into a new era which I termed the Adaptive Age. The features of the Adaptive Age include renewed attention to ends as values, and away from the focus on means to ends. Another reality evident in the Adaptive Age is the growing awareness of our interrelatedness and interconnectedness. As this awareness grows our interconnectedness grows. We see unveiled before us more and more of the strands of our interconnectedness. Once we start this process it cannot be stopped. We are a world-wide web of interrelatedness, and understanding our nature and how we function necessitates taking a systemic view. Understanding new realities requires systems thinking.

Globalization

We need no longer discuss what globalization will look like. The recent crash of some Asian countries places the evidence before us. The effects of the collapsed economies and many of their key businesses has had a ripple effect which has reached every corner of the globe. Falling stockmarkets, collapsing businesses, and devalued currencies are some of the more obvious consequences of very large systemic problems. The political, social, religious, and environmental crises that have yet to follow will exceed that of a Chernobyl. What about the strides made toward democracy? What about the social infrastructural issues? What about the potential religious backlash? What about the polluted and devastated environment for which there is no time, money, or attention? These questions are not restricted to the Asian countries in question. These questions relate to the world-wide web. *The definition of globalization is awareness that we are part of a world-wide web.*

How is the community of the world-wide web going to respond? It cannot be the responsibility of the IMF to get these countries' 'houses' in order. 'House' is an outdated metaphor. Being in a house implies being apart, bounded by walls, self-standing and independent. How are we going to repair the broken networks of this web? Who is going to exercise leadership? Who is going to help the people do their adaptive work? Who is going to ensure that these countries are not forced to implement technical fixes for adaptive problems? Who is going to hold steady during the times of distress?

Globalization is teaching us that we are 'our brothers' and sisters' keepers'. Are we going to take up our responsibilities? The reality is that we have no choice. We may try to defer this for a while, but as the Adaptive Age reaches maturity we will have to respond to the challenge. All realities are global in their effect. There is no thing that is apart from the world-wide web.

Globalization means:

- growing awareness of our interrelatedness;

- understanding that we are always in relationship with one another;

- knowing that the global macrocosm is reflected in the local microcosm, hence we need to think globally and act locally;

- valuing compromise and co-operating without losing what we stand for, yet understanding what others stand for;

- paying attention to the five principles of leadership – the world does not revolve around us; evolution occurs through co-evolution; our baggage and our sub-conscious processes are part of each microcosm that together constitutes the fabric of the global macrocosm; and all things are relative and network relationships are of paramount importance.

The Move to Capitalism

One feature of our global world-wide web is that there is a move by non-capitalistic countries to capitalism. Whether the problems being experienced by some Asian countries will halt or slow down this trend poses an interesting question. I personally doubt it, largely because it suits the capitalist countries not to encourage the slowdown. Some countries, for example Malaysia, may try to protect themselves from the rampant capitalism of the west, but protecting local industries, as proved in the case of South Korea, is not the solution.

The mark of business leadership will be the assistance that businesses provide to their counterparts, partners, or alliances in the emerging capital markets. The World Trade Organization needs to be encouraged to take a more systemic rather than a competition-based view when arguing for capitalist 'free-market' policies in emerging economies. Mature capitalistic countries with business leaders who understand the complexities inherent in the capitalist structure should take note of their global systemic role. Keeping the capitalist system healthy has to be a priority.

Communication

The development of communication channels between parts of the world is an important reality. The growth and speed of communication is destined to accelerate. The development of the Internet and the world-wide-web (WWW) is a manifestation of who we are. We can now use the WWW to communicate to other parts of our world-wide web. The development and growing dependence on the WWW has many implications. We can no longer pretend that communication is not possible or is outside of our reach. Our mode of delivering information and services is already changing rapidly. What value-tensions will this trend create or surface? Strategic planners should be paying great attention to this emerging reality.

Religious Conflicts

While religious conflicts have been a feature of every age, as Samuel Huntington (1996) points out, the fault lines have never been bolder than now. This foreshadows future upheavals, conflicts, and heightened tensions between civilizations. The issues will be around values. The search for self-identity and meaning will be based on competing values. The demand to be included but to remain apart will increase. The development of the European Community has been characterized by these tensions. For example, Turkey wants to be part of the EC but wants to be respected for having a different identity, different values and different ways of doing things. How will religious co-operation occur in the future?

Businesses need to build these tensions into their scenarios. They need to consider the effects of these tensions on their world-wide stakeholders and to factor this into their identification of strategic growth opportunities and threats. Businesses need to pay attention to multi-cultural management issues which includes understanding the nature of religious tensions. The strategic planning function should research the effects of religious values on consumer behaviour and consumer values.

The Environment

The environment remains a major systemic pressure point for all businesses. Now that we have come to heed our symbiotic relationship with our environment, neglect is a short-term and irresponsible stance to take. Environmental issues are destined to escalate. The strategic planning function should ensure that the organization plays its part in the adaptive work that needs to be done in the face of this new reality.

Demographics

Population growth and population shifts affect the size, shape, and profile of the communities in which the organization operates. Tracking the world's demographic characteristics is particularly important for large global organizations. This will influence their perception of strategic growth opportunities and threats. It will inform them of the changing character of their consumers and it will alert them to the changing profile of the workforce. Demographics is a key input to strategic planning assumptions.

Who are We and Who do we want to Become?

These age old questions remain eternally relevant. Part of the reason is that being is about becoming. Being is a process, not a state. We are on the road. Becoming is being on the road.

Being on the road requires self-awareness, mindfulness, and attentiveness. Who we are and what we want to become is reflected in our institutions and organizations. They are a communal statement of who we are and who we want to become. We shape them and they shape us. They are manifestations of our aims and aspirations and they speak volumes about our understanding of our systemic roles and responsibilities. Businesses are informed by our value systems and inform our value systems. They are with us on the road. They present us with defining moments, ask us to consider our ethical priorities, and invite us to exercise our leadership skills. If we pay attention to businesses as an extension of ourselves we can influence them to become systemically-attuned learning organizations. It is unwise to look upon businesses only as a means to short-term ends. Business organizations are a significant part of the socio-economic fabric of life.

In conclusion, businesses are invited to exercise leadership. They are challenged to take up their systemic responsibilities and to face the adaptive work that new realities present. Evidence of their leadership skills will be their ability to influence rather than use their power to alter the status quo. Through the efforts of the strategic planning function, businesses should guide new visions that are commonly desired visions of the future. By fostering the spirit of a learning organization, leadership through strategic planning will help the organization to continuously recreate itself. Through the co-creation and co-evolution of new steps and new dances with new partners, businesses will share and promote life in the world-wide web.

Note

1 Title of the book written by Jim Rohwer (1996).

References

Allison, M. and Kaye, J. (1997) *Strategic Planning for Non-Profit Organisations*, John Wiley & Sons, New York.

Armour, A. and Browning, D. (1995) *Systems-Sensitive Leadership*, College Press Publishing, Missouri.

Badaracco Jr., J.L., (1997) *Defining Moments*, Harvard Business School Press, Boston, MA.

Badaracco Jr., J.L., (1991) *The Knowledge Link*, Harvard Business School Press, Boston, MA.

Bell, D. (1976) *The Cultural Contradictions of Capitalism*, Basic Books, New York.

Bellah, R.N. *et al.* (1996) *Habits of the Heart*, University of California Press, Berkeley, CA.

Bennis, W. (1989) *On Becoming a Leader*, Addison-Wesley Publishing Company, New York.

Bennis, W. (ed.) (1992) *Leaders on Leadership*, Harvard Business School Publishing, Boston, MA.

Bennis, W. *et al.* (1994) *Beyond Leadership*, Blackwell Publishers, Cambridge, MA.

Block, P. (1996) *Stewardship*, Berrett-Koehler Publishers, San Francisco.

Burns, J.M. (1978) *Leadership*, Harper & Row Publishers, New York.

Capra, F. (1991) *The Tao of Physics*, Shambala, Boston, MA.

Capra, F. (1996) *The Web of Life*, Doubleday, New York.

Carter, S.L. (1993) *The Culture of Disbelief*, Basic Books, New York.

Daly, H.E. and Cobb, J.B. (1994) *For the Common Good*, Beacon Press, Boston, MA.

Daloz, L.A.P., Keen, C.H., Keen, J.P. and Parks, S.D. (1996) *Common Fire*, Beacon Press, Boston, MA.

De Pree, M. (1989) *Leadership is an Art*, Dell Publishing Division, New York.

De Pree, M. (1992) *Leadership Jazz*, Dell Publishing Division, New York.

Drucker, P.F. (1989) *The New Realities*, HarperBusiness, New York.

Drucker, P.F. (1992) *Managing for the Future*, Butterworth-Heinemann Ltd, Oxford.

Drucker, P.F. (1993) *Post-Capitalist Society*, HarperBusiness, New York.

DuBrin, A.J. (1998) *Leadership: Research Findings, Practice, and Skills*, Houghton Mifflin Company, Boston, MA.

Eccles, R.G. and Nohria, N. (1992) *Beyond the Hype*, Harvard Business School Press, Cambridge, MA.

Ferguson, M. (1982) *The Aquarian Conspiracy*, Granada Publishing Limited, London.

The Financial Times (1997) Weekend edition, 26/27 July.

Fombrun, C.J. (1994) *Leading Corporate Change*, McGraw-Hill, Inc. New York.

Glass, N. (1996) *Management Masterclass*, Nicholas Brealey Publishing, London.

Haas, H.G. (1992) *The Leader Within*, Harper Collins, New York.

Halal, W.E. (1996) *The New Management*, Berrett-Koehler Publishers, San Francisco.

Handscombe, R. and Norman, P. (1993) *Strategic Leadership*. McGraw-Hill Book Company Europe, Maidenhead.

Heifetz, R.A. (1994) *Leadership Without Easy Answers*, Harvard University Press, Cambridge, MA.

Heider, J. (1985) *The Tao of Leadership*, Wildwood House Ltd, Aldershot.

Heilbroner, R. (1993) *21st Century Capitalism*, W.W. Norton & Company, New York.

Hesselbein, F., Goldsmith, M. and Beckhard, R. (eds) (1996) *The Leader of the Future*, The Drucker Foundation, Jossey-Bass, San Francisco.

Hill, L. (1992) *Becoming a Manager*, Harvard Business School Press, Boston, MA.

Hoecklin, L. (1996) *Managing Cultural Differences: Strategies for Competitive Advantage*, Addison-Wesley Publishers Ltd.

Hofstede, G. (1997) *Cultures and Organizations: Software of the Mind*, McGraw-Hill, New York.

Howard, P.K. (1994) *The Death of Common Sense*, Warner Books, New York.

Howard, R. (1993) *The Learning Imperative*, Harvard Business Review.

Huntington, S.P. (1993) *The Third Wave: Democratization in the Late Twentieth Century*, University of Oklahoma Press, Oklahoma.

Huntington, S.P. (1996) *The Clash of Civilizations and the Remaking of the World Order*, Simon & Schuster, New York.

Hutton, W. (1996) *The State We're In*, Vintage, London.

Jaworski, J. (1996) *Synchronicity: The Inner Path of Leadership*, Berrett-Koehler Publishers. San Francisco.

Kanter, R.M. (1990) *When Giants Learn to Dance*, Unwin Paperbacks, London.

Kao, J. (1997) *Jammimg: The Art and Discipline of Business Creativity*, HarperBusiness, New York.

Kaplan, R.S. and Norton, D.P. (1996) *The Balanced Scorecard*, Harvard Business School Press, Boston, MA.

Kegan, R. (1994) *In over our Heads: The Mental Demands of Modern Life*, Harvard University Press, Cambridge, MA.

Kennedy, P. (1993) *Preparing for the Twenty-First Century*, Random House, New York.

Korten, D.C. (1995) *When Corporations Rule the World*, Berrett-Koehler Publishers, San Francisco.

Kouzes, J.M. and Posner, B.Z. (1995) *The Leadership Challenge*, Jossey-Bass Inc., San Francisco.

Lele, M.M. (1992) *Creating Strategic Leverage*, John Wiley & Sons, New York.

Locke, E.A. and associates (1991) *The Essence of Leadership*, Lexington Books, New York.

MacGregor Burns, J. (1978) *Leadership*, Harper & Row Publishers, USA.

Mason, R.O. and Mitroff, I.I. (1981) *Challenging Strategic Planning Assumptions*, John Wiley & Sons, Chichester.

McRae, H. (1994) *The World in 2020*, Harvard Business School Press, Boston, MA.

Maynard, H.B. and Mehrtens, S.E. (1993) *The Fourth Wave*, Berrett-Koehler Publishers, San Francisco.

McCollough, T.E. (1991) *The Moral Imagination and Public Life*, Chatham House Publishers, New Jersey.

Meadows, D., Meadows, D., Randers, R. (1992) *Beyond the Limits*, Chelsea Green Publishing Company, Vermont.

Mintzberg, H. (1994) *The Rise and Fall of Strategic Planning*, The Free Press, New York.

Moingeon, B. and Edmondson, A. (eds) (1996) *Organizational Learning and Competitive Advantage*, Sage Publications Ltd, London.

Moore, J.F. (1996) *The Death of Competition: Leadership & Strategy in the age of Business Ecosystems*, HarperBusiness, New York.

Morgan, G. (1997) *Images of Organization*, Sage Publications Ltd, London.

Naisbitt, J. (1996) *Megatrends Asia*, Simon & Schuster, New York.

Neuhauser, P.C. (1988) *Tribal Warfare in Organisations*, HarperCollins Publishers.

Northouse, P.G. (1997) *Leadership: Theory and Practice*, Sage Publications, London.

Ohmae, K. (1995) *The End of the Nation State*, The Free Press, New York.

O'Toole, J. (1995) *Leading Change*, Jossey-Bass Publishers, San Francisco.

Peters, T.J. and Waterman, R.H. (1982) *In Search of Excellence*, Harper & Row, New York.

Piper, T. *et al.* (1993) *Can Ethics Be Taught?* Harvard Business School, Cambridge, MA.

Porter, M.E. (1985) *Competitive Advantage*, The Free Press, New York.

Porter, M.E. (1980) *The Competitive Advantage of Nations*, The Macmillan Press Limited, London.

Prahalad, C.K. and Hamel, G. (1990) The Core Competence of the Corporation, *Harvard Business Review*, May-June, pp. 79–91.

Ray, M. and Rinzler, A. (eds) (1993) *The New Paradigm in Business*, G.P. Putnam's Sons, New York.

Rifkin, J. (1995) *The End of Work*, G.P. Putnam's Sons, New York.

Rohwer, J. (1996) *Asia Rising*, Simon & Schuster, New York.

Sackmann, S.A. (1991) *Cultural Knowledge in Organizations: Exploring the Collective Mind*, Sage Publications Ltd, London.

Sandel, M.J. (1996) *Democracy's Discontent*, Harvard University Press, Cambridge, MA.

Saul, J.R. (1995) *The Unconscious Civilization*, Anansi Press Limited, West Concord, Ontario.

Schein, E.H. (1995) *Organizational Culture and Leadership*, second edition Jossey-Bass Publishers, San Francisco.

Schultz, H. (1997) *Pour Your Heart into It*, Hyperion, New York.

Senge, P.M. (1990) *The Fifth Discipline*, Century Business, London.

Senge, P. *et al.* (1994) *The Fifth Discipline Fieldbook*, Doubleday, New York.

Shaler, L.E. (1993) *Strategies for Change*, Abingdon Press, Nashville.

Schoen, D.A. (1998) *The Reflective Practitioner*, Basic Books, New York.

Schwartz, P. (1992) *The Art of the Long View*, Century Business, London.

Solomon, R.C. (1994) *The New World of Business*, Littlefield Adams Quality Paperbacks, Maryland.

Sowell, T. (1996) *Migrations and Cultures*, BasicBooks, New York.

Swimme, B. (1984) *The Universe is a Green Dragon*, Bear & Company, New Mexico.

Terry, R. (1995) *Economic Insanity: How Growth Driven Capitalism is Destroying the American Dream*, Berrett-Koehler Publishers, San Francisco.

Thompson, A.A. and Strickland, A.J. (1996) *Strategic Management Concepts and Cases*, Irwin Publishers, New York.

Thurow, L.C. (1996) *The Future of Capitalism: How Today's Economic Forces Shape Tomorrow's World*, William Morrow and Company, Inc. New York.

Van der Heijden, K. (1996) *Scenarios: The Art of Strategic Conversation*, John Wiley & Sons Ltd, Chichester.

Weidenbaum, M. and Hughes, S. (1996) *The Bamboo Network*, The Free Press, New York.

Wheatley, M.J. (1992) *Leadership and the New Science: Learning about Organization from an Orderly Universe*, Berrett-Koehler Publishers, Inc., San Francisco.

White, R.P., Hodgson, P. and Crainer, S. (1996) *The Future of Leadership*, Pitman Publishing, Maryland.

Index